EAST WEST
ASTROLOGY

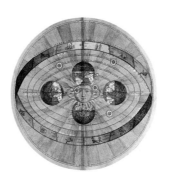

EAST WEST ASTROLOGY

COMBINING THE CHINESE AND WESTERN
TRADITIONS TO CHART YOUR DESTINY

LORI REID

ELEMENT

Shaftesbury, Dorset • Boston, Massachusetts • Melbourne, Victoria

First published in Great Britain in 1999 by
ELEMENT BOOKS LIMITED
Shaftesbury, Dorset SP7 8BP

Published in the USA in 1999 by
ELEMENT BOOKS INC
160 North Washington Street, Boston MA 02114

Published in Australia in 1999 by
ELEMENT BOOKS
and distributed by Penguin Australia Ltd
487 Maroondah Highway, Ringwood, Victoria 3134

Designed and created with
THE BRIDGEWATER BOOK COMPANY LIMITED

ELEMENT BOOKS LIMITED
Managing Editor MIRANDA SPICER
Senior Commissioning Editor CARO NESS
Production Manager SUSAN SUTTERBY

THE BRIDGEWATER BOOK COMPANY
Art Director KEVIN KNIGHT
Designer/Page Production JANE LANAWAY
Editorial Director SOPHIE COLLINS
Managing Editor ANNE TOWNLEY
Project Editor CAROLINE EARLE
Picture research VANESSA FLETCHER

Printed and bound in Great Britian by
Butler & Tanner Ltd.

Library of Congress Cataloging in Publication
data available

ISBN 1 86204 462 7

*For Caro, for being the most enlightened editor and for
moving heaven and earth to bring this book into the
light of day. Thank you.*

With thanks to
Jonathan Ayres, Clare Bayes, Brian Beard, Rosanna Beard, Stephanie
Brotherstone, Chris Burgess, David Burton, Adam Carne, Yana Casquero,
Robert Chappell, Joanna Christie, Henry Colthurst, Roger Cooper, Rebecca
Drury, Angela Enahoro, Maggie de Freitas, Helen Furbear, Anette Gerlin,
Trevor Gunn, Mary-Anne Harding, Samantha Hollingdale, I. Kaskero, Chloe
Knight, Julia Knight, Pat Knight, Tim Kingswood, Cassandra Leigh, Alasdair
Mackay, Sarah McGowan, Norman McLean, Aylla McPhail, Wendy Oxberry,
Max Rashand, Sharon Rashand, Caron Riley, Emma Scott, Frances Selkirk,
Doug Streeter, Andrew Stemp, Neil Strowger, Sue Wallace, Charlotte Walsh,
for help with photography

With thanks to:
Bright Ideas, Lewes, East Sussex
Courts, Shoreham-by-Sea, East Sussex
S.E. Harris, Hove, East Sussex
Harry's English Restaurant, Hove, East Sussex
Sarah Jamieson and Jenny Turtill, The Workshop, Lewes,
East Sussex
InterSport Lewes, Lewes, East Sussex
Jevoncraft, Lewes, East Sussex
Katherine Tanswell, Walk in Wardrobe, Hove, East Sussex
Wyevale Garden Centres plc, Kingston, East Sussex
for the kind loan of props

Picture Credits

Archiv für Kunst und Geschichte, London: 6b, 10b.
The Image Bank: 50bl, 51tr, 61tr, 64bl, 66ml, 84tr, 86tl, 93tr, 100t, 103t, 128b,
137ml, 156b, 158ml, 166t, 167ml, 178t, 183b, 191t, 193t, 196b, 209t.
Images Colour Library, London: Cover pictures,
Fortean Picture Library: 7tr.
NASA: 7b, 10tl, 11(all planets), 26bl, 182t.
The Science Photo Library: 218.
The Stock Market: 11tl, 26m, 46t, 54tr, 59t, 60t, 70m, 71t, 74t, 75tr, 78m, 79t,
80t, 81b, 82t, 87t, 89tr, 94t, 96t, 98b, 107b, 108t, 109ml, 115tr, 120ml, 124t,
126t, 131b, 134t, 136t, 140t, 149t, 155t, 159t, 162t, 164t, 169b, 172t, 173b,
176t, 180t, 185b, 187t, 190b, 194b, 198t, 207b, 208t, 211t, 212b, 215t.
Tony Stone: 171t.

CONTENTS

THE HISTORY OF ASTROLOGY

Precisely when the study of astrology began is uncertain. What we can be sure of, however, is that people have been fascinated by the stars since early times. Discoveries of bone, engraved with the phases of the Moon and belonging to the Cro-Magnon era, suggest that observations of planetary movements were being made as far back as the dawn of human civilization.

The sages of the East saw the destiny of the Emperor written in the stars.

CHARTING THE SKIES

It is interesting to wonder if Early Man made any sort of connection between celestial patterns and events that simultaneously took place on Earth. In his writings, Cicero, the Roman orator and statesman, referred to Babylonian astronomical records that had fallen into the hands of the conquering Roman armies. He claimed that these records, containing *exact* movements of the planets, reputedly stretched back some 47,000 years.

Certainly, it must be assumed that cyclical patterns were recognized fairly early on: day succeeding night; season following season; birth and death; the growth, decay, and regrowth of vegetation; the migration of birds; the ebb and flow of the tides; and so on. And, at some point, a matching cyclical pattern in the skies overhead must have been perceived: the interchange of Sun and Moon; the monthly lunar phases; the rising and setting of planets; and the yearly movement across the heavens of the different clusters of stars.

At first, as the earliest people began to cultivate the land and domesticate livestock, they must have recognized a need to predict seasonal changes and to forecast weather conditions. Counting lunar phases and watching the Sun's apparent progress through the sky, for example, enabled them to calculate the passage of time. But another connection, rightly or wrongly, was eventually made. Eclipses, the appearance of comets and the recurrence of other cosmic phenomena became linked to earthly catastrophes, such as

Believed to have traveled from Chaldea, the Magi followed the star to the birthplace of the infant Jesus.

pestilence and floods. The ability to foretell when such celestial events were to occur, and thereby prepare for any accompanying cataclysmic consequences upon their lives, must have been considered highly advantageous.

It would seem that, from these early observations of planetary movements, there developed a deeper realization of synchronicity, out of which astrology was born.

FROM ANCIENT BEGINNINGS

It is generally believed that the form of astrology used today originated in Mesopotamia six to eight thousand years ago. It was there that the Chaldeans and Babylonians acknowledged that an affinity existed between the movement of the planets and events that took place on Earth. It was the job of the learned scribes, all versed in astronomical and astrological lore, to keep calendrical records, to announce the beginning and ending of the seasons, to interpret the implication of the changing celestial patterns, and, most importantly, to use these findings to make predictions concerning their king and country.

From Mesopotamia, astrological knowledge spread to Egypt, Ancient Greece, and the Roman Empire and from there to the rest of the known Western world.

Incidentally, it was three astrologers from Chaldea who followed the star that led them, the Magi, to the stable where the infant Jesus was born.

ASTROLOGY IN THE EAST

At the same moment in time, in widely different geographical locations, observations of celestial bodies, calendrical record-keeping, and the study of planetary portents were taking place independently in lands further to the East. Some authorities, however, maintain that divination using planetary influences developed in China well before it did in central Asia and Europe. Indeed, chronological records in China, that date back to around 2500 B.C.E., suggest that Chinese sages must have had extensive knowledge of astronomy long before this date, and that they were already well versed in astrological lore at this time.

Interestingly, although some of the principles differ fairly fundamentally between the astrological systems of East and West, their evolution and progress seem to have followed similar lines. Each originally used the art exclusively to make prophecies concerning the emperor and his state. It was not until hundreds of years later that astrology became a divinatory tool for the use of the masses.

STONEHENGE

Around 2500 B.C.E., Stonehenge is thought to have been built as a giant observatory. The special alignment of the stones enabled observers to plot the movements of the Sun and the Moon,

Oriented to the heavens, the ring of monoliths at Stonehenge marked the planetary movements across the skies.

thereby forecasting astronomical phenomena, including the solstices and, in particular, eclipses, which were believed to presage doom and disaster. Such a sophisticated construction stands as evidence that the inhabitants of northern Europe already possessed advanced knowledge of astronomy by this time.

ASTRONOMY VS. ASTROLOGY

Taken from the Greek word "astron," which means "star," astronomy and astrology both study the solar system and the constellations that make up our universe. Essentially, astronomy deals mathematically with the measurement of the celestial bodies, while astrology interprets their meaning and possible influences on life on Earth.

Originally, the two systems were interrelated, neither being taught without the other. In fact, right up to our present millennium, no self-respecting physician would have practiced medicine without a firm grounding in both disciplines, and certainly would not have treated an individual without having consulted the natal chart of the patient first.

Planet Earth in its glory, as seen from space.

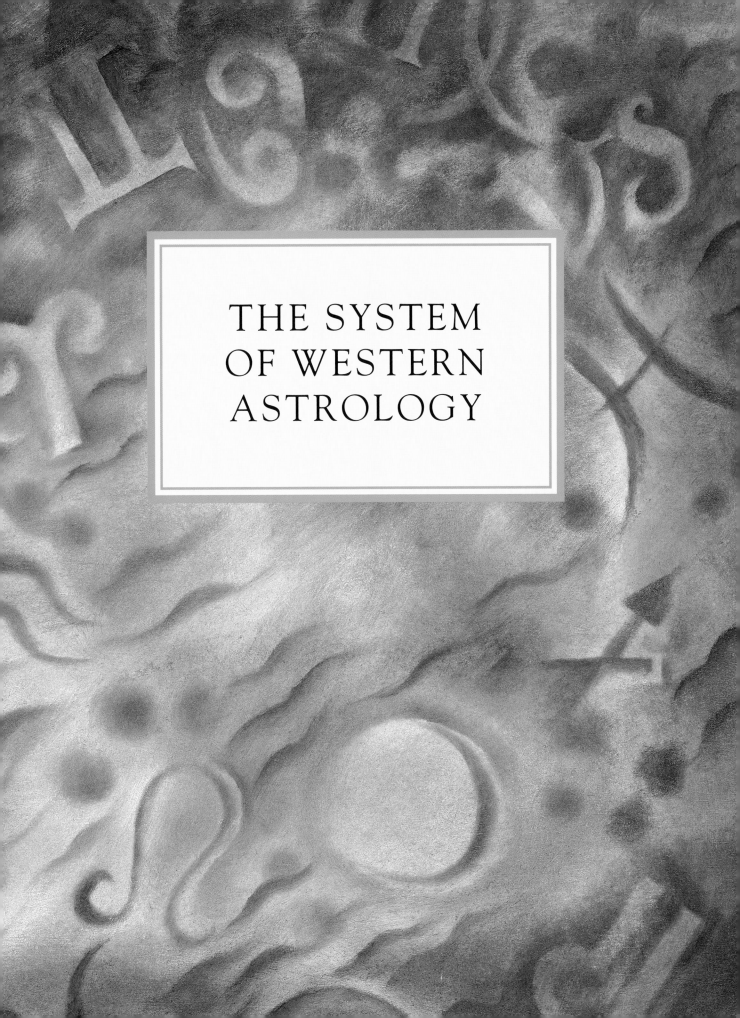

THE SYSTEM
OF WESTERN
ASTROLOGY

WESTERN ASTROLOGY: AN OVERVIEW

Western astrology is based on the movements of the planets in our solar system. It places the Earth at the center of an imaginary ring around which the Sun and planets appear to travel. Although we know, of course, that it is the Earth that spins around the Sun, and not the Sun around the Earth, when we stand on the Earth and look up into the sky, it appears to us that the Sun is, indeed, moving.

As the vital force, the Sun represents creative power.

Like clockwork, the planets make their way across the sky in precise motion, returning to the same spot with unfailing regularity, according to their orbit and individual speed.

As these bodies move around the heavens, they create changing and repeating patterns, forming relationships with each other, sometimes tense, other times harmonious.

Everyone and everything that comes into being will be characterized individually, or "stamped," by the pattern that prevails at the moment of birth.

WHAT IS A HOROSCOPE?

From Ancient Greek, "Horoscope" literally means to "watch and record time." Mapping the exact position of the planets at the moment of birth will produce a symbolic representation of the individual or event. This map is known as a Horoscope or birth chart.

THE ZODIAC

Fundamental to the system of Western astrology, the Zodiac is a device for locating the position of the planets as they travel, at different speeds, across the sky. The word literally means, a "ring of animals." It is an imaginary belt in space encircling the Earth, made up of the twelve familiar astrological signs. Each sign takes up a space of 30°, with Aries starting the circuit. From Earth, it appears to us that the Sun, Moon, and planets weave their way through this ring of signs. It is the Sun, apparently moving at about 1° per day, that determines which sign of the Zodiac a person

In Ancient times Western astrologers believed the Earth was the pivot around which the heavens revolved.

belongs to. For example, while the Sun is traveling through the 30° section that makes up the sign of Libra, all people born within those thirty days are Librans.

THE PLANETS AND THEIR MEANINGS

While the sign in which the Sun is traveling on the day we are born determines our general characteristics, the Moon and planets provide substance to our personalities by adding "color" and "flavor" to our make-up. Moreover, the positions of the planets and the specific relationships they form with each other on the day we are born are believed to exert particular energies, which directly affect our lives, guiding and shaping them from the outset.

In astrological language, though the Sun is strictly speaking a star, and the Moon is astronomically a satellite of the Earth, both are referred to as planets.

Just as similar physical characteristics run through a family, so the same planetary patterns are often repeated in the birth charts of parents and their children.

ASTROLOGICAL SYMBOLS

When compiling a horoscope, symbols are used as a form of shorthand to denote the names of the signs and planets.

SIGNS		PLANETS	
ARIES	♈	SUN	☉
TAURUS	♉	MOON	☽
GEMINI	♊	MERCURY	☿
CANCER	♋	VENUS	♀
LEO	♌	MARS	♂
VIRGO	♍	JUPITER	♃
LIBRA	♎	SATURN	♄
SCORPIO	♏	URANUS	♅
SAGITTARIUS	♐	NEPTUNE	♆
CAPRICORN	♑ OR ♑	PLUTO	♇ OR ♇
AQUARIUS	♒		
PISCES	♓		

PLANETARY INFLUENCES

Having observed the movements of the individual planets and noted the corresponding events on Earth, the ancient astrologers gave particular attributes to each of the heavenly bodies. In addition, each was said to "rule" a particular zodiacal sign and thus imbue it with its own characteristics. Since there are twelve signs and only ten "planets," two of the faster-moving planets perform dual duty and take rulership of two signs each. These are Mercury, which governs both Gemini and Virgo, and Venus, which rules Taurus as well as Libra.

PLANET	RULES	SYMBOLIZES
THE SUN	Leo	vital energy, physical strength and power, creativity, love, happiness, the masculine principle
THE MOON	Cancer	feelings, emotions, sensitivity, the feminine principle, the mother
MERCURY	Gemini and Virgo	the intellect, ideas, communications, language, wit, skill, commerce, medicine
VENUS	Taurus and Libra	affection, harmony, music, beauty, grace, charm, lesser fortune
MARS	Aries	power, energy, activity, aggression, leadership, impulsiveness, adventure
JUPITER	Sagittarius	greater fortune, optimism, generosity, luck, expansion
SATURN	Capricorn	limitation, restriction, duty, steadfastness, consolidation, caution, self-control
URANUS	Aquarius	originality, drama, revolution, sudden change, renunciation, eccentricity
NEPTUNE	Pisces	dreaminess, imagination, inspiration, confusion, mysticism, prophecy
PLUTO	Scorpio	regeneration, transformation, rebirth, subconscious processes

ARIES

BORN BETWEEN: **MARCH 21—APRIL 20**

RED ROSE

LIFE DRIVES

Since Aries is the leading sign in the roll-call of the Zodiac, is it any wonder that people born in this group strive to win, to be the best, to come first in every activity they undertake? This is the impetus that gives members of this sign the competitive streak, which drives them to the forefront of the action. Courageous, energetic, confident, and bold, they like to be the ones who take the initiative and they have the reputation of jumping in where lesser mortals fear to tread. Adventurers par excellence, Aries people like to live life very positively in the fast lane.

AT WORK AND AT PLAY

Tough cookies, Aries' competitiveness is legendary. They like to set the pace, working fast and furiously, and they only respect those who keep up with them. Colleagues or employees who fall by the wayside get short shrift. These people are essentially pioneers and they excel in any occupation that takes them to the cutting edge, which strives to push forward the boundaries of knowledge and experience. The armed forces are a natural draw, as is engineering. Cars and sports of all types are a particular passion.

LOVE AND RELATIONSHIPS

Impulsive lovers, those born under this sign usually follow their hearts rather than their heads. Indeed, most of them suffer from "love at first sight" syndrome—again, and again, and again, throughout their lives.

PERSONALITY KEYNOTES

active, dramatic, bold, impulsive, competitive, courageous, pioneering, like to be leaders, quick to learn, full of initiative, loads of enthusiasm, aggressive, impatient, tactless, insensitive, hot-headed, quick-tempered

ASSOCIATIONS

❊ Symbol *Ram* ❊ Planetary Ruler *Mars* ❊ Element *Fire*
❊ Color *Scarlet* ❊ Flower *Red Rose*
❊ Stone *Diamond*
❊ Lucky Number *1*
❊ Lucky Day *Tuesday*

For them, the excitement is in the thrill of the chase and, when they spot the person of their dreams, they burn with ardor until they fell their quarry. If they can control that strong streak of ego-centricity, Aries can become some of the most stimulating and passionate lovers one is ever likely to meet.

Robust and headstrong, the ram personifies Aries as leader of the pack.

HEALTH AND WEALTH

Aries rules the head, and as such, headaches and eye-strain tend to be common complaints among the natives of this sign. Being impulsive types, they have a tendency to do things on the run, always rushing from one task to the next, which unfortunately makes them more prone than others to accidents, sudden falls, and burns. Moreover, with fiery Mars as their ruling planet, it is not surprising that high temperatures and feverish conditions are also associated with this sign.

Aries-born folk never mind sticking their necks out, so taking chances with their finances comes as second nature to them. They will readily invest money into a friend's enterprise, or gamble on share investments. Fortunately, many of these risks pay off. However, Aries subjects are not the sort who will hang around bemoaning their fate when their luck runs out. There's always another exciting challenge on the horizon.

ARIES SHOULD

• learn to share

• think about things from their partners' points of view

ARIES SHOULDN'T

• be too hasty in making judgments about others

• be too pushy when forming relationships

TAURUS

LIFE DRIVES

Security and stability are the driving forces for all Taureans. They seek a life which will provide a steady and comfortable existence. Possessions are therefore very important, acting as they do as anchors, keeping their lives on a steady, even keel. Patience is a strong suit and they like to take their time to consider their options fully. But, determined and steadfast, once members of this sign have a goal in mind, there is very little that will deflect them from their chosen course of action.

AT WORK AND AT PLAY

Solid, stable and hard-working, Taureans make reliable and responsible members of the workforce—as long as they are allowed to go at their own pace. Being harried and hassled are pet hates, and no self-respecting Taurean will be pushed around against his or her volition. Back them into a corner and there's a danger they will turn into raging bulls! Their talents can take them into a wide range of occupations, from farming and horticulture, architecture and finance, to singing, dancing, and design.

LOVE AND RELATIONSHIPS

Members of this sign are some of the most sensual people in the entire Zodiac. Taurus is a physical sign, which means its natives enjoy basic pleasures and creature comforts. As lovers, they are some of the most loyal and committed of partners, never entering relationships lightly, but committing themselves only after having envisaged every conceivable situation from every conceivable angle. Once they give their heart to a partner, though, they give it for life. Their gritty determination means they are prepared to hang on through thick and thin, even long, long after a relationship has come to an end.

HEALTH AND WEALTH

Taurus rules the neck and throat, anatomical areas which are particularly vulnerable in Taurean subjects who tend to suffer from sore throats, hoarseness, and colds that settle in the chest. A tendency to overindulge, coupled with a penchant for rich food and good wine, invariably piles on the weight, especially around middle-age. Trips to the gym would help if only Taureans weren't quite so averse to exercise!

Not renowned for gambling with their money or risking their possessions, natives of this sign tend to accumulate wealth slowly but surely throughout their lives. For them, money in the bank provides security and they take comfort in seeing their pennies grow. They do particularly well with long-term investments and possess a brilliant eye for seeking out objects that accrue in value over the years.

Placid unless aroused, the bull characterizes the Taurean personality.

PERSONALITY KEYNOTES

hard-working, charming, sensible, practical, patient, affectionate, emotionally stable, loyal, needy of material comforts, sensual, plodding, reliable, artistic, musical, stubborn, self-indulgent, possessive, resentful, greedy, materialistic

ASSOCIATIONS

Symbol *Bull* · Planetary Ruler *Venus*
Element *Earth*
Color *Pastel shades of Green and Blue*
Flower *Carnation*
Stone *Emerald*
Lucky Number *6*
Lucky Day *Friday*

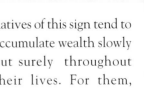

CARNATION

TAUREANS SHOULD
• *allow themselves to be swept off their feet*
• *build their relationships on love, not on material security*

TAUREANS SHOULDN'T
• *always be thinking about the practicalities in a love affair*
• *be stiflingly possessive*

GEMINI

BORN BETWEEN: **MAY 21—JUNE 20**

LIFE DRIVES

Blessed with intelligence and wit, most Gemini people are born with a special talent for putting difficult concepts and ideas into words. In short, they have a gift for communication and many members of this sign excel in languages and literature. Most Gemini, too, have a passion and natural understanding of technological gadgets, filling their homes with the latest in hi-fi equipment, computers, and time-saving machinery to take the boredom out of everyday routines. Above all else, these are social creatures, with butterfly minds, which need constant stimulation, entertainment, and amusement from a multitude of interests and a wide circle of friends.

AT WORK AND AT PLAY

Because of their inborn inventiveness and gift for communication, Gemini people often gravitate to the world of media. Many will find their way into journalism and broadcasting, perfect outlets for their coruscating wit. The travel industry and IT provide other equally suitable occupations for these technological whizz-kids. Sales and commercial retail are also excellent avenues for their sharp patter and persuasive talents. Routine, however, is the pet hate of Gemini people, so a job that allows them flexitime will get the best from their ingenious minds.

LOVE AND RELATIONSHIPS

Bright and breezy by nature, Gemini has the reputation of being the most flirtatious sign of the Zodiac. It's true that, emotionally, members of this sign

A desire to do everything and to be everywhere is manifested in the dual image of the Gemini twins.

GEMINI SHOULD

• *follow their hearts rather than constantly rationalizing their feelings*
• *cuddle their partners*

GEMINI SHOULDN'T

• *flirt quite so outrageously with other people when they're already committed in a relationship*
• *be so cool and off-hand*

can sometimes be fickle, but that is because they have such a low boredom threshold. However, with the right partner who knows how to stimulate their minds and hold their interests, Gemini natives can be the wittiest, most intelligent, and therefore rewarding of lifetime companions.

HEALTH AND WEALTH

The upper limbs and the lungs come under the rulership of Gemini, so respiratory problems can occur. They are also prone to injuries to their hands and arms.

In addition, because these restless individuals are likely to expend more nervous energy than most, they tend all too easily to suffer from nervous exhaustion. Therefore, a balanced routine, combining plenty of sleep with a moderate amount of exercise in the fresh air, is highly recommended for their well-being.

As long as Gemini folk have a wide circle of friends and enough money to enjoy their hobbies, they are happy. They're not especially interested in hoarding cash or chasing investments, although timely financial advice from some of their many contacts can often prove extremely fruitful. In general, however, Gemini make a good living from their quick wits, literary talents, and highly inventive minds.

HONEYSUCKLE

PERSONALITY KEYNOTES

stimulating, entertaining, clever, quick-witted, vivacious, versatile, adaptable, inquisitive, inventive, changeable, talkative, unpredictable, possessing the gift of the gab, restless, deceitful, unreliable, nervous, superficial

ASSOCIATIONS

❦ Symbol *Twins* ❦ Planetary Ruler *Mercury* ❦ Element *Air*
❦ Color *Yellow* ❦ Flower *Honeysuckle*
❦ Stone *Agate*
❦ Lucky Number *5*
❦ Lucky Day *Wednesday*

CANCER

BORN BETWEEN: **JUNE 21—JULY 22**

LIFE DRIVES

Of all the star signs, Cancer harbors the most family-oriented members. For these people, home is the center of their universe. Many Cancerians are happy to devote themselves exclusively to the care and protection of their loved ones, striving hard to create a warm and harmonious domestic life so essential to their well-being. These are gentle, sentimental, and emotional creatures, who learn early on in their lives that it is sometimes better to hide their sensitive feelings under the protective covering of a crab-like shell.

MOONSTONE

AT WORK AND AT PLAY

Cancerians' inborn instinct for nurturing others finds a natural outlet in the caring professions, such as medicine and nursing. People belonging to this group are inherently empathetic and many have a wonderful bedside manner, which others find magically healing and soothing. Their domestic talents, too, can turn them into master chefs and experts

PERSONALITY KEYNOTES

domesticated, home-loving, protective, affectionate, understanding, instinctive, caring, sensitive, supportive, thoughtful, cautious, security-conscious, kind, compassionate, shy, moody, clingy, unforgiving

ASSOCIATIONS

❧ Symbol *Crab*
❧ Planetary Ruler *Moon*
❧ Element *Water* ❧ Color *Silver and White* ❧ Flower *Lily*
❧ Stone *Moonstone*
❧ Lucky Number *2*
❧ Lucky Day *Monday*

in the hotel or catering trades. Moreover, brilliant flashes of intuition, coupled with a phenomenal memory, puts these natives head and shoulders above any competitor in the world of business or in the financial sector.

LOVE AND RELATIONSHIPS

Cancerians are true romantics. They adore body contact, so enjoy nothing better than snuggling up to the person they love. Whether male or female, the

nurturing instinct comes naturally to members of this sign and deep affection for their loved ones flows naturally from a seemingly bottomless well. As partners, they are warm and emotional, protective, and supportive. But, if their feelings are hurt, they can become moody and irrational, retreating into their shells until such time as they feel it is safe to face life once again.

HEALTH AND WEALTH

This sign rules the chest, the breasts, and the stomach. A tendency to worry, which leads to digestive problems, is typical of people born at this time of year. The kidneys, too, can be one of their weaker links. Thus the health message for Cancerians is that they need to learn to relax, to eat healthy natural foods, and generally to take care of their diets.

Family treasures handed down from generation to generation often form the basis of Cancerian wealth. These are nostalgic people who prize antiques and may astound themselves when they discover the value of the pieces they possess. Other than that, Cancerians are notorious collectors and can make a handsome profit from this hobby.

Just like the crab, Cancerians build themselves a sturdy outer shell to protect their inner sensitivity.

CANCERIANS SHOULD

• *tell their partners about their hurt feelings*
• *let go of their mothers' apron strings and learn to be more independent*

CANCERIANS SHOULDN'T

• *harbor grudges forever*
• *sit around at home all the time when there's so much adventure to be had in the world*

LEO

BORN BETWEEN: **JULY 23—AUGUST 22**

SUNFLOWER

LIFE DRIVES

With the Sun as the ruler of this sign, how can any Leo fail to be a star! Dynamic, charismatic, and flamboyant by nature, these people are some of life's natural performers, always turning in a class act to the delight of their family and friends. Proud as peacocks, their stately bearing and noble manner confers upon them a regal presence which attracts respect from others. Just as well, since they thrive on praise and adulation—so much so, in fact, that many are all too often taken in by empty flattery. But, warm and generous, open and passionate in all they do, the sunny disposition of the Leo usually cheers the hearts of those they touch.

AT WORK AND AT PLAY

The colorful and extroverted personalities of this group lend themselves quite readily to the worlds of fashion and design. The entertainment business, too, calls these expansive folk who turn to the limelight as a flower turns to the sun. At work, they make popular team members and are respected by their colleagues. In business, they make fine executives, often ending up on the board. For it is their in-bred powers of leadership and ability to command that invariably sees the Leo rise to the top in his or her chosen career.

LEOS SHOULD
• *give their partners space to be themselves*
• *learn to compromise*

LEOS SHOULDN'T
• *let pride come between them and their partners*
• *always hog the limelight or compete with their loved ones*

LOVE AND RELATIONSHIPS

Leos make generous, demonstrative lovers. They're warm, sensual people, who are prepared to give themselves, body and soul, to the person they love. But they need constant reassurance from their partners and suffer miserably from wounded pride if they are not patently admired and respected in return. In partnerships, they do like to be the dominant force, and a partner who knows how to make a Leo feel about ten feet tall will be rewarded with unswerving loyalty and a lifetime of devotion.

HEALTH AND WEALTH

A huge appetite for living life to the full can lead natives of this sign to over-indulge in rich, creamy, or spicy foods—all guaranteed to wreak havoc on their cholesterol levels. And this is precisely what Leos need to keep in check since they are prone to rheumatic-type diseases, circulatory problems, and heart ailments. Fortunately their love of red wine may dilute some of their worst excesses. Gentle and regular exercise is recommended, but they must beware not to strain their backs which is another of their vulnerable areas.

There isn't a Leo who does not, in one way or another, enjoy the five-star treatment. Consequently, a lot of the Leonine salary will go toward maintaining a comfortable lifestyle. However, since Leos are a lucky group, gifted and generally highly regarded, they are usually able to command a good income which keeps them in the manner to which they have been accustomed.

As the lion is king of the jungle, so Leo's natural inclination is to rule.

VIRGO

SARDONYX

LIFE DRIVES

High standards of excellence characterize the members of this sign. Cool, careful, and analytical, their razor-sharp mentality can pick things up at a glance and focus in on minutiae in a flash. It's true they can be fussy but, on the other hand, all Virgos display great intelligence and are blessed with powers of reasoning which are hard to match. Moreover, many have a sharp wit and a sense of humor that is often wry and surprisingly unexpected. Practical, prudent, modest, and hard-working, these people have their feet firmly on the ground and own a maturity that, more often than not, belies their years.

PERSONALITY KEYNOTES

logical, realistic, practical, faithful, wise, perceptive, analytical, tactful, discreet, orderly, clean, neat, tidy, loyal, industrious, fussy, house-proud, perfectionist, hypercritical, wry, hard-working, achievement-motivated

ASSOCIATIONS

❦ Symbol *Maiden*
❦ Planetary Ruler *Mercury*
❦ Element *Earth*
❦ Color *Dark Blue, Red-Brown*
❦ Flower *Anemone* ❦ Stone *Sardonyx*
❦ Lucky Number *5* ❦ Lucky Day
Wednesday

AT WORK AND AT PLAY

With such honed critical faculties, no other group is better placed to succeed in any occupation that requires discipline, patience, and skill in minute precision. Careers in engineering, scientific research, statistics, and record-keeping of all descriptions attract the members of this sign. The social sciences and the public health services equally beckon and offer a suitable outlet for Virgos' methodical minds and their extraordinary organizational talents.

VIRGOS SHOULD

• *learn to relax*
• *accept people for what they are*

VIRGOS SHOULDN'T

• *quibble over the details*
• *be quite so logical in matters of the heart*

LOVE AND RELATIONSHIPS

Even in love, Virgos never quite lose their sense of reality. Practical and logical, they can spot falsehood at twenty paces. And, although they are discriminating, they realize that perfection is an illusion. Nevertheless, details remain important to them and members of this sign are unlikely to commit themselves to a partner until they are sure of their ground. To them, intelligence and honesty are essential prerequisites for the long-term success of an intimate relationship.

HEALTH AND WEALTH

Virgos have a tendency to suffer from stress and tension, often manifested by intestinal problems such as stomach cramps and ulcers. They are notorious for fretting and worrying which can result in headaches. In particular, they are discriminating when it comes to what they eat and they often opt for natural or organic produce.

Many Virgos turn to complementary therapies—acupuncture and homeopathy—which they find more suitable than conventional medicines. Generally, though, natives of this sign tend to have strong and healthy constitutions.

Not the greatest risk-takers in the world, Virgos tend to build up their resources slowly but surely. They favor safe investments, especially if their money is tied up with ethical companies or with those that support environmentally conscious products. Naturally hard-working and frugal, Virgos save enough money to ensure a comfortable existence for themselves and for those they love.

A drive for perfection is personified by Virgo, the maiden.

LIBRA

BORN BETWEEN: **SEPTEMBER 23—OCTOBER 22**

LIFE DRIVES

Cultured and urbane, Librans ooze sophistication and good taste. Appearances are important to them and they will go to great lengths to ensure that their surroundings are esthetically pleasing. More than anything else in life, they aspire to gracious living and enjoy good company. They themselves make excellent companions, for they are affable, keen to please, and always have something interesting to say. All Librans find discord deeply unsettling and will avoid disagreements at all costs, often being prepared to give in even when they know they are right, simply to restore peace and harmony.

AT WORK
AND AT PLAY

As the peacemakers of the Zodiac, Librans make naturally skilled negotiators and so excel in occupations where tact and diplomacy are required. Nothing depresses their spirits more than uncongenial surroundings, so working in a pleasant and attractive environment is essential to their well-being. Easygoing and composed, they fare best in a team or where joint projects are required. Many Librans find a suitable outlet for their talents in the world of music and the arts.

LOVE AND
RELATIONSHIPS

Because relationships are so important to Librans, people belonging to this sign are really only happy when they have a soulmate at their side. But they do find making decisions very difficult and may vacillate for years before committing themselves to a partner. Just as they require beauty and harmony in their lives and environment, so they look for beauty and elegance in the people with whom they choose to share their lives.

HEALTH AND WEALTH

Health problems affecting Librans often tend to manifest themselves in urinary disorders. Drinking plenty of water every day will flush out residual toxins. The key to Libran well-being is maintaining a balance—a balanced diet, a balance between work and recreation, between exercise and rest. When this delicate equilibrium becomes upset, their whole metabolic system is thrown out of kilter. Paying attention to this need for harmony in physical, psychological, and spiritual terms should keep the Libran healthy and content.

ROSE

PERSONALITY KEYNOTES

cool, elegant, artistic, fair, impartial, broad-minded, diplomatic, sophisticated, charming, sociable, intelligent, eye for beauty, tolerant, indecisive, vain, extravagant, sycophantic

ASSOCIATIONS

❦ Symbol *Weighing Scales*
❦ Planetary Ruler *Venus*
❦ Element *Air* ❦ Color *Lavender*
❦ Flower *Rose*
❦ Stone *Opal*
❦ Lucky Number *6*
❦ Lucky Day *Friday*

Librans tend to attract money, which is just as well since they enjoy spending it in large quantities! Encouragement to save from a young age and to spread their investments are two rubrics that will stand the Libran finances in good stead.

LIBRANS
SHOULD
• *look beneath a potential partner's pretty facade*
• *stick to the decisions they make*

LIBRANS
SHOULDN'T
• *expect their partners to be perfect in every way*
• *always try to please others at their own expense*

Fashionably poised, Librans strike a balance in all they do.

SCORPIO

TOPAZ

LIFE DRIVES

There is little doubt that, with their intense and powerful demeanors, Scorpios come across as forceful personalities with deep-rooted, labyrinthine passions. They carry around them an aura of mystery and intrigue, which others find compellingly attractive. Yet, no matter how much they try, it is unlikely that anyone will succeed in completely penetrating a Scorpio's enigmatic soul, for members of this group are secretive individuals, fiercely protective of their own privacy. Whether at home, at work, or in love, Scorpios need to be the ones in control. They despise any shallowness, hypocrisy, weakness of character, and, above all else, betrayal. With their perspicacity and penetrating gaze, they have the power to read between the lines and see into the heart of the matter in a trice.

Intense and powerful, Scorpio's gaze can penetrate one's soul.

AT WORK AND AT PLAY

Whatever they take on, Scorpios involve themselves one hundred percent. Their powers of concentration and ability to focus on the job in hand are unequaled. They have an urgent "need to know," which drives many of them into investigative or forensic occupations. Some are drawn to psychology and psychoanalysis, others to scientific research. Surgery and dentistry also attract, but so too do the mystical arts and the occult.

LOVE AND RELATIONSHIPS

Passionate and intense, Scorpio has the reputation of being the sexiest sign of the Zodiac. Certainly, when they fall in love, these people give their all. However,

they do expect their love and devotion to be returned in the same depth and quantity. Woe betide a partner who is disloyal or, worse still, one who cheats on a member of this sign. For a Scorpio never forgets and never ever forgives!

PERSONALITY KEYNOTES

deep, sexy, passionate, strong, discerning, intense, magnetic, protective, supportive, penetrative, committed, forceful, determined, possessive, supersensitive, obsessive, jealous, envious, secretive, suspicious, ruthless

ASSOCIATIONS

Symbol *Scorpion* Planetary Ruler *Pluto* Element *Water* Color *Magenta, Claret* Flower *Chrysanthemum* Stone *Topaz, Jasper* Lucky Number *8* Lucky Day *Tuesday*

HEALTH AND WEALTH

Scorpio rules the reproductive system and sexual organs. Problems in these areas are common and may range from menstrual complications in women to hernia or urological complaints in men. Although Scorpios have been described as wiry in constitution, when ill, they can make difficult and demanding patients, rebelling against medical advice which can complicate treatment. Fortunately, however, they are blessed with good powers of recovery.

When it comes to savings and making investments, following whatever their intuition tells them to do often pays off handsomely for members of this sign. This inborn savvy, combined with their astute business sense, will ensure that money stockpiles nicely for them in the bank. But remember, Scorpios are secretive individuals and they like to keep their financial affairs under wraps—even from those they consider to be their nearest and dearest.

SCORPIOS SHOULD

- *learn to be less jealous*
- *trust their partners*

SCORPIOS SHOULDN'T

- *be so suspicious*
- *become so vindictive when hurt in love*

SAGITTARIUS

BORN BETWEEN: NOVEMBER 22—DECEMBER 21

TURQUOISE

LIFE DRIVES

Incorrigibly cheerful and optimistic, Sagittarian enthusiasm gives the members of this sign a massive zest for life. Sporty and brave, these dynamic people are driven by seemingly blind faith, telling themselves that all is for the best in the best of possible worlds. And indeed, for them, it usually does turn out for the best in the end. These are born extroverts who, whether physically or metaphorically, like to roam free. Moreover, there's something of the visionary in every Sagittarian and, though natives of this group are often blunt and tactless, very often their words and ideas hit the mark.

AT WORK AND AT PLAY

Religion, politics, and the law are the traditional occupations that suit the nature and talents of this sign. But many Sagittarians find their way into schools and universities where they become dedicated and well-loved teachers and lecturers. Publishing, too, attracts these people, and if they write, there will be a strong philosophical or spiritual slant to their work. Whether it be as a main career or as a spare-time pursuit, one way or another, sport will figure highly in these people's lives.

PERSONALITY KEYNOTES

enthusiastic, optimistic, open, independent, warm, friendly, sociable, adventurous, excitable, open-minded, easy-going, lucky, idealistic, sincere, positive, tactless, impulsive, untidy, unpunctual

ASSOCIATIONS

❦ Symbol *Archer* ❦ Planetary Ruler *Jupiter* ❦ Element *Fire*
❦ Color *Purple* ❦ Flower *Narcissus*
❦ Stone *Turquoise*
❦ Lucky Number *9*
❦ Lucky Day *Thursday*

LOVE AND RELATIONSHIPS

Not the most constant of the signs, members of this group value their freedom and hate to be tied down. They are restless souls with a strong idealistic streak, which makes them seek knights in shining armor or damsels in distress. A partner who is prepared to share their dream and their sense of adventure will win the Sagittarian heart forever. In intimate relationships, love and laughter are essential, and a light-hearted attitude to life's problems will help to smooth the bumps through the inevitable ups and downs of life.

HEALTH AND WEALTH

Sagittarius governs hips and thighs, areas which tend to become overweight among natives of this sign, especially as middle-age approaches. Walking and riding, pursuits particularly associated with the Archer, form suitable exercises for this problem. However, accidents may affect their hips, so they should take precautions against any serious falls. In general strong and hearty types, the Sagittarian appetite for rich, spicy food can all too often take its toll on the liver.

Reputed to be the luckiest sign of the Zodiac, Sagittarians somehow always manage to land on their feet. This propitious streak follows them in their financial dealings and can, in some, fuel an urge to gamble or take heady risks. However, whether it is their happy-go-lucky natures, or whether Lady Luck especially smiles upon these, her favorites, the Sagittarian does seem to live a charmed and fortunate life.

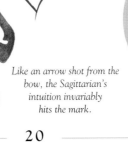

Like an arrow shot from the bow, the Sagittarian's intuition invariably hits the mark.

SAGITTARIANS SHOULD

• *learn to be more tactful*
• *use intuition when forming new relationships*

SAGITTARIANS SHOULDN'T

• *be so trusting*
• *reveal their innermost selves quite so readily to all and sundry*

CAPRICORN

BORN BETWEEN: DECEMBER 22—JANUARY 19

LIFE DRIVES

Arguably the most mature sign of the Zodiac, belonging to this group means that Capricorn natives are serious and sober individuals with a strong sense of built-in responsibility to protect and provide for others. These are solid-as-a-rock individuals who aim for the top—and usually get there. Ambitious and achievement-motivated, in their books, striving to attain and maintaining quality and high standards are essential. This pursuit of excellence can be interpreted, by some, as snobbishness, but, to the Capricorn, presenting a good self-image to the world is critically important.

CAPRICORNS SHOULD

• learn to let their hair down
• make a point of telling their loved ones how much they love them

CAPRICORNS SHOULDN'T

• put work before their emotional needs
• be quite so insensitive to the foibles of others

AT WORK AND AT PLAY

Success is life's driving force for this group of people. Few Capricorns will sit idly by when there is a job to be done, especially when the job in question will enable them to climb up one more rung of the ladder. For success means money and power and prestige—the essential ingredients that reward a life's work, according to the members of this sign. To their colleagues, they are rocks, towers of strength, who never flinch from their responsibilities. They are able to carry out their work with cool efficiency, often over and above the call of duty.

Tough and sure-footed like a mountain goat, Capricorns pick their way to the top.

LOVE AND RELATIONSHIPS

Creating a stable and secure environment for their partners and dependants is top of the agenda for members of this sign. So busy do they become in fulfilling this obligation, that Capricorns often forget the lighter side of life, or they neglect the emotional and spiritual needs of their loved ones. But, though they may come across as dour and unsentimental, make no mistake, these people have a soft and tender heart beating beneath their seemingly crusty exterior.

HEALTH AND WEALTH

Bones and, in particular, knees are the most vulnerable areas for Capricorns. In fact, problems with joints and cartilage are especially prevalent. The skin, too, can be a bugbear with allergies and nervous rashes breaking out at times of stress. Psychologically, black moods and depression can sometimes get the better of these natives when emotional problems can make them inward-looking, bringing to the fore a strong introspective streak which seems to be a characteristic of this sign.

With excellent money-making skills, Capricorns do well financially. They are instinctive savers, prepared to work hard and invest their earnings in safe, blue-chip companies. For these careful individuals, taking any sort of financial gamble is anathema. As far as they are concerned, money is far too difficult a commodity to come by, and they are not prepared to risk—and they never squander—a single penny of it without a very good reason.

GARNET

PERSONALITY KEYNOTES

practical, industrious, cautious, dependable, loyal, staunch, ambitious, determined, undemonstrative, self-controlled, honest, image-conscious, aloof, austere, loner, obsessed, conventional, conservative, old-fashioned, blunt

ASSOCIATIONS

⚜ Symbol *Goat*
⚜ Planetary Ruler *Saturn*
⚜ Element *Earth* ⚜ Color *Mid-Green*
⚜ Flower *Carnation*
⚜ Stone *Garnet, Onyx*
⚜ Lucky Number *7*
⚜ Lucky Day *Saturday*

AQUARIUS

BORN BETWEEN: **JANUARY 20—FEBRUARY 18**

LIFE DRIVES

Eccentric and individualistic are the adjectives that best describe those born at this time of the year. And indeed these are some of the most original and inventive people that one is ever likely to meet. As a whole, Aquarians have a tendency to challenge the norm, to shake people out of their cozy complacency. For they themselves have a strong streak of rebellion in their natures and, refusing to conform to society's mandate, many choose to lead less than conventional lives. Nevertheless, blessed with far-sighted ideas, Aquarians are driven by an extraordinary humanitarian zeal. Fueled by altruistic motives, they will lend support to those who are less fortunate than themselves.

AT WORK AND AT PLAY

An eye for innovation gives Aquarians the ability to become great social reformers. Many take their progressive ideas into broadcasting or else into the halls of academic life, since writing, researching, and experimenting come naturally to these gifted people. However, it is as inventors that they truly excel, often spotting the gap in the market, or recognizing the need for a product that will totally revolutionize our lives.

AQUARIANS SHOULD
• apologize when they're in the wrong
• avoid coming across as too detached

AQUARIANS SHOULDN'T
• be afraid of their feelings
• automatically assume partners will tolerate an "open" relationship

PERSONALITY KEYNOTES

altruistic, democratic, humanitarian, eccentric, rebellious, independent, sincere, inventive, intelligent, ingenious, communicative, lively, witty, emotionally detached, unconventional

ASSOCIATIONS

❆ Symbol *Water Bearer* ❆ Planetary Ruler *Uranus* ❆ Element *Air* ❆ Color *Electric Blue* ❆ Flower *Snowdrop* ❆ Stone *Amethyst* ❆ Lucky Number *6* ❆ Lucky Day *Saturday*

AMETHYST

LOVE AND RELATIONSHIPS

In all types of relationships, Aquarians are sincere, loyal, and truthful. However, when it comes to showing their emotions, it is apparent, time and time again, that they are simply not comfortable about laying their feelings bare. This is because they tend to intellectualize their emotions and, as a result, they can appear cool and remote. Yet, despite this aloofness, deep down the Aquarian is an intensely caring person. They make very good "shoulders to cry on" as they are very good listeners. More often than not, they will be able to give considered and impartial reasoning. When all is said and done, members of the Aquarian sign can make some of the most loving, caring, and solicitous partners one could ever wish to have.

HEALTH AND WEALTH

Those born under this sign are particularly vulnerable to twisted ankles, sprains, pulls to the hamstrings, and damage to

Pouring water on the Earth symbolizes the Aquarian's flow of imaginative ideas.

the muscles in the legs. Psychologically, any form of restriction, whether mental or physical, is bad for these types as they have a fear about being hemmed in. Vigorous sports, such as running, pumping iron, or aerobic workouts, are especially beneficial, particularly because a sluggish circulation is another weakness associated with this sign. Exercising out in the fresh air is recommended for boosting the circulation and toning the heart.

The world of high finance and business holds no thrills for the majority of Aquarians who prefer to save their income in secure deposit accounts. Risks, on the rare occasions they are taken, are usually thought through logically first, thereby limiting the chances of disaster. In general, these natives make their money through intellectual work, progressive ideas, or brilliant inventions.

PISCES

BORN BETWEEN: **FEBRUARY 19—MARCH 20**

LIFE DRIVES

Pisces folk are ruled by their feelings. This means that they go through life following their emotions, instinctively steering their way rather than working things out logically and rationally. Intuition is one of their strongest assets and they possess an inherent talent for tapping into other people's feelings and automatically sensing their states of mind and soul. This makes them sensitive and gentle creatures, as well as wonderfully sympathetic companions. Essentially dreamy and romantic, members of this sign tend to construct a fairytale world into which they can escape when their own lives get too tough to handle.

AT WORK AND AT PLAY

A wide range of professions suit the gifted and intuitive talents of this group. For a start, the Piscean sensitivity and empathy call many of these natives into counseling, clinical psychology, and alternative therapies. Some find their forte working for charitable organizations or for other caring institutions. Yet others turn to the world of music, literature, and the arts, where they can express their considerable artistic and imaginative abilities and find fulfilment through creative endeavor.

LOVE AND RELATIONSHIPS

Perhaps the most tender-hearted sign of the Zodiac, belonging to this group makes these natives sensitive and vulnerable. But, because they are so easy-going and, all too often adoring of their partners, Pisceans can be easily put upon. Loneliness is their biggest fear and they tolerate a lot so as not to be alone. In the right relationship, however, their romantic, understanding, and compassionate natures will know no bounds.

Like the fish swimming in opposite directions, Pisceans are torn between logic and emotion.

PERSONALITY KEYNOTES

impressionable, sensitive, intuitive, kind, creative, artistic, sympathetic, giving, understanding, dreamy, romantic, sensual, tender, soft-hearted, spiritual, passive, vague, irrational, hapless

ASSOCIATIONS

❧ Symbol *Fish* ❧ Planetary Ruler *Neptune* ❧ Element *Water* ❧ Color *Sea Green* ❧ Flower *Lilac* ❧ Stone *Aquamarine* ❧ Lucky Number *3* ❧ Lucky Day *Thursday*

AQUAMARINE

HEALTH AND WEALTH

Pisces rules the feet and many Pisceans suffer miserably with foot problems throughout their lives. Consequently, good-fitting shoes, even if expensive, are essential for their well-being. Pisceans are also prone to fretfulness and worry, which can take their toll on the stomach and digestive system, leading to ulcers. They succumb to disease more quickly than most if they follow a poor diet. Psychologically, members of this sign can all too easily become depressed and some may resort to alcohol or drugs in an attempt to lift their spirits.

They are trusting souls and in money matters they really need to be sure of those in whom they place their trust, for many Pisceans have been conned out of their life savings by unscrupulous "friends" or "advisers." However, members of this sign are indeed capable of generating wealth, usually through their prodigious creative talents, and they are best advised to put their money away safely in a bank.

PISCES SHOULD
• *sometimes take off their rose-colored spectacles*
• *learn to stand on their own two feet*

PISCES SHOULDN'T
• *always follow their emotions*
• *see themselves as a victim, or play the martyr quite so often*

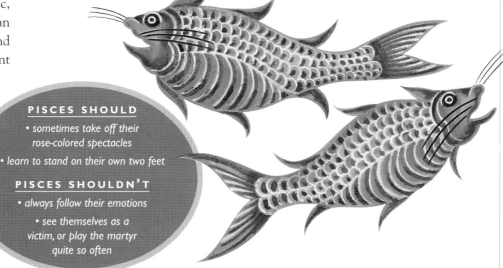

THE SYSTEM
OF CHINESE
ASTROLOGY

A BRIEF INTRODUCTION TO CHINESE ASTROLOGY

The astrology of the East is an intricate, complex science that requires a good deal of time and patience to fully appreciate its many intriguing subtleties. The system works on a multiplicity of levels, each fascinating in its own right. As a whole, it offers a wealth of information and invaluable insights into every aspect of an individual's character and way of life.

CYCLES WITHIN CYCLES

At the heart of its complexity lies the Oriental system of reckoning time, the key players being the Sun, Moon, and Jupiter, which are seen to traverse the heavens at vastly different speeds to one another.

The year is based on the movement of the Moon and calculated according to the lunar phases. So, New Year's Day can fall between late January and the end of February. Days are arranged into groups of ten, with twenty-four fortnights, each fifteen days long, forming a solar year.

To confuse matters further, the twelve-year period it takes Jupiter to orbit the Sun is known as a "Great Year." Five Great Years group together to form a grand sexagesimal cycle, which, once it has run its course, begins the process all over again.

All over the world the Chinese celebrate the New Year with a Spring Festival.

THE TWELVE ANIMAL SIGNS OF THE GREAT YEAR

Familiar to all Chinese people are the exotic Animals of Oriental astrology, each representing one year of the twelve-yearly cycle. The Animals run in strict sequence, beginning with the Rat, and followed in turn by the Ox, Tiger, Rabbit, Dragon, Snake, Horse, Monkey, Sheep, Rooster, Dog, and finally, the Pig.

Each Animal stands as a symbol, denoting the essential "character," "color," and "flavor" that influences all things that come into being in any one year. For example, people born in the Year of the Ox will have markedly different natures, talents, temperaments, and even different destinies to those who are born, say, in the Year of the Snake, Monkey, or Rooster. This notion of one's character being influenced by the year of birth is absolutely fundamental to Chinese astrology since it is the framework upon which an individual's personal horoscope is built.

ADDING THE LEVELS OF COMPLEXITY

Of course, to describe a person solely by the characteristics of his or her Animal sign would be to paint with a very broad brush, for no two Tigers are identical or two Dogs exactly alike, even though they may have been born in the same year. So, then, in order to explain what causes the subtleties of personality that differentiate one person from another, it is on the refinements of the sophisticated Oriental system that one must concentrate.

Most salient of these are the Elements that govern the years, the Yin-Yang polarity of each year and the hour in which an individual is born.

Jupiter, the planet of fortune, takes roughly twelve years to orbit the sun.

THE ELEMENTS

According to Chinese philosophy, five Elements—Wood, Fire, Earth, Metal, and Water, in that order—form the essential building blocks of all living things. Each Animal sign within its sixty-year framework is ruled by a different Element. So, for example, a person born in 1938 would be an Earth Tiger, one born in 1950 is a Metal Tiger, and in 1962 a Water Tiger, and so on. Each successive appearance of the Animal sign is modified by the characteristics of the next Element in turn, which help to distinguish one year's nativity from another under the same Animal sign.

The characteristics that are conferred by each of the Elements are as follows:

The twelve Chinese Animals divided into the yin-yang polarities.

ELEMENT	KEY CHARACTERISTICS
WOOD	warm, generous, considerate, elegant, cooperative
FIRE	dynamic, decisive, innovative, joyful, lucid
EARTH	honest, patient, responsible, industrious, prudent
METAL	strong, moral, ambitious, energetic, independent
WATER	flexible, persuasive, diplomatic, creative, kind

YIN AND YANG

The dynamic complementary forces that keep the universe in balance are known as Yin and Yang. Yin, seen as feminine and receptive, is associated with water, night, and the Moon. Yang, considered to be masculine and active, is associated with day, fire, and the Sun. Yin contains a seed of Yang, and vice versa, as represented by the central spots in the Yin-Yang symbol. The two forces interrelate, dominating and yielding by turn, waxing and waning like the day and night, summer and winter, birth and death. Balance between the two is the key to harmony.

Each Animal year is designated either as Yin or Yang, and therefore confers either a receptive or dominating undercurrent to the nature according to when an individual is born. Since the aim is to achieve equilibrium, recognizing which force underpins our birth time will enable each one of us to find ways of avoiding excesses, or shoring up a dearth of either in our lives.

THE HOUR OF BIRTH

The hour in which we are born adds yet another differentiating facet to our character. Like the years, the twelve double hours are also ruled by the same sequence of Animals, beginning with the Rat who rules the time between 11pm–1am. So, an individual who is born in a Tiger Year and in the hour of the Rabbit will have Tiger characteristics tempered by those of the Rabbit.

ANIMAL PROFILES

RAT	charming, charismatic, active, intuitive, lucky
OX	honest, solid, practical, steadfast, down-to-earth
TIGER	courageous, passionate, enthusiastic, optimistic
RABBIT	imaginative, sensitive, artistic, fussy, wise
DRAGON	dynamic, colorful, original, confident, popular
SNAKE	subtle, shrewd, perspicacious, stylish, proud
HORSE	busy, volatile, witty, vivacious, independent
SHEEP	arty, cultured, gentle, loving, self-indulgent
MONKEY	ingenious, intelligent, versatile, quick-witted
ROOSTER	passionate, focused, industrious, tidy
DOG	reliable, caring, honest, devoted, unselfish
PIG	sincere, gregarious, generous, materialistic

THE CHINESE YEAR CHART

By observing recurring planetary patterns, the Ancient Chinese sages devised a system for reckoning time. Based principally on the phases of the Moon, but taking into account the rotations of Jupiter and Earth around the Sun, they drew up a precise, but complex, calendar.

In later years, the calendar was simplified by grouping the years into blocks of twelve and, later still, by introducing the twelve Animals which now give their names to each of the years.

The twelve years run in strict sequence and in rotation: Rat, Ox, Tiger, Rabbit, Dragon, Snake, Horse, Sheep, Monkey, Rooster, Dog, and, finally, Pig.

The events of each year, the Chinese believe, are affected by cosmic or universal influences specific only to that twelve-month period so that any one year will be very different from the next. Those influences are symbolized by the Animal that "governs" the year so when we understand the nature of each Animal, we start to see what sort of year lies in store.

A clever and ingenious mind is represented by the Monkey—the ninth sign of the cycle.

YEAR	FROM—TO	ANIMAL	ELEMENT		ASPECT
1912	Feb 18, 1912—Feb 5, 1913	Rat	Water	+	Yang
1913	Feb 6, 1913—Jan 25, 1914	Ox	Water	–	Yin
1914	Jan 26, 1914—Feb 13, 1915	Tiger	Wood	+	Yang
1915	Feb 14, 1915—Feb 2, 1916	Rabbit	Wood	–	Yin
1916	Feb 3, 1916—Jan 22, 1917	Dragon	Fire	+	Yang
1917	Jan 23, 1917—Feb 10, 1918	Snake	Fire	–	Yin
1918	Feb 11, 1918—Jan 31, 1919	Horse	Earth	+	Yang
1919	Feb 1, 1919—Feb 19, 1920	Sheep	Earth	–	Yin
1920	Feb 20, 1920—Feb 7, 1921	Monkey	Metal	+	Yang
1921	Feb 8, 1921—Jan 27, 1922	Rooster	Metal	–	Yin
1922	Jan 28, 1922—Feb 15, 1923	Dog	Water	+	Yang
1923	Feb 16, 1923—Feb 4, 1924	Pig	Water	–	Yin
1924	Feb 5, 1924—Jan 24, 1925	Rat	Wood	+	Yang
1925	Jan 25, 1925—Feb 12, 1926	Ox	Wood	–	Yin
1926	Feb 13, 1926—Feb 1, 1927	Tiger	Fire	+	Yang
1927	Feb 2, 1927—Jan 22, 1928	Rabbit	Fire	–	Yin
1928	Jan 23, 1928—Feb 9, 1929	Dragon	Earth	+	Yang
1929	Feb 10, 1929—Jan 29, 1930	Snake	Earth	–	Yin
1930	Jan 30, 1930—Feb 16, 1931	Horse	Metal	+	Yang
1931	Feb 17, 1931—Feb 5, 1932	Sheep	Metal	–	Yin
1932	Feb 6, 1932—Jan 25, 1933	Monkey	Water	+	Yang
1933	Jan 26, 1933—Feb 13, 1934	Rooster	Water	–	Yin
1934	Feb 14, 1934—Feb 3, 1935	Dog	Wood	+	Yang
1935	Feb 4, 1935—Jan 23, 1936	Pig	Wood	–	Yin
1936	Jan 24, 1936—Feb 10, 1937	Rat	Fire	+	Yang
1937	Feb 11, 1937—Jan 30, 1938	Ox	Fire	–	Yin
1938	Jan 31, 1938—Feb 18, 1939	Tiger	Earth	+	Yang
1939	Feb 19, 1939—Feb 7, 1940	Rabbit	Earth	–	Yin
1940	Feb 8, 1940—Jan 26, 1941	Dragon	Metal	+	Yang
1941	Jan 27, 1941—Feb 14, 1942	Snake	Metal	–	Yin
1942	Feb 15, 1942—Feb 4, 1943	Horse	Water	+	Yang
1943	Feb 5, 1943—Jan 24, 1944	Sheep	Water	–	Yin
1944	Jan 25, 1944—Feb 12, 1945	Monkey	Wood	+	Yang
1945	Feb 13, 1945—Feb 1, 1946	Rooster	Wood	–	Yin
1946	Feb 2, 1946—Jan 21, 1947	Dog	Fire	+	Yang
1947	Jan 22, 1947—Feb 9, 1948	Pig	Fire	–	Yin
1948	Feb 10, 1948—Jan 28, 1949	Rat	Earth	+	Yang
1949	Jan 29, 1949—Feb 16, 1950	Ox	Earth	–	Yin
1950	Feb 17, 1950—Feb 5, 1951	Tiger	Metal	+	Yang
1951	Feb 6, 1951—Jan 26, 1952	Rabbit	Metal	–	Yin
1952	Jan 27, 1952—Feb 13, 1953	Dragon	Water	+	Yang
1953	Feb 14, 1953—Feb 2, 1954	Snake	Water	–	Yin
1954	Feb 3, 1954—Jan 23, 1955	Horse	Wood	+	Yang
1955	Jan 24, 1955—Feb 11, 1956	Sheep	Wood	–	Yin
1956	Feb 12, 1956—Jan 30, 1957	Monkey	Fire	+	Yang
1957	Jan 31, 1957—Feb 17, 1958	Rooster	Fire	–	Yin
1958	Feb 18, 1958—Feb 7, 1959	Dog	Earth	+	Yang
1959	Feb 8, 1959—Jan 27, 1960	Pig	Earth	–	Yin

YEAR	FROM—TO	ANIMAL	ELEMENT	ASPECT	
1960	Jan 28, 1960—Feb 14, 1961	Rat	Metal	+	Yang
1961	Feb 15, 1961—Feb 4, 1962	Ox	Metal	–	Yin
1962	Feb 5, 1962—Jan 24, 1963	Tiger	Water	+	Yang
1963	Jan 25, 1963—Feb 12, 1964	Rabbit	Water	–	Yin
1964	Feb 13, 1964—Feb 1, 1965	Dragon	Wood	+	Yang
1965	Feb 2, 1965—Jan 20, 1966	Snake	Wood	–	Yin
1966	Jan 21, 1966—Feb 8, 1967	Horse	Fire	+	Yang
1967	Feb 9, 1967—Jan 29, 1968	Sheep	Fire	–	Yin
1968	Jan 30, 1968—Feb 16, 1969	Monkey	Earth	+	Yang
1969	Feb 17, 1969—Feb 5, 1970	Rooster	Earth	–	Yin
1970	Feb 6, 1970—Jan 26, 1971	Dog	Metal	+	Yang
1971	Jan 27, 1971—Feb 15, 1972	Pig	Metal	–	Yin
1972	Feb 16, 1972—Feb 2, 1973	Rat	Water	+	Yang
1973	Feb 3, 1973—Jan 22, 1974	Ox	Water	–	Yin
1974	Jan 23, 1974—Feb 10, 1975	Tiger	Wood	+	Yang
1975	Feb 11, 1975—Jan 30, 1976	Rabbit	Wood	–	Yin
1976	Jan 31, 1976—Feb 17, 1977	Dragon	Fire	+	Yang
1977	Feb 18, 1977—Feb 6, 1978	Snake	Fire	–	Yin
1978	Feb 7, 1978—Jan 27, 1979	Horse	Earth	+	Yang
1979	Jan 28, 1979—Feb 15, 1980	Sheep	Earth	–	Yin
1980	Feb 16, 1980—Feb 4, 1981	Monkey	Metal	+	Yang
1981	Feb 5, 1981—Jan 24, 1982	Rooster	Metal	–	Yin
1982	Jan 25, 1982—Feb 12, 1983	Dog	Water	+	Yang
1983	Feb 13, 1983—Feb 1, 1984	Pig	Water	-	Yin
1984	Feb 2, 1984—Feb 19, 1985	Rat	Wood	+	Yang
1985	Feb 20, 1985—Feb 8, 1986	Ox	Wood	–	Yin
1986	Feb 9, 1986—Jan 28, 1987	Tiger	Fire	+	Yang
1987	Jan 29, 1987—Feb 16, 1988	Rabbit	Fire	–	Yin
1988	Feb 17, 1988—Feb 5, 1989	Dragon	Earth	+	Yang
1989	Feb 6, 1989—Jan 26, 1990	Snake	Earth	–	Yin
1990	Jan 27, 1990—Feb 14, 1991	Horse	Metal	+	Yang
1991	Feb 15, 1991—Feb 3, 1992	Sheep	Metal	–	Yin
1992	Feb 4, 1992—Jan 22, 1993	Monkey	Water	+	Yang
1993	Jan 23, 1993—Feb 9, 1994	Rooster	Water	–	Yin
1994	Feb 10, 1994—Jan 30, 1995	Dog	Wood	+	Yang
1995	Jan 31, 1995—Feb 18, 1996	Pig	Wood	–	Yin
1996	Feb 19, 1996—Feb 6, 1997	Rat	Fire	+	Yang
1997	Feb 7, 1997—Jan 27, 1998	Ox	Fire	–	Yin
1998	Jan 28, 1998—Feb 15, 1999	Tiger	Earth	+	Yang
1999	Feb 16, 1999—Feb 4, 2000	Rabbit	Earth	–	Yin
2000	Feb 5, 2000—Jan 23, 2001	Dragon	Metal	+	Yang
2001	Jan 24, 2001—Feb 11, 2002	Snake	Metal	–	Yin
2002	Feb 12, 2002—Jan 31, 2003	Horse	Water	+	Yang
2003	Feb 1, 2003—Jan 21, 2004	Sheep	Water	–	Yin
2004	Jan 22, 2004—Feb 8, 2005	Monkey	Wood	+	Yang
2005	Feb 9, 2005—Jan 28, 2006	Rooster	Wood	–	Yin
2006	Jan 29, 2006—Feb 17, 2007	Dog	Fire	+	Yang
2007	Feb 18, 2007—Feb 6, 2008	Pig	Fire	–	Yin
2008	Feb 7, 2008—Jan 25, 2009	Rat	Earth	+	Yang
2009	Jan 26, 2009—Feb 13, 2010	Ox	Earth	–	Yin
2010	Feb 14, 2010—Feb 2, 2011	Tiger	Metal	+	Yang
2011	Feb 3, 2011—Jan 22, 2012	Rabbit	Metal	–	Yin
2012	Jan 23, 2012—Feb 9, 2013	Dragon	Water	+	Yang
2013	Feb 10, 2013—Jan 30, 2014	Snake	Water	–	Yin
2014	Jan 31, 2014—Feb 18, 2015	Horse	Wood	+	Yang
2015	Feb 19, 2015—Feb 7, 2016	Sheep	Wood	–	Yin
2016	Feb 8, 2016—Jan 27, 2017	Monkey	Fire	+	Yang
2017	Jan 28, 2017—Feb 15, 2018	Rooster	Fire	–	Yin
2018	Feb 16, 2018—Feb 4, 2019	Dog	Earth	+	Yang
2019	Feb 5, 2019—Jan 24, 2020	Pig	Earth	–	Yin

Sixth in the order of the Animal signs, the Snake represents inscrutability.

In the same way, all the people born in one particular year will also be affected by those influences and so they will have characteristics and personality traits in common—but they will be very different from people born the year before or the year after them. And because the same trends recur every twelve years, so they will also share similarities with others born under the same Animal year sign, although they may be 12, 24, 36, or even 144 years apart.

Solid and hardworking, the Ox is second in the Animal sequence.

RAT

ESSENTIAL NATURE

Leadership sits well on the shoulders of those who are born in the year of the Rat. For, just as this is the first sign of the twelve, so Rats like to be at the head of the game, at the forefront of the action, and where they can give the orders. Restless and inquisitive, these are busy people whose minds are constantly on the go. Above all, they are clever and instinctively shrewd. As the Chinese say, even in times of scarcity, Rats somehow always know where sacks of grain can be found. No wonder, then, that these remarkably resourceful creatures are the supreme opportunists and arch survivors of the Animal signs.

DREAMS AND DRIVES

Rats can never let a challenge pass, for these excitable people are born with a keen sense of adventure and enjoy the frisson that comes with living on the edge. Foreign travel is their particular joy. But, in truth, it is power and money that are the underlying motivating forces in the lives of those who belong to this sign.

The Rat is the resourceful leader of the pack.

THE YEAR OF THE RAT

This year is auspicious for all new beginnings. It is a time to turn over a new leaf and take a fresh look at the world. Spirits rise in Rat years and market economies begin to show an upward turn. Discoveries and inventions are especially prevalent and, for all, opportunities abound.

SIGN DATA

Rank First in order
Symbol of Charm
Chinese Name SHU
Ruling hour 11pm–12.59am

IN THEIR HABITAT

Happy homemakers, members of the Rat sign put the comfort of themselves and their family above fashions and the latest trends. The members of this sign are domesticated people who rejoice in their family and home. Avid collectors, the Rat household will be stuffed to the gunwales with their acquisitions and souvenirs—the amassing of which appears to be a lifetime pursuit, picked up from antique shops, bric-a-brac stalls, and their foreign destinations. Blue is the color associated with this sign, which is likely to be evident in the decor and furnishings of their comfortable homes.

IN THE WORLD

Blessed with inventive minds, members of the Rat sign are known for living by their wits. The tedium of routine dulls their senses, so these people need to work in careers that will stimulate their minds, and in occupations that offer flexible working conditions. They will not enjoy a nine-to-five desk job, as Rat folk need space and flexibility to meet their potential. In fact, they function best as bosses, allowing them the freedom to use their sixth sense to steer them toward opportunities and away from any potential trouble. Invaluable as advisers, shrewd in the financial sector, daring in sports, whatever they do, the members of the Rat fraternity will bring innovation and fresh insight into their work.

CHARM

AS FRIENDS AND LOVERS

Undeniably charming, the Rats are popular and everybody's friend. Generally cheerful and sociable, they always have an interesting tale to tell. Fiercely loyal, Rats are ardent lovers and generous to those they hold dear.

Ox

ESSENTIAL NATURE

Blessed with sterling qualities, members of this sign are noted for their diligence and industriousness. These are strong, solid, and practical individuals, reputed for their common sense and their ability to keep their feet firmly on the ground. Characteristically, Ox-born folk are resolute and persistent, possessing a seemingly indefatigable endurance that enables them to keep on going through thick and thin. At times, this very determination can verge on the stubborn, for once they have made up their minds on a course of action, very little will deter them from reaching their objective.

DREAMS AND DRIVES

Members of the Ox fraternity are staunch citizens who believe in tradition and who fight to maintain the status quo. Security is, in fact, one of their main drives in life. In general, they are not risk-takers since it is the safe and the familiar that draws them. Because of this, many tend to return again and again to favorite haunts, places where they are assured they can find solace and peace of mind.

INDUSTRY

IN THEIR HABITAT

A rural rather than urban setting appeals to members of this sign. But if an Ox were to live in town, a garden would be essential because they like to be close to Nature. For this group, home is very definitely where the heart is, and home must not only be comfortable, but also a safe haven and retreat. Violet is the Ox color but so too are the muted shades of the countryside—golds, greens, and russet brown.

THE YEAR OF THE OX

These years are characterized by steady growth. They are times of harvest when we reap what we have sown in previous years. Essentially conservative, tastes and fashions veer toward the classical and value for money is the order of the day.

SIGN DATA

Rank Second in order
Symbol of Industry
Chinese Name NIU
Ruling hour 1am–2.59am

IN THE WORLD

Dutiful and reliable, the Ox is born with broad shoulders capable of bearing responsibility well. Employers will rely increasingly on these individuals, knowing that they will carry out their designated tasks with thoroughness and efficiency. While many members of this sign choose to work for large organizations and corporate institutions, they are likely to find a small niche for themselves, as they work best on their own rather than as part of a team. Although they may toil away, seemingly in the background, their industriousness does not go unnoticed. Sooner or later, the Ox does make it to the top.

AS FRIENDS AND LOVERS

This is not the most out-going of the signs, for people who are born in the Year of the Ox tend to keep themselves to themselves. Usually, they have a small, but select and trustworthy circle of friends to whom they are very loyal. In love, they are not overly romantic or sentimental, but they are deeply devoted to their mates and, once they have given their hearts, the chances are they will not roam.

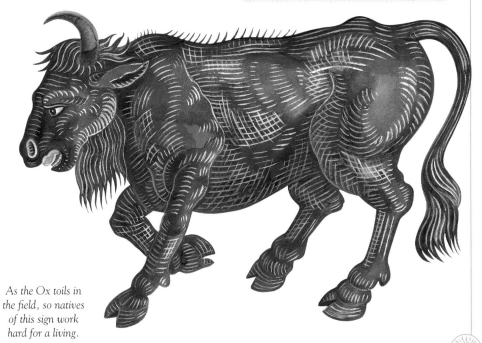

As the Ox toils in the field, so natives of this sign work hard for a living.

TIGER

ESSENTIAL NATURE

Assertive and courageous, Tigers cannot pass up a challenge. Where lesser mortals demur, the Tiger rushes in. Where others would look the other way, the Tiger confronts the situation head on. And when no one else will defend the weak, the neglected, and the downtrodden, the Tiger, fearless of danger, will wield a sword against the oppressor. For these are truly humanitarian creatures—impetuous and fiery perhaps—but always warm-hearted, open, and honest as the day is long. According to the Chinese, having a plucky Tiger in the house is the best insurance against fire, theft, and all manner of things that go bump in the night.

DREAMS AND DRIVES

The righting of injustice fires the Tiger's soul. People born in this year are endowed with a protecting spirit and will fight for their own rights and for the rights of those they love. Arch tacticians, Tigers can be unpredictable and should never be underestimated. They like to have their fingers on the pulse and need to feel they are always several moves ahead of the game. Driven by an old-fashioned code of honor and chivalry, they are fair-minded people and honest brokers who always show good manners to anyone with whom they deal.

COURAGE

IN THEIR HABITAT

Originality is one of the Tiger's trademarks and this is reflected in Tigers' homes. Members of this sign are not afraid to experiment with color, texture, and light. They like to be different from the crowd and will decorate their interiors adventurously. Here

THE YEAR OF THE TIGER

Drama, tension, upheaval, and disaster often accompany a Tiger year. This is a time when unusual weather conditions can be expected, when daring deeds take place, and when the unexpected in politics and finances becomes the norm. It is an exciting year when the vibrancy of life quickens the pulse and the winners are the daring and the brave.

SIGN DATA

Rank Third in order
Symbol of Courage
Chinese Name HU
Ruling hour 3am–4.59am

is found the unusual—innovative ideas and eclectic collections all blended together with truly inimitable style.

IN THE WORLD

Intelligent, alert, and far-sighted, members of this sign are quick learners and can pick up a skill in the twinkling of an eye. They find it easy to move between jobs, juggling several tasks in the air at the same time and changing careers completely at least once, but usually more, in a lifetime. These people are happiest working with a varied portfolio and at their best when they are in charge.

True to the animal that represents their year, Tiger people are brave and bold.

AS FRIENDS AND LOVERS

Genial and likeable, Tigers will always collect friends and admirers wherever they go throughout their lives. As lovers they are ardent and passionate, the true romantics of the Zodiac, who are also endowed with a healthy sex drive. These people carry about them a frisson of excitement and

even a hint of danger, which members of the opposite sex find irresistibly appealing. Warm and generous-hearted, Tigers are at their happiest in a close and loving relationship, but one in which their partner is prepared to turn a blind eye to the odd peccadillo here and there.

RABBIT

ESSENTIAL NATURE

The least aggressive of all the 12 signs, Rabbits are sensitive people and known as the peacemakers of the world. They abhor violence in all its forms and will use any means at their disposal to avoid confrontation and unpleasantness. Rabbits are wise people, born with an innate understanding of the world and a deep perspicacity that belies their seemingly nonchalant behavior. Highly cultured and abundantly gifted with creative talent, members of this group have refined tastes. They are stylish people with a huge capacity for appreciating art and an exquisite eye for beauty.

DREAMS AND DRIVES

A strong sense of belonging and an intense love of family are the driving forces that underlay the Rabbit psyche. Essentially, these people need to feel part of a group and will while away many a happy hour in conversation. Indeed, it's no secret that Rabbits especially delight in gossip!

IN THEIR HABITAT

Home, for Rabbits, is the center of their universe. It is because of this that they pour immense energy, love, and money into creating the loveliest of environments in which to live. Their good taste and excellent sense of style guarantees that the Rabbit's house will be chic and elegant. And, since Rabbits are some of the greatest collectors of art, fine prints, porcelain, antiques, and artistic treasures of all kinds will be in evidence all around. Green, the color associated with the Rabbit, is often used in the shades of eau de nil, jade, or sage to produce the cool, chic refinement that characterizes the sophistication of this sign.

Refined and sensitive, those born in the Year of the Rabbit are creative souls.

庭
和

PEACE

THE YEAR OF THE RABBIT

A comparatively peaceful time in which conciliatory measures, agreements, and diplomatic settlements will make headline news. Family matters and issues concerning women and children come to the fore. Medical advances can be expected, welfare reforms will be debated, and the arts will be given greater prominence.

SIGN DATA

Rank Fourth in order
Symbol of Peace
Chinese Name TU
Ruling hour 5am–6.59am

IN THE WORLD

With their intelligence, their psychological penetration, and their formidable powers of persuasion, Rabbits make supreme diplomats and fine negotiators. Hence, many gravitate toward the diplomatic services, public relations, and the legal profession. Alternatively, their creative talents lend themselves to the world of music and the arts, so that Rabbits will be found in the media, design studios, orchestras, and fashion. Another positive side to their nature, their nurturing and caring instinct, often takes members of this sign into the medical or counseling fields. With their ability to listen to people's problems and their excellent bedside manner, people in the Rabbit fraternity make sensitive doctors and nurses, and some of the best psychotherapists in the business.

AS FRIENDS AND LOVERS

Rabbits are just happy to be one of the crowd. Simply being accepted as a member of the group or the club is reward enough for these social creatures who take great comfort in being with like-minded individuals. As friends, they are sympathetic, understanding, and always ready with a wise or comforting word. Aloofness masks a soft, romantic, and nostalgic heart and, as lovers, Rabbits tend to be sensual and considerate. Their mothering instinct is ever present beneath the surface and, on occasion, may spill over the top and turn into smothering and possessiveness as far as partners and loved ones are concerned.

DRAGON

YEARS OF THE DRAGON: 1904 * 1916 * 1928 * 1940 * 1952 * 1964 * 1976 * 1988 * 2000 * 2012

ESSENTIAL NATURE

Exotic and dynamic, Dragons are free spirits and essentially a law unto themselves. All members born into this sign tend to be extremely charismatic. They invariably lead a high-profile existence, since they like to court the limelight. They are fortunate individuals, seemingly watched over by Lady Luck for, no matter what mishap occurs, they always seem to land on their feet and walk away smiling. Truly original and extroverted, their enthusiasm is contagious and their optimism has the power to brighten even the gloomiest day.

DREAMS AND DRIVES

To the Chinese, the Dragon has traditionally been the symbol of power and this, indeed, is the potent motivating force that underlies the dreams and actions of people born under this sign. To be in the driving seat, to carry authority, to be honored, respected, and to become a person of influence are overriding ambitions of these dynamic folk. "No" is one of the biggest

THE YEAR OF THE DRAGON

Usually a dramatic year, this is a time to think big. The more spectacular, the more unusual, and the more bizarre, the better the chances of success. With an undercurrent of luck and the feel-good factor sweeping through the year, the auspices are favorable for marriage, for starting a business or launching a brand new idea.

SIGN DATA

Rank Fifth in order
Symbol of Luck
Chinese Name LONG
Ruling hour 7am–8.59am

spurs to their energy. To be told that a pet project will not work, that a cherished plan cannot be implemented, or that an idea they have been considering is simply unfeasible is enough to send the Dragon into overdrive. Then, he or she will work like fury, even moving mountains if necessary, just to prove that the task can be done.

IN THEIR HABITAT

Dragons are not the most domestic of creatures, their place being out in the big wide world among their adoring public. Consequently, they may not spend as much time at home as other Animal signs might. But, entirely consistent with their mega personalities, their homes, too, must have a sense of the grand and the imposing about them. Interiors belonging to the Dragon, therefore, are often opulent with rich colors, such as red and gold, to create a sumptuous ambiance that reflects their own prestige.

IN THE WORLD

Success and the Dragon go together. These are people with big ideas, who are supremely confident and utterly irrepressible. Dragons, it appears, have the power to make the impossible possible. They are complete dynamos of energy who blast their way through life, and for them no challenge is too large to be met and conquered. They are big spenders and they are not afraid to take risks with their finances as well as their careers, but somehow they always manage to win through. The Dragon's original mentality brings a fresh approach into any career they choose, but their talents are perhaps best suited to the world of entertainment.

LUCK

Symbol of money and luck, a Dragon in the house brings good fortune.

AS FRIENDS AND LOVERS

Magnetic personalities, Dragon-born folk are affable types and never short of friends, despite the fact that they are perfectly capable of relying on themselves. Fundamentally loyal and true, they cannot forgive treachery or disloyalty from partners or friends. Though there is a tendency for the free-spirited Dragon to remain single, a partner who is intelligent, witty, and amusing stands a good chance of winning the Dragon's heart.

SNAKE

Subtle and seductive, people born in this year possess bewitching charm.

ESSENTIAL NATURE

Shrewd and subtle, the Snake watches and waits. This is not an impulsive sign. Instead, its members tend to be private people, calm, secretive, and reserved. Moreover, behind their observant gaze lies a careful, analytical mind, which gives this group an exquisite eye for detail and an almost infallible ability to get straight to the crux of the matter. These thoughtful people are endowed with wisdom and a deep philosophical understanding of the vagaries of life. It is for this talent, and for the fact that they need a life which is financially secure, that Snakes are known as "the guardians of the treasure."

DREAMS AND DRIVES

The world of the cut and thrust is definitely not for the Snake, since members of this sign crave peace and tranquility. For it is mental energy rather than physical dynamism that drives the Snake on. Sitting in quiet contemplation is their preferred state of being. Snakes do not like to be rattled.

IN THEIR HABITAT

Quality rather than quantity prevails in the Snake household. And, while style and elegance are important, it is deep comfort and luxury that these people most want to achieve. One house never seems to be enough for Snakes. They either move several times throughout their lives or they have more than one house to their names.

IN THE WORLD

Intuitive when handling people and astute in their dealings, there's a bit of the Machiavelli in the heart of every Snake. These people work in subtle ways, playing their cards close to their chests until the last moment. Capable of psychological insights that can penetrate the very depths of a person's soul, members of the Snake sign make excellent psychotherapists. Other branches of science and technology draw them too, and so do philosophy and politics. A talent for gathering information and assimilating facts of all kinds stands them in good stead in any form of research in which they invariably excel.

THE YEAR OF THE SNAKE

Snakes are arch scandalmongers and, in this year, all sorts of indiscretions will come to light. Political intrigue, sexual peccadillos, and improper dealings will hit the news. Reading the small print is essential as duplicity in all aspects of life appears to be rife. Issues concerning morality will be aired, as will matters connected with fertility and reproduction. Economically, the financial markets will be buoyant.

SIGN DATA

Rank Sixth in order
Symbol of Sagacity
Chinese Name SHE
Ruling hour 9am–10.59am

SAGACITY

AS FRIENDS AND LOVERS

Snakes make powerful friends but potent enemies. Should they ever be crossed, they will simply bide their time until they can strike the most effectively—and strike they will, with deadly aim and no quarter given. These are extremely selective people with exceptionally high standards, and when it comes to choosing a partner, they make sure that it is done with care and discernment. Once committed, though, they can become jealous and possessive. Prime sensualists, Snakes are very intense lovers and delight in the pleasures of the flesh.

HORSE

YEARS OF THE HORSE: 1906 ✳ 1918 ✳ 1930 ✳ 1942 ✳ 1954 ✳ 1966 ✳ 1978 ✳ 1990 ✳ 2002 ✳ 2014

ESSENTIAL NATURE

Bright, social, and bursting with energy, Horse individuals can be the life and soul of the party. They are blessed with sparkling wit and a scintillating mind, and can carry on four or five conversations at the same time without losing the thread of any for a single moment. Vivacious, lively, and full of irrepressible enthusiasm, they take life at a gallop and cram more into one day than others do in a week. Freedom and independence are as essential to them as the air they breathe. The members of this sign need to feel free to come and go as they please and, should they ever feel the reins tightening, they will simply kick up their heels and gallop off to pastures new.

DREAMS AND DRIVES

Members of the Horse fraternity can be erratic and volatile creatures who cannot tolerate a routine, humdrum existence. A low boredom threshold keeps them busy and drives them to act on impulse. Travel is a particular love, since they are born with itchy feet, sometimes taking off on a whim, just pausing long enough to throw a toothbrush and change of clothes into a bag.

THE YEAR OF THE HORSE

Trading is brisk and emotions are volatile in this fast-paced and exciting year. Fluctuating fortunes, both on a global and personal level, can be expected with spending and borrowing running out of control. Sports and outdoor pursuits, however, do well.

SIGN DATA

Rank Seventh in order
Symbol of Fervor
Chinese Name MA
Ruling hour 11am–12.59pm

IN THEIR HABITAT

A lively, stimulating environment tends to surround Horse-born folk, who extend a warm welcome to all and sundry who drop in to visit. For these people love to chat and make excellent hosts, providing a convivial atmosphere with friendly informality. Members of this sign are highly skilled with their hands and evidence of their handiwork is all around—although all too often in the form of half-finished projects that were abandoned in midair when something more exciting came along to grab their attention! Colors associated with this sign are golds, yellows, and oranges, all blended imaginatively to produce comfort and practicality with flair. Rigorous housework, however, is not a favored pastime.

IN THE WORLD

Versatility, a razor-sharp mentality, and the ability to pick up new skills at a glance make these people infinitely suitable for almost any profession that they care to take up. However, their verbal acuity and brilliant linguistic talents lend themselves best to the media and to the world of communication. Guiding tours, or working in sales, translation, journalism, or information technology are all careers that attract these agile minds.

AS FRIENDS AND LOVERS

The good humor and easy-going disposition that is characteristic of this sign ensures that its members are popular, guaranteeing them a good following of friends. Despite their frequently whimsical nature, they do like to feel they are part of a group and are staunchly loyal to their friends and family. In matters of the heart, the Horse is blind and tends to throw all caution to the wind, falling in love too quickly and too often for comfort.

The need to kick up their heels and gallop off into the sunset is ever present in Horse-born people.

FERVOR

SHEEP

ESSENTIAL NATURE

Gentle and cultured, people born in the Year of the Sheep are artistic souls. This is a passive and receptive group and its members are instinctively the nurturing and caring kind. It is not in their nature to protest, rebel, or buck the system since disagreement and aggression seriously upset their systems. They want life to be "neat and tidy," with no raw edges, no roughness or unpleasantness of any description. Kind, helpful, and considerate to others, their thoughtfulness is often repaid throughout their lifetimes. Indeed, fortune favors these folk who somehow manage to attract success and money wherever they go.

DREAMS AND DRIVES

Members of the Sheep clan make contented followers, for these people are not born to lead and are, in fact, uncomfortable if they have to take the reins into their own hands. To be cossetted and protected, cushioned from strife, and sheltered from the ills of the world is a fundamental need of this sign. Taking life at a gentle pace, enjoying the tranquility of Nature, and absorbing the beauties of music and the arts, are all their hearts desire.

IN THEIR HABITAT

Most Sheep are contentedly domesticated and revel in homely pursuits. Whether male or female, both are homemakers par excellence. They derive great pleasure in pottering around their homes, making jam, arranging flowers, cooking for the family, and generally making a cozy nest for themselves and their loved ones. Traditionalists at heart, their environment tends toward the classical, sumptuous but at the same time elegant. These are people who love ease, so they will invest in all manner of modern conveniences to take the drudgery out of housework and give themselves more time to pursue their artistic passions.

IN THE WORLD

The inborn artistic sensitivity associated with this sign draws its members to the world of the arts. Many become gifted performers, excelling in singing, acting, or playing a musical instrument. Design and painting, too, are talents in which they shine. Whatever they do, these people are never short of fans or patrons. Moreover, their work tends to be popular with the masses, which is good news for their bank accounts, and just as well, since Sheep do have expensive tastes and spend money quite liberally! If they choose not to gravitate toward an artistic career, then their nurturing instincts may well point them in the direction of the caring professions. Social work, alternative therapies, and complementary medicine all appeal.

THE YEAR OF THE SHEEP

In general, a tranquil time when fashion and the arts come under good auspices. People will attend to domestic matters, issues concerning personal relationships, and the family unit will be discussed. Politically, this is a year of reconciliation, of diplomatic moves, and the healing of rifts.

SIGN DATA

Rank Eighth in order
Symbol of The Arts
Chinese Name YANG
Ruling hour 1pm–2.59pm

Of a passive disposition, those born in Sheep years are essentially gentle souls.

妍 美
狡 術

THE ARTS

AS FRIENDS AND LOVERS

Most Sheep-born individuals have a huge network of acquaintances, but a small coterie of true friends. Perhaps this is because it is not in the nature of the Sheep to talk intimately or to get close to other people without being very, very sure of their ground. Or perhaps it is that they do not easily trust others for fear of being hurt or let down. However, those they do trust remain their friends for life. Interestingly, these family-oriented people are made for marriage and are at their happiest in a close-knit unit, preferably as part of an extended clan.

MONKEY

ESSENTIAL NATURE

With one of the sharpest minds of all the Animal signs, the clever, quick-witted Monkey is able to dance rings around everyone else. Members of this group are bright, alert creatures, who are able to size up a situation in the twinkling of an eye and comfortably adapt to any circumstance or company in which they find themselves. Masters and mistresses of psychological penetration, they have an inborn understanding of what makes people tick. Of course this is a talent that comes in handy in their everyday social dealings, but it also enables them to manipulate people and engineer situations to their own advantage. Charming, funny, and full of high jinks, there's never a dull moment when a Monkey is around.

IMAGINATION

DREAMS AND DRIVES

In life, Monkeys seek amusement. For them, monotony is a killer, so it's a racy, pacy sort of life they're after—plenty of action, plenty of people, plenty to entertain themselves with. It's well-known that Monkeys are mischievous, and because they are arch manipulators, they enjoy stirring up people and situations simply to see what happens next. For these people, life is too short to hang around digging deeply for facts. Instead, they want to take in a little of everything because they cannot bear to miss a single trick.

IN THEIR HABITAT

The noisy hubbub of urban life thrills the senses of the Monkey so these folk are made for the frenetic activities of the city. Even when they go on vacation, it's the bright lights that draw

THE YEAR OF THE MONKEY

A progressive, upbeat swing usually accompanies the Year of the Monkey, with communications high on the agenda. But to succeed at this time, it is essential to keep one's wits well honed since a good deal of chicanery abounds. Nothing in the Monkey year is straightforward, so plans must be double-checked and extra insurances taken out for good measure.

SIGN DATA

Rank Ninth in order
Symbol of Imagination
Chinese Name HOU
Ruling hour 3pm–4.59pm

them and they are more likely to head for the excitement and buzz of New York than to the serenity of the prairies. At home, Monkey-born people are not the most domesticated of creatures, since housework is far too dull a business in their minds. They do, however, make wonderfully stimulating parents, with their wealth of general knowledge. With many tricks up their sleeves and endless amusing stories on the tips of their tongues, Monkeys have very little trouble bridging the age gap.

IN THE WORLD

It's the razor-sharp mentality of the clever Monkey that enables these people to process all kinds of information in a trice and pick up a skill at a glance. Consequently, the members of this sign can fit into, and make a success of, almost any occupation that grabs their interest. Imaginative and insatiably curious, these inquisitive people are natural problem-solvers, who are constantly looking for new experiences and fresh challenges to stimulate their minds and their senses.

Witty, amusing, and full of life, Monkeys are highly entertaining people.

AS FRIENDS AND LOVERS

Young at heart and with youthful spirits maintained throughout their lives, Monkeys are fun to be with. More than anything, these people like to amuse and to be amused, so being in the company of like-minded souls is essential for members of this sign. Perhaps this is why Monkeys have bulging address books filled with names of friends and acquaintances they *can call on at the touch of a button. With their coruscating wit and talent for mimicry, Monkeys are in their element when entertaining a rapt audience. Even as lovers these people need variety, which means that, when it comes to personal relationships, they are not generally reputed for their faithfulness.*

ROOSTER

ESSENTIAL NATURE

Tough, resilient, and strong-minded, Roosters are feisty creatures, who respect those who match their own strengths and indomitable spirit but do not have much patience with those who can't keep up the pace. With their honest and forthright nature, they don't have time to stroke people's egos or to take the sensibilities of more sensitive souls into account. These people like to deliver the unvarnished truth and feel that others can take it or leave it as they wish. But there is a good deal more to the Rooster than meets the eye, for they are indeed colorful individuals, stylish, and even prone to showing off. Pithily witty, masters and mistresses of the one-liner, Roosters are highly amusing people, brilliant joke-tellers, and excellent after-dinner speakers.

DREAMS AND DRIVES

Details are important for these people who are driven by extremely high standards. Indeed, nothing short of perfection will do for Rooster-born folk who demand only the best from other people and from the situations in which they involve themselves. They make highly effective managers. Their status in the community is important to them and they will work long hours to climb, slowly and methodically, to the top of the ladder. They have a love of pomp and pageantry and adore grand occasions when they can dress up in their finery. But their true passion is being at one with Nature, and environmental conservation is an important part of their lives.

IN THEIR HABITAT

Roosters are house-proud and run their homes with super efficiency—lists and rotas will be the order of the day. Everything in the Rooster household must be in the right

THE YEAR OF THE ROOSTER

Fashion is big in Rooster Years when image is of the essence. Politically, the downtrodden make themselves heard and, economically, measures are taken to ensure that financial institutions run more efficiently. Relationships are perhaps not so well starred this year when differences between couples could finally become intolerable.

SIGN DATA

Rank Tenth in order
Symbol of Honesty
Chinese Name JI
Ruling hour 5pm–6.59pm

The fine feathers of the Rooster are reflected in the image-conscious natives of this sign.

place because clutter will not be tolerated under any circumstance. As far as Roosters are concerned, cleanliness as a virtue is next to godliness, so keeping the kitchen and bathrooms hygienic is essential—every surface, nook, and cranny is not only cleaned but disinfected as well. The old-fashioned, muted shades of apricot are associated with this sign, which blend well with the stylish Rooster's love of classical furniture and traditional decor.

IN THE WORLD

Practically and logically minded, the clear, unsentimental nature of the Rooster makes those belonging to this group excellent scientists and statisticians. The financial sector appeals to them as well, since they are truly gifted when it comes to accounting, handling money, and dealing with budgets. Shrewd, super-efficient, and brilliant at strategy in all fields, it is their talent for organization and delegation that often brings Roosters the recognition they deserve in whatever profession they have chosen.

AS FRIENDS AND LOVERS

Shirkers and second-raters have no place in the Rooster's heart. Friends and lovers who want to share life with members of this sign will have to develop a thick skin or at least understand that Roosters do mean well, despite their sometimes tactless and abrasive manner. Deceit in particular is a pet hate. As friends, Roosters are generous and sincere, and as lovers they are caring, steadfast and as loyal as the live-long day.

HONESTY

DOG

Just like the animal symbolizing this sign, people born in these years make true and trusted friends.

ESSENTIAL NATURE

Those born in the Year of the Dog are essentially kind and caring individuals who put others before themselves. They are the true altruists of the Animal signs, ever prepared to make time to listen to others, to provide a shoulder to cry on, and to offer a wise word or two of comfort and reassurance. Solid citizens, members of this sign are endowed with inherent sterling virtues of integrity, honesty, and moral fortitude. This is precisely what makes those born in the Year of the Dog staunchly respected in the community and why they become pillars of society. Some, though, might say the Dog is too conservative and prudish, or someone with a tendency to poke his or her nose in where it is not welcome. However, this is rare, and it is their generosity of spirit and their genuine concern for others that ultimately shines through.

DREAMS AND DRIVES

When members of this group are loved and contented, their needs are simple indeed. Money, power, and prestige come way down the list on the Dogs' agenda for, as far as these people are concerned, top priority is given to family and loved ones who constitute all the treasure they desire in life.

IN THEIR HABITAT

At heart, people born under this sign are traditionalists and this is reflected in their lifestyles and in the way they run their households. Their interiors and decor tend to be classical in style, giving their homes a timeless feel. Everything is neat and tidy, but comfortable at the same time. Here, the family and the needs of their offspring come first, so there will always be a well-stocked larder, a warm fire, and a welcoming smile for them to look forward to.

THE YEAR OF THE DOG

Family life, domestic security, property, and defense are all salient in the Year of the Dog. Concerns regarding the environment and humanitarian issues come to the fore. Conservation, animal welfare, and civil liberties will make the news. According to the Chinese, getting married or starting a family this year will bring lasting happiness and good fortune.

SIGN DATA

Rank Eleventh in order
Symbol of Fidelity
Chinese Name GOU
Ruling hour 7pm–8.59am

IN THE WORLD

Because those belonging to this group are generally set in their ways, they are in no hurry to change the system or the modus operandi of the organizations in which they work. But they are cheerful and industrious, and always prepared to give their colleagues a helping hand. They are responsible people, intelligent, fair-minded, and willing to take on extra commitment when necessary. As a result, Dogs are always popular and respected members of the workforce.

FIDELITY

AS FRIENDS AND LOVERS

Dog-born folk make true and trusted friends. They especially like to mix socially, and to be part of a group sharing similar interests. Especially keen on outdoor activities, they enjoy sports events and other gatherings, particularly if their loved ones are also involved. When it comes to *personal relationships, they are innately shy and it takes a long time for them to feel confident enough to entrust their affections to another person. Once they have found their soulmates, however, they become kind and gentle lovers, ever supportive and anxious to please.*

PIG

FAMILY

ESSENTIAL NATURE

With their sunny natures and cheerful dispositions, people born in the Year of the Pig are jovial characters who are obliging and outgoing. They are relaxed and unpretentious individuals, inherently kind, caring, and generous to a fault. There is always a meal for the hungry at their table, a word of encouragement when others are low, and a hand ready to help for those in need. Honest as the day is long, they expect honesty in return and are therefore perhaps naively trusting. If, at times, the unscrupulous do take advantage of these people's good nature, the Pig will not bear a grudge for long. However, if put upon for too long, even these easy-going souls will finally draw the line, and a pig in a rage is not a pleasant sight.

DREAMS AND DRIVES

Although members of this group are no laggards when it comes to hard work, deep down it is a life of luxury that these people crave. So it is that, among the Animal signs, the Pig has perhaps the greatest reputation for sybaritic desires. They dream of easy living, of five-star hotels, or servants at hand to attend to their every whim. But though a life of flowing champagne and plentiful caviar is only available to a few, they will, nevertheless, find ways within their own means to treat themselves to the little indulgences they believe they deserve.

IN THEIR HABITAT

Sensual and home-loving, Pigs are creatures of comfort so it is inevitable that their homes will be warm, deeply comfortable, and inviting. Members of this sign oscillate between bouts of industriousness akin to workaholism, and total and complete indolence. At these times, housework is not high on their agenda so their homes can appear messy and untidy. Devoted to hearth and home, Pig-born people are nevertheless domestic creatures who strive to create tight bonds within a close-knit family unit.

IN THE WORLD

Adaptable, patient, and intelligent, people belonging to this sign tend to excel in creative occupations. They especially make excellent designers and craftworkers, as they enjoy fashioning beautiful objects with their hands. Their patience and caring instincts often draw them into teaching or the medical professions. Though people born in the Year of the Pig do have extravagant tastes, they are, however, also canny when it comes to money matters and, one way or another, they do usually end up comfortably off.

THE YEAR OF THE PIG

Auspicious for the leisure industry, for gambling, and for trade in luxury goods, this is a year for conspicuous consumption. As the sign of the family, the Year of the Pig favors all domestic matters. But, since this is the last in the cycle, it is principally a year in which priority should be given to tying up loose ends and to putting one's affairs in order, ready to start afresh with the new cycle beginning in the following year.

SIGN DATA

Rank Twelfth in order
Symbol of The Family
Chinese Name ZHU
Ruling hour 9pm–10.59pm

AS FRIENDS AND LOVERS

With their kindly nature and undemanding ways, Pigs have very few enemies and in fact continue to make friends throughout their lifetimes. A close social circle is important and, since many of them are gifted with culinary skills, they adore giving dinner parties and make excellent hosts. Warm and loving, people born in the Year of the Pig are made for married life and derive great pleasure from the physical contact of intimate relationships.

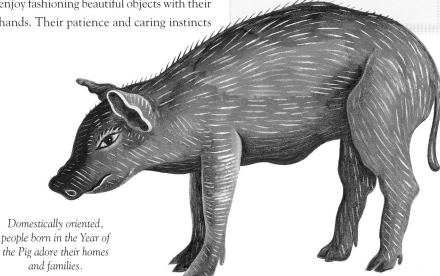

Domestically oriented, people born in the Year of the Pig adore their homes and families.

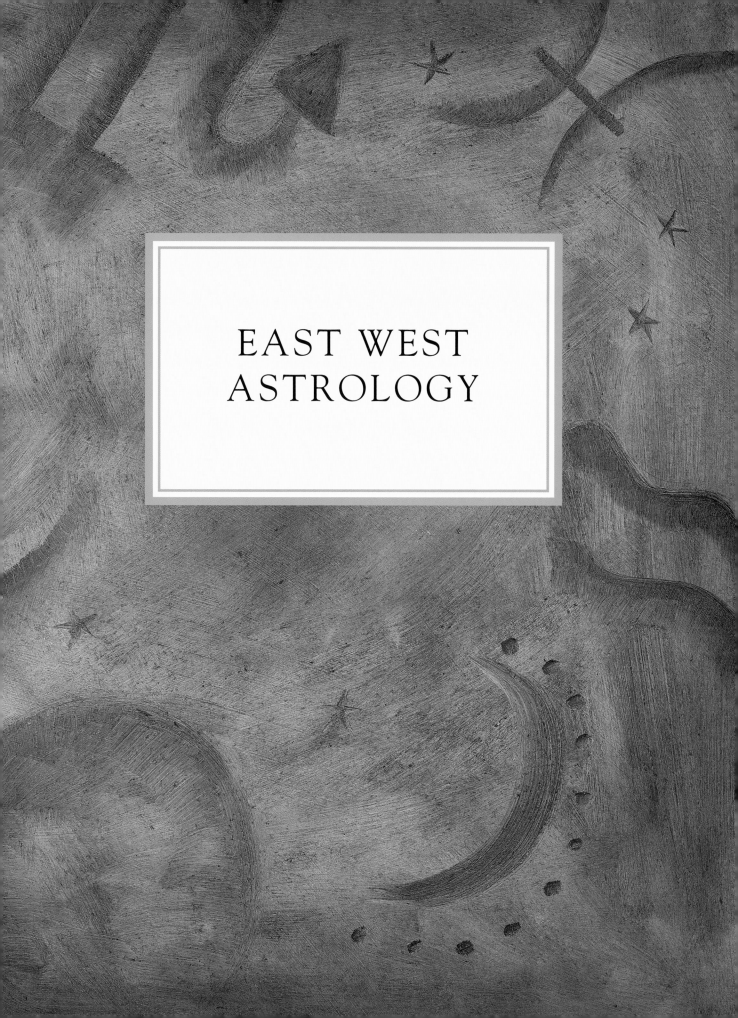

EAST WEST
ASTROLOGY

EAST WEST COMPARISONS

Two systems that essentially analyze people's characters and trace patterns of potential future events, Oriental and Western astrology take vastly different routes to reach similar conclusions. Yet each system offers invaluable insights into every aspect of an individual's character and way of life.

PERHAPS THE MOST fundamental discrepancy lies in the actual charting of the heavens. Oriental astrologers base their findings around the Pole Star, while Western tradition places the Earth at the center of the Ecliptic, or apparent motion of the Sun through the Zodiac. Some of the characteristics associated with the planets differ too. Venus, for example, has a feminine quality in the West but is essentially masculine in the Oriental tradition.

Each of the twelve Animals, like the courageous Tiger, symbolizes the characteristics of the year.

Discrepancies also exist between the two calendars, the West based on the Sun and the East based on the phases of the Moon. However, the first similarity between the two systems is found in the twelve groupings— twelve Chinese Animal signs and twelve signs of the Zodiac. But, even here their differences are interesting because, according to the Chinese system, each of their Animal signs lasts for an entire year, while in the West, each

In Western astrology, the signs, such as Aquarius, were named after the heavenly constellations.

sign of the Zodiac spans an average of thirty days, with the Sun "whizzing" through all twelve in just one year. Another shared link may be found in the concept of the Elements (see opposite), a classification that puts a "spin" on each of the signs and so modifies the general character or disposition of its natives.

A final similarity held in common is the notion of a dualistic principle that underlies the forces of Nature. According to the Chinese, this is the philosophy of Yin and Yang, whereby half the Animal signs pertain to the Yin qualities and the other half to the attributes of Yang. This equates fairly closely to the Western tradition of dividing the Zodiac into signs that are considered Masculine or Feminine in nature. Those that are either Yang or Masculine tend to take an assertive, dynamic approach to life. Yin or Feminine signs are more instinctive and intuitively gifted.

Both Oriental and Western astrologers read the heavens but their methods are very different.

EAST VS. WEST

Although the two astrological systems are fundamentally very different, they do share some interesting—and coincidental—similarities.

EASTERN ASTROLOGY	WESTERN ASTROLOGY
calendar governed by the moon	calendar governed by the sun
12 signs spanning a 12-year cycle	12 signs spanning a 12-month cycle
Elements (Five)	Elements (Four)
Yin and Yang forces	Masculine and Feminine forces

THE ELEMENTS

The use of the elements in both Eastern and Western astrological systems is fundamental to the understanding of the signs. They not only modify character and nature, but they also act as umbrellas, grouping together people who are mentally on the same wavelength and emotionally compatible with each other.

WESTERN ASTROLOGY

In Western astrology, each Element governs three signs. All signs under the same Element share similar elemental characteristics.

ELEMENT	SIGNS	KEY CHARACTERISTICS
EARTH	Taurus, Virgo, Capricorn	practical, stable, level-headed, industrious
AIR	Gemini, Libra, Aquarius	talkative, witty, sociable, logical
FIRE	Aries, Leo, Sagittarius	warm, friendly, dynamic, enthusiastic
WATER	Cancer, Scorpio, Pisces	emotional, receptive, intuitive, sensitive

EASTERN ASTROLOGY

In Chinese astrology, the Elements work in two ways. Firstly, each Animal sign has a fixed association with one or other of the Elements which becomes that sign's signature. And secondly, each year is ruled by one of the Elements in turn.

ELEMENT	ANIMAL SIGNS	KEY CHARACTERISTICS
WOOD	Tiger, Rabbit	warm, generous, considerate, elegant, cooperative
FIRE	Snake, Horse	dynamic, decisive, innovative, joyful, lucid
EARTH	Ox, Dragon, Sheep, Dog	honest, patient, responsible, industrious, prudent
METAL	Monkey, Rooster	strong, moral, ambitious, energetic, independent
WATER	Rat, Pig	flexible, persuasive, diplomatic, creative, kind

The twelve-yearly cycles are repeated five times, making a grand cycle of sixty years. So, for example, a person born in 1938 would be an Earth Tiger, someone born in 1950 is a Metal Tiger, and in 1962 a Water Tiger, and so on. Each successive appearance of the Animal sign is modified by the characteristics of the next Element in turn which helps to distinguish one year's nativity from another under the same Animal sign. In addition each person born in a particular Animal Year is further modified by the year's Yin-Yang polarity and by their hour of birth.

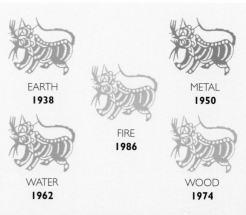

EARTH
1938

METAL
1950

FIRE
1986

WATER
1962

WOOD
1974

INTRODUCING THE COMBINATION SIGNS

As well as marking out the year according to the Moon's phases, the Ancient Chinese also noted the path the Sun tracked across the skies. As the Sun's heat grew stronger, so the crops grew higher, birds flew, and insects buzzed. Then, as the Sun's heat began to wane, so the corn ripened, the rains came, and frost covered the land. Solstices and equinoxes partitioned the year and conveniently marked out the agricultural seasons to guide the farmers through their monthly tasks.

In similar fashion, Western farmers, too, noted the Sun's progress through the skies and utilized the same solar pointers.

Independently, both in the East and West, astrologers reading the celestial movements framed a timetable that took account of these annual changes.

In the East, the year was divided into twenty-four sections. Known as fortnights, each one denoted a cosmological or seasonal event that described a change in the weather, or the next agricultural stage in the year. In the West, the year was divided into twelve sections, each lasting four weeks and known by the signs of the Zodiac.

So, for every Western Zodiac sign that takes up one month, there are two Oriental fortnights covering the same time of year.

Here, we can begin to see how the two systems can intertwine to give us a broader picture of the influences that affect an individual born at any particular time of the year.

Virgo and the fortnight called "End of Heat" both mark harvest time.

THE EAST AND WEST SOLAR DIVISIONS OF THE YEAR

THE CHINESE FORTNIGHTS	WESTERN ZODIACAL SIGNS	APPROXIMATE CALENDAR DATES
Spring Equinox/Clear and Bright	Sun in Aries	March 21—April 20
Grain Rain/Summer Commences	Sun in Taurus	April 21—May 20
Grain Sprouting/Grain in Ear	Sun in Gemini	May 21—June 20
Summer Solstice/Lesser Heat	Sun in Cancer	June 21—July 22
Greater Heat/Autumn Commences	Sun in Leo	July 23—August 22
End of Heat/White Dews	Sun in Virgo	August 23—September 22
Autumn Equinox/Cold Dews	Sun in Libra	September 23—October 22
Descent of Hoar Frost/Beginning of Winter	Sun in Scorpio	October 23—November 21
Lesser Snow/Greater Snow	Sun in Sagittarius	November 22—December 21
Winter Solstice/Lesser Cold	Sun in Capricorn	December 22—January 19
Greater Cold/Beginning of Spring	Sun in Aquarius	January 20—February 18
Rain Waters/Insects Awaken	Sun in Pisces	February 19—March 20

THE LUNAR MONTHS

On top of this combination can equally be superimposed the Lunar months, each one following the same cycle governed by the Animal signs. The first month begins with the first New Moon of the year and since this occurs between late January and mid-February, the month equates with the Western astrological sign of Aquarius and the Oriental sign of the Tiger. Thereafter, the months run through the sequence of Animal signs in exactly the same way as the twelve Animal year cycle.

The months, in turn, also take their characteristics from the Animal at the helm. It may be said that it is here that East and West can comfortably come together, blending the qualities of one with the influences of the other.

THE ZODIAC SIGNS COMBINED WITH THE ORIENTAL ANIMAL YEARS

Whether of the Eastern or Western tradition, astrology essentially concerns itself with the study of character and motivation. By combining the attributes of our Western Zodiacal sign with the characteristics of our Chinese Animal, we can appreciate the subtle modifications that help to refine our understanding of personality and destiny. Moreover, it is this very synthesis, this interweaving of the best of both philosophies, that enables us to build up a picture of ourselves which, just like the facets on the surface of a jewel, reflects the complex and multidimensional qualities that make each one of us unique.

In order to uncover your own unique blend of characteristics, you must first find your Western astrological sign (also known as your Sun sign) and then run through the sequence of years until you find your Chinese Animal year.

Then, you may like to look at some of the other facets of your make-up, those other dimensions to your psyche and your life. Take a look at the combination of your Sun sign with the Animal sign that rules your Chinese Lunar month. And, if you know your hour of birth, you can even combine your Sun sign with the Animal ruling that hour and read up about that aspect of yourself.

The sequence of the Animal years repeat through the great cycle of time.

Each combination will reveal more about you, enriching your understanding of your loves and desires, your needs and drives, and offering deeper psychological insights into what makes you the person you are.

THE EAST AND WEST LUNAR MONTHS

CHINESE MONTHS	ANIMAL SIGN RULER	MONTHLY NAME	SUN SIGN	WESTERN MONTHS
1st	Tiger	Tiger Moon	Aquarius	January–February
2nd	Rabbit	Rabbit Moon	Pisces	February–March
3rd	Dragon	Dragon Moon	Aries	March–April
4th	Snake	Snake Moon	Taurus	April–May
5th	Horse	Horse Moon	Gemini	May–June
6th	Sheep	Sheep Moon	Cancer	June–July
7th	Monkey	Monkey Moon	Leo	July–August
8th	Rooster	Rooster Moon	Virgo	August–September
9th	Dog	Dog Moon	Libra	September–October
10th	Pig	Pig Moon	Scorpio	October–November
11th	Rat	Rat Moon	Sagittarius	November–December
12th	Ox	Ox Moon	Capricorn	December–January

ARIES

BORN BETWEEN: **MARCH 21—APRIL 20**
FIRE SIGN

*A*ries, *the sign that begins the Western astrological year, roughly corresponds to the Chinese month known as the Dragon Moon.*

If you were born at this time of the year you can either call yourself an Aries, or a native of the Peach Blossom Moon, which is a very beautiful alternative name the Chinese give to this month.

According to the Chinese, this time of year is also broken up into two fortnights, each describing an aspect of the weather, or a feature relevant to the agricultural year. The first fortnight is called the Spring Equinox and this corresponds to the first two weeks of Aries. If you were born in the second half of the sign, though, you belong to the second Chinese fortnight, Clear and Bright.

But it is, of course, when both your month and your year of birth are combined that the various influences begin to interweave themselves in a way that is essentially unique for you.

In whatever combination, as a bold and dynamic force, Aries will add passion and verve to the mix.

ARIES-RAT

Arguably one of the busiest and most energetic of the Rat tribe, combining the characteristics of Aries with this sign produces self-confident, adventurous, go-getting individuals who like to be at the forefront of the action. They are a courageous group of people, who cannot pass up a challenge if they meet one, and who always prefer to be in the driving seat. Renowned for their charm and affability, Aries-Rats, however, can also be irritable and short-tempered, especially with those who cannot keep up the pace. With typical drive and enthusiasm, these lively individuals will happily party till midnight and boogie till dawn.

KEY CHARACTERISTICS

- clever
- astute
- daring
- active

YOUR COMPATIBLE SIGNS

Sagittarius-Monkey
Leo-Dragon

EAST WEST FUSION

EAST
Aries brings strength and staying power to the Rat

WEST
The Rat adds charm to temper Aries' fiery nature

OBSERVATIONS
Insensitivity is perhaps the biggest blind spot of this combination. The need constantly to have the reins firmly in their own hands can rankle with family and friends.

Beating the opponent is a fundamental need of the Aries-Rat.

THE ESSENTIAL YOU

WORK, HEALTH, HOBBIES
Hard-working and ambitious, Aries-Rats are restless people, never quite satisfied until they feel they have reached the pinnacle of success. Brilliant organizers and not afraid to take a risk or three, it's just as well that they invariably have luck on their side.

Travel, especially to out-of-the-way places, is a great delight, and particularly so if they can bring back unusual artifacts which become talking points back home. All the better if this can be turned into a lucrative career, such as import and export.

♥ ♥ ♥

LOVES, LIKES, DISLIKES
In life, these tough, resilient creatures give as good as they get and they appreciate those who can stand their ground. They do not understand nor respect weakness of any kind, so friends and partners who can match their abundant spirit and energy will get their approval. In love, members of this dual sign are ardent, terrific fun, passionate, and a laugh a minute.

CHILDREN AND PARENTS
Aries-Rat children are busy little things. They have so many interests and hobbies, but alas never enough time to finish one thing before embarking on another. Sports are a passion which they carry with them into adulthood. As parents, these people are immensely enthusiastic, joining in with their children's hobbies, encouraging their talents and guiding them with a loving, but firm, hand.

Travel is a passion for all Aries-Rats.

ARIES-OX

Aries-Oxen are driven, achievement-oriented individuals who attain their success by dint of plugging away at their ambitions. With the combination of the fiery Ram and the dogged persistence of the tenacious Ox, people of this dual sign cannot be other than bold and fearless. The impulsive Ram brings dynamic energy to this partnership, which means that Aries-Oxen charge through life, brooking no opposition, until they reach their goal. In love too, they are just as dominant, since subtlety is not their game. Only a strong, honest, practical and down-to-earth partner will make an ideal match for the Aries-Ox.

OBSERVATIONS

Intolerance can be a negative trait of this duality, possibly because Aries-Oxen are resourceful people who are happy to plow their own furrows.

Decision-making and hard-headed negotiations do not daunt the industrious Aries-Ox.

KEY CHARACTERISTICS
- indomitable
- serious
- practical
- reserved

YOUR COMPATIBLE SIGNS
Sagittarius-Rooster
Leo-Snake

THE ESSENTIAL YOU

WORK, HEALTH, HOBBIES
Ever ready to roll up their sleeves, these solid workaholics do their best to tackle whatever they take on. Without a doubt, Aries-Oxen are hard workers and don't give up easily when they smell success at the end of the trail. But they do like to go it alone, so are happier self-employed than having to take orders, especially from those whom they do not respect. Health-wise, these are robust individuals who enjoy hands-on work and home renovation.

LOVES, LIKES, DISLIKES
Aries-Oxen loathe small-talk and superficiality of all sorts. They are not party-goers but stay-at-homes. In fact, their home is very much their castle and here they can lose themselves in their gardens. Nest-building crafts, such as cooking, sewing, and mending, give them a great deal of pleasure and satisfaction. Creating a cozy home for themselves and their loved ones quietly fills the Aries-Oxen's hearts with joy.

CHILDREN AND PARENTS
Young Aries-Oxen are reserved little people who take information in without necessarily making a song and dance of things. They like their food, though they could happily leave the savory course and tuck straight into the dessert. As adults, members of this group are good providers, they instil respect for authority into their children, and expect their offspring to behave—or else!

Gardening, a special delight of the Ox, can help members of this group to unwind.

EAST WEST FUSION

EAST
The Aries brings fire and passion to stir the stolid Ox

WEST
Caution is the gift the Ox gives to the otherwise impulsive Ram

ARIES: **MARCH 21–APRIL 20**
YEARS OF THE TIGER: 1902 ∗ 1914 ∗ 1926 ∗ 1938 ∗ 1950 ∗ 1962 ∗ 1974 ∗ 1986 ∗ 1998 ∗ 2010
HOUR OF THE TIGER: 3AM – 4.59AM

ARIES-TIGER

Fiery, restless, and impetuous, Aries-Tigers like living life in the fast lane. Excitement and adventure draw them like magnets, for most are intrepid explorers, born with a pioneering zeal. Fueled by high octane energy, these are mini tornadoes who whizz through life cramming as many activities into the day as they possibly can. Being trapped, feeling hemmed in and unable to follow their star at a moment's notice is the Aries-Tiger's worst nightmare. Perhaps larger than life, people belonging to this dual sign are nevertheless caring, truly heroic figures, ever ready with equal measures of courage and passion to fight for those in need.

Aries-Tigers love to lend their formidable strength to those less fortunate than themselves.

OBSERVATIONS

Restlessness and impatience are perhaps the chinks in the Aries-Tiger armor

With strength, stamina, and a lack of self-doubt, Aries-Tiger natives will go far.

EAST WEST FUSION

EAST
Aries imbues the Tiger with staying power

WEST
The Tiger brings a strong humanitarian drive to the ardent Ram

KEY CHARACTERISTICS
- fiery
- passionate
- humanitarian
- courageous

YOUR COMPATIBLE SIGNS
Leo-Dog

Sagittarius-Horse

WORK, HEALTH, HOBBIES
A talent for innovation and seemingly endless energy will take the members of this duality far, ensuring they do well in whatever occupation they choose to follow. They possess a strong humanitarian zeal, which urges them to work in areas that help to improve the lot of humankind. And if this means they will never be rich, so be it—they will tighten their belts philosophically. They're happy to give any spare time or cash to charity.

♥   ♥   ♥

LOVES, LIKES, DISLIKES
The Aries-Tiger combination produces a charismatic personality, someone who attracts the opposite sex like moths to a flame. Dashing and passionate, sexy and alluring, both the men and women of this dual sign are never short of admirers, nor is their love life ever dull. These people are attention-seekers and will always gravitate toward center stage. With their impressive and irrepressible personalities, Aries-Tigers will make as many friends as they do enemies throughout their lives.

CHILDREN AND PARENTS
Wide-eyed and interested in everything that makes the world go round, these children are a pleasure to teach and popular with everyone. With typical Aries-Tiger enthusiasm, they launch themselves into whatever activity is taking place and hugely enjoy life. A low boredom threshold and a need for variety in their lives increase as these people mature. It is possible that Aries-Tiger parents will have several children from different marriages in their households, all of whom they will love immensely. In return, these parents are respected for their warmth and fair-mindedness.

ARIES: **MARCH 21–APRIL 20**
YEARS OF THE RABBIT: 1903 ∗ 1915 ∗ 1927 ∗ 1939 ∗ 1951 ∗ 1963 ∗ 1975 ∗ 1987 ∗ 1999 ∗ 2011
HOUR OF THE RABBIT: 5AM – 6.59AM

ARIES-RABBIT

Active and independent, the Aries-Rabbit's tendency to be constantly searching for new opportunities means several changes of direction throughout his or her life. More energetic than the average Rabbit, those who are born under this dual influence will pursue their ambitions actively while apparently coming across as cool and relaxed. Careerwise, Aries-Rabbits are best suited to artistic or creative occupations and many gravitate toward the media, although they may have interests in all these areas. The spunky Aries' input means that those born under this dual sign are the least constant of the Rabbit clan. They are sometimes hard to read and, essentially, what they need is to be given their own space.

KEY CHARACTERISTICS
- connoisseur
- home-loving
- considerate
- lucky

YOUR COMPATIBLE SIGNS
Sagittarius-Pig
Leo-Sheep

OBSERVATIONS
Wrapping themselves up in the pursuit of their own interests can be a distinct disadvantage when forming close personal relationships

Image is important to the Aries-Rabbit who knows how and when to impress.

EAST WEST FUSION

EAST
The active Ram fires the normally placid Rabbit with energy and verve

WEST
The Rabbit smoothens the rougher edges of the Aries personality

Aries-Rabbits fill their homes with all manner of artistic trinkets.

WORK, HEALTH, HOBBIES
The art world, cultural events, and communications in general draw the Aries-Rabbits, both professionally and in their leisure hours. Healthwise, these are more robust and vigorous than most other Rabbits, but they also require a softer, more comfortable life than one might in general expect of a typical Aries. A huge appetite for knowledge is a personal quest that drives these people on.

LOVES, LIKES, DISLIKES
The Aries-Rabbits' abiding passion for beauty spurs them to fill their homes with books, paintings, curios, and objects d'art of all description. In love, these refined creatures are not the most cuddly people on the face of the planet. Certainly, they come across as attentive and sympathetic, but their deep dislike of embroilment of any kind means that, emotionally at least, they like to keep their distance.

CHILDREN AND PARENTS
Keen to learn, children of this duality are never bored, for they like to shape their own environment with a creative hand. So they surround themselves with all manner of artistic projects and have distinctive ideas when it comes to taste and fashion. As adults, these people do love their homes, but they also like to pursue their own interests. Consequently, the Aries-Rabbit parent, though undoubtedly loving, may tend nevertheless to be somewhat remote from his or her family.

ARIES-DRAGON

Life for those born under the dual sign of the Aries-Dragon is full of activity. With their high-octane drive and enthusiasm, members of this fraternity cram as much as they can into their day, never letting anything or anyone stand in the way of what they want. These are upwardly-mobile individuals, setting their sights higher than would seem humanly possible. And yet, such is the determination, pushiness, and sheer bravado of this personality, that the Aries-Dragon always seems to get there one way or another. Or perhaps it is down to luck, for Dragons do tend to attract an equal measure of good fortune as they do bad.

A charismatic personality will take Aries-Dragons to the top of their chosen careers.

KEY CHARACTERISTICS
- ❦ optimistic
- ❦ feisty
- ❦ outgoing
- ❦ popular

YOUR COMPATIBLE SIGNS
Leo-Monkey
Sagittarius-Rat

EAST WEST FUSION

EAST
Aries heightens the Dragon's determination to win through

WEST
The Dragon brings pizzazz into the life of the Ram

OBSERVATIONS
Excessive self-confidence can make members of this dual sign appear arrogant and pompous

THE ESSENTIAL YOU

WORK, HEALTH, HOBBIES

Aries-Dragons are made for leadership. They possess a natural ability to inspire others with their special brand of enthusiasm. Businesses simply thrive under their imaginative control. For they are bold and daring individuals who think big and who will not be thwarted. For them, no job is ever too challenging to take on and conquer. And conquer they will, whether it is to get to the top of K2, become a grand master at chess, or turn an ailing company into a multi-million dollar spinner. Members of this sign have the will, the strength and the power to do it—no problem!

LOVES, LIKES, DISLIKES

Attractive and oozing charisma, members of this duality act as magnets to the opposite sex. They have a courtly notion of love and tend to play the knights in shining armor or the fair damsels in distress. When they do fall in love, they burn with great passion and give every ounce of themselves to the object of their desire. But they tend to fall in love too readily, it seems, and with a different person every time. Their constant and abiding love affair, it is fair to say, is with themselves.

CHILDREN AND PARENTS

Challenge is everything in the life of an Aries-Dragon so, even as children, whatever these people do, they like to win. This double sign confers a huge ego, which means these youngsters are not shy, retiring types. A need for a high-profile existence is ever present here from cradle to grave. Consequently, as adults and parents, they are drawn by the wonders of the world at large, which means that they tend to be out and about a good deal rather than around their hearths and families.

At work as well as in life, Aries-Dragons like to be one move ahead.

ARIES: **MARCH 21–APRIL 20**
YEARS OF THE SNAKE: 1905 ✱ 1917 ✱ 1929 ✱ 1941 ✱ 1953 ✱ 1965 ✱ 1977 ✱ 1989 ✱ 2001 ✱ 2013
HOUR OF THE SNAKE: 9ᴀᴍ – 10.59ᴀᴍ

THE ESSENTIAL YOU

ARIES-SNAKE

Combining the Sun sign of Aries with the Moon sign of Snake is a positive formula that mixes courage and enterprise with shrewdness and intelligence. With such a mixture as this, success is guaranteed. Active and plucky, members of this dual sign have a good deal more get-up-and-go than the average Snake. At work, the Aries-Snake is an achiever and possessed of an astuteness that enables him or her to make money fairly easily. This is just as well, since members of this tribe are generous and fairly liberal when it comes to parting with their hard-earned cash. In love, Aries-Snakes are ardent and passionate, never afraid to take the initiative. Domestically, they are happy home-makers too.

KEY CHARACTERISTICS

- intelligent
- astute
- possessive
- profound

YOUR COMPATIBLE SIGNS

Sagittarius-Ox
Leo-Rooster

Music comes as a balm to ease the tensions of the Aries-Snake.

EAST WEST FUSION

EAST
Aries provides energy for the otherwise sluggish Snake

WEST
The Snake brings wisdom to the incautious Ram

OBSERVATIONS

An inability to laugh at their own foibles and mistakes means that these people take themselves far too seriously

Aries enterprise and Snake intuition make a formidable business combination.

WORK, HEALTH, HOBBIES

Excellent organizers, Aries-Snake individuals work best from a position of authority where they can give the orders. These people are shrewd and astute and know precisely how to earn a fast buck. In business and sales, they have the Midas touch, so it is no wonder that members of this duality invariably end up wealthy. But life is a serious matter for these intense people who really need to learn to unwind and lighten up a little.

♥ ♥ ♥

LOVES, LIKES, DISLIKES

In personal relationships, Aries-Snakes tend to be constant and faithful companions. They have a deep-rooted need to love and to be loved in return and, with the right person at their side, will spend their days and nights in happy domesticity. The Snake half of this duality brings to the partnership a joy of reading and listening to music—a chance to sit back and take things easy for a while.

CHILDREN AND PARENTS

At school, Aries-Snake children are fond of their studies. But, because members of this dual sign are terrific researchers and brilliant detectives, these youngsters particularly shine at the sort of project work that involves digging and delving for facts. Some will show a particular aptitude for sports, some for academic subjects, and others will enjoy both. It all depends on which half of their dual natures is inspired first. As adults, Aries-Snakes make devoted parents.

EAST WEST FUSION

ARIES-HORSE

EAST
The fiery Ram endows the Horse with courage

WEST
The Horse brings grace and elegance to the erstwhile rough-and-ready Ram

Active, enthusiastic, and energetic, the Aries-Horse takes life at a gallop. New ideas and fresh adventures constantly grab the attention of these natives but, with such a low boredom threshold, they are in danger of leaving a trail of half-finished projects behind them. Consequently, in the Aries-Horse's household, there is always the danger that many plans are made but few are brought to ultimate fruition. However, Aries-Horses excel in any situation where bold strokes and innovative approaches are called for. For these people can be relied on for their courage to lead and their boldness to direct. Sexually ardent, Aries-Horses are pushy people with a tendency to come on strong.

KEY CHARACTERISTICS

- witty
- lively
- rash
- easily side-tracked

YOUR COMPATIBLE SIGNS
Leo-Tiger
Sagittarius-Dog

OBSERVATIONS
Aries-Horses can all too easily be distracted from the job in hand

Impulsive and extravagant, Aries-Horses have a passion for shopping.

THE ESSENTIAL YOU

WORK, HEALTH, HOBBIES

Articulate and persuasive talkers, these people are good at thinking on the hoof and making rapid decisions under fire, which means they excel in public relations and they make brilliant spin doctors. Indeed, any sort of career as spokesmen and women would suit their talents admirably. The world of journalism and television, too, draws many members of this extrovert sign. Extravagant, but all too often imprudent, money flows through their hands like water, often leaving little to show for all their hard work.

Journalism makes a suitable career for these quick-thinking individuals.

LOVES, LIKES, DISLIKES

When it comes to affairs of the heart, the impulsive Aries-Horse has a tendency to fall in and out of love at the drop of a hat. The problem is that members of this dual sign simply hate to be hemmed in and the thought of commitment leaves them cold. And yet, when they do settle down, these people find immense comfort and encouragement from a close intimate partnership. Socialites par excellence, given their ready wit and amusing repartee, they are a godsend for the party hostess.

CHILDREN AND PARENTS

Just as a parent Aries-Horse likes to do everything in double-quick time, so the youngsters of this duality also conduct their lives in a fast and furious fashion. All too often, however, this can mean they don't give themselves enough time to fully appreciate whatever activity they are undertaking, or else that more projects get started than ever get finished. Parents and teachers alike will throw up their hands in dismay at their lack of commitment to any one activity, be this learning the violin or tidying their bedroom.

Love and romance are vital ingredients in the life of the Aries-Sheep.

ARIES-SHEEP

Although Aries is the sign of leadership, those born under the Oriental sign of the Sheep tend to be of a more retiring nature, not accustomed to pushing themselves forward, but preferring to take their cue from others. Nevertheless, people belonging to this dual rulership are indeed more spirited than the average Sheep, but even so they are better working in the wings, and, as such, they are brilliant at providing power behind the throne. In love, Aries-Sheep are possessive and emotionally demanding. They are at their best when in a stable relationship because, as long as they have a strong, adoring partner at their side, they feel they can conquer the world.

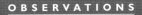

OBSERVATIONS

A tendency to let others take advantage of their ideas can lead to both loss of money and opportunity

KEY CHARACTERISTICS

- security-oriented
- loving
- supportive
- talkative

YOUR COMPATIBLE SIGNS
Sagittarius-Rabbit
Leo-Pig

THE ESSENTIAL YOU

WORK, HEALTH, HOBBIES
Working in the arts suits the gentle and sensitive members of this duality. These people are not cut out to run the show themselves but are best in a supportive role. As creative partners, for instance, they fare very well indeed. Fashion, design and the beauty business are excellent avenues for these people's talents, whether as a main occupation or a spare-time pursuit. Cooking, arranging flowers, and all manner of handicrafts remain life-long joys.

LOVES, LIKES, DISLIKES
A close, one-to-one, loving and reciprocally supportive partnership is the be-all and end-all of the Aries-Sheep's existence, for members of this dual sign are born for love and marriage. But it is

also important that their partners are good providers because these people love to surround themselves in comfort and need to be protected from the harsher realities of life.

CHILDREN AND PARENTS
Youngsters of this duality are tender little lambs who need to be cossetted and protected. Routine and the close bond of family life is essential to their well-being. These children need to be nurtured and encouraged to value their talents and develop their skills. Being taught from a young age to stand on their own two feet would help them in adult life. Since helping the ones they love is a mission for them in life, these people make very supportive parents to their offspring.

EAST WEST FUSION

EAST
The Ram brings a steely strength to the oversensitive Sheep

WEST
The Sheep softens the tougher sinews of the Ram

Aries-Sheep appreciate being acknowledged for the support they give to others.

ARIES: **MARCH 21–APRIL 20**
YEARS OF THE MONKEY: 1908 ✳ 1920 ✳ 1932 ✳ 1944 ✳ 1956 ✳ 1968 ✳ 1980 ✳ 1992 ✳ 2004 ✳ 2016
HOUR OF THE MONKEY: 3PM – 4.59PM

THE ESSENTIAL YOU

ARIES-MONKEY

Aries-Monkeys are always happy to meet their friends.

Where the Aries Monkey is concerned, life is a constant round of social events, partying, meeting new people, telephoning contacts, and talking to friends. As with all Monkeys, communication is the key, and these people are some of the most garrulous folk around. Those born under this twin rulership are high-profile people for whom being in the company of others is all important. Amusing and fun-loving, but also active and go-getting, boredom is the biggest enemy of this group. Popular with their colleagues and equally at home whether as boss or employee at work, these bright sparks excel at the cutting edge of technology.

KEY CHARACTERISTICS

- talented
- competitive
- efficient
- talkative

YOUR COMPATIBLE SIGNS

Sagittarius-Dragon
Leo-Rat

OBSERVATIONS

The incessant chatter of the Aries-Monkey can be annoying and extremely wearing for their companions

EAST WEST FUSION

EAST
Aries teaches the Monkey the meaning of honesty

WEST
The Monkey imparts shrewdness to the trusting Ram

Mysteries and surprises delight the natives of this dual sign.

WORK, HEALTH, HOBBIES

Versatile, adaptable, quick, and intelligent, members of this dual sign are able to pick up a new skill in a trice. Because they are so articulate, lecturing or demonstrating comes as second nature to them. But they have a brilliant eye that enables them to size up a system, find its faults, and make the necessary changes that will radically improve it. With this ability, coupled to their boundless energy, Aries-Monkeys can get through their workload in half the time of others, thus freeing themselves to pursue their many other interests.

❤ ❤ ❤

LOVES, LIKES, DISLIKES

Ever young at heart, Aries-Monkeys like to have fun. They especially adore surprises, so clever lovers know the way to these people's hearts is simply to keep them guessing. Staying in to watch a video with a take-out pizza is not a favorite pastime. Instead, these social butterflies like to be where the action is, and if they're not entertaining their friends, then they're probably out and about with one group or another, or else generally absorbing the buzz of the city.

CHILDREN AND PARENTS

"Talks too much in class" is perhaps the most frequently written comment in the school reports of young Aries-Monkeys. Perhaps that is because these children are so bright and alert that they can take in the lesson in the blink of an eye and then, well, what is there left to do but turn to their friends and chat? Aries-Monkeys never truly grow up, but simply become big kids—even when they have children of their own.

ARIES-ROOSTER

Clever, witty, and blunt, for the Aries-Rooster, a spade is a spade. People born under the combination of these two forthright signs are plain speakers, who have no time to stand around embellishing the truth. In short, Aries-Roosters are uncompromisingly honest, but equally they expect others to deliver the plain, unvarnished truth too. Members of this double sign are tough enough to take it on the chin and they respect those who can give as good as they get. Careerwise, people of this combination are formidable. They can master any task they take up and become recognized experts in each. And, with energy to spare, Aries-Roosters make it all look so easy.

KEY CHARACTERISTICS

✳ full of integrity
✳ impressive
✳ enthusiastic
✳ candid

YOUR COMPATIBLE SIGNS

Sagittarius-Snake
Leo-Ox

Art is just one of the hobbies Aries-Roosters can cram into their activity-packed lives.

Aries-Roosters enjoy demonstrating their expertise to others.

EAST WEST FUSION

EAST
Aries provides the fuel that powers the Rooster's drive to accomplish

WEST
The Rooster refines the Ram's abilities

OBSERVATIONS

While laudable, candor can sometimes hurt those whose skin is considerably thinner than that of the tough Aries-Rooster

THE ESSENTIAL YOU

WORK, HEALTH, HOBBIES

One job is rarely enough for the versatile and intelligent Aries-Rooster. For members ruled by this duality are dynamic creatures with far-ranging talents and the mentality to absorb facts and figures as blotting paper does ink. Physically and mentally, these truly Renaissance men and women, human dynamos with the capacity to play several roles, become expert in a raft of skills and, seemingly, live several lifetimes all at once.

LOVES, LIKES, DISLIKES

Practically talented, Aries-Roosters like to turn their hands to anything, invariably with stunning success. So, they will paint and refurbish, cook cordon bleu, play violin like Paganini, and thoroughly enjoy every varied minute of their day. The only thing Aries-Roosters truly dislike is having time on their hands. With every minute thus accounted for, partners of these busy folk will obviously have their work cut out to get any attention!

CHILDREN AND PARENTS

Children belonging to this duality tend to respect their parents and are generally obedient. They show signs of their multifaceted talents from a young age and are eager to pursue all their interests. Exposing them to the richness of art, music, and literature when still young will help their own talents to flourish. Since there is so much to do and time is of the essence, starting a family and becoming a parent gets very low priority ranking in the life agenda of the average Aries-Rooster.

ARIES: **MARCH 21–APRIL 20**
YEARS OF THE DOG: 1910 * 1922 * 1934 * 1946 * 1958 * 1970 * 1982 * 1994 * 2006 * 2018
HOUR OF THE DOG: 7PM – 8.59PM

ARIES-DOG

OBSERVATIONS

Good intentions can sometimes be misinterpreted as meddling in other people's affairs

Aries-Dogs choose their soulmates with care.

Dog quietens the brashness of the Ram, producing a group of people who are confident of their abilities but not pushy in nature. Moreover, Aries-Dogs enjoy their independence and are less likely to stay with the pack. Their search for true spiritual rapport prevents them from settling down too early in life. When they do find their life partners, they will have to learn that a little tact facilitates a relationship far more than does the delivery of the cold, hard truth.

EAST WEST FUSION

EAST
Aries teaches the Dog to be more enterprising

WEST
The Dog inspires the Ram with kindness

KEY CHARACTERISTICS
- caring
- responsive
- fair-minded
- sincere

YOUR COMPATIBLE SIGNS
Sagittarius-Tiger
Leo-Horse

Like man's best friend, Aries-Dogs are faithful and true.

The Aries' energy and dash gives the normally reticent Dog a goodly amount of spirit, making those born under this combination some of the more dynamic people of the Dog clan. But the kindness and generosity of the

THE ESSENTIAL YOU

WORK, HEALTH, HOBBIES
Loyal and responsible workers, members of this sign are blessed with honesty and good judgment, which makes them trusted and valued by their bosses and colleagues. Occupationally it is their strong sense of justice that often leads these people into politics or else into a career in the legal profession. Fighting the good fight and championing the down-trodden are the driving forces that keep these people on their toes.

LOVES, LIKES, DISLIKES
As a rule, Aries-Dogs are not especially materialistic types. Amassing possessions or living life in five-star fashion are not strong motivating drives as far as these people are concerned. For members of this sign are essentially realists and they like to carve out an existence that, to them, is basic and honest and true. Potential partners can find it difficult to share such austere values and this can seriously affect the viability of a long-term relationship.

CHILDREN AND PARENTS
The kindly disposition of young Aries-Dogs means they develop a love of animals and Nature from a young age. They also like to look after their siblings and friends, and if they do fall out, it is probably because children of this duality have an unfortunate tendency to be tactless. Although said inadvertently, their remarks can sting. As parents, these people are dedicated to their families and their homes.

60

ARIES-PIG

People born under the twin rulership of this sign are energetic and full of joie de vivre. Aries-Pigs make warm and affectionate friends and, if the truth be told, lusty lovers too. In fact, Aries-Pigs are lusty in every sense—vigorous and strong, passionate and energetic. They have huge appetites both physically and mentally, and are able to take on any task that is thrown at them. Apart from their big appetites, Aries-Pigs also have a vast capacity for adventure. These people are leaders and pioneers, especially in the world of the arts. In life, Aries-Pigs are open and trusting, and when it comes to love they are enthusiastic and optimistic.

OBSERVATIONS

The tendency for Aries-Pigs to give up on a situation or a task at hand can undermine any potential success due to them

KEY CHARACTERISTICS
- cheerful
- optimistic
- unfocused
- bawdy

YOUR COMPATIBLE SIGNS
Sagittarius-Sheep
Leo-Rabbit

The sunny nature of the Aries-Pig makes the natives of this group fun to be with.

EAST WEST FUSION

EAST
Aries endows the Pig with more get-up-and-go

WEST
The Pig mellows the aggressive push of the Ram

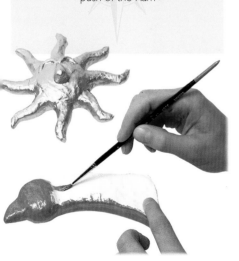

The artistic talents of the Aries-Pig find a fulfilling outlet in creative projects.

THE ESSENTIAL YOU

WORK, HEALTH, HOBBIES
Aries-Pigs are full of bright ideas, hugely talented people who especially appreciate the visual arts. They can work in great fits of enthusiasm, only to give up before the task is completely finished, thereby minimizing their chances of great success. They are not loners and are happiest when working with other people, preferably in a creative environment where they can let their impressive imaginations run free.

♥ ♥ ♥

LOVES, LIKES, DISLIKES
Mightily popular, Aries-Pigs make wonderful companions and invariably have a vast circle of people they can call their friends. Here are some of life's true helpers, for there is little that members of this dual sign will not do for those they love. In fact, they really don't mind putting themselves out at all for their partners and families. What's more, they do it willingly and cheerfully. They are trusting souls and expect others to be kind and fair in return—treachery and disloyalty wounds them to the core.

CHILDREN AND PARENTS
Lovable bundles of fun, children of this duality show artistic flair from an early age. Teaching them the importance of finishing whatever they take on would stand them in good stead in adult life. Members of this sign are born with naturally sunny dispositions, which makes them easy to raise, except for the occasional tantrum when they think someone has been unfair to them. Aries-Pigs make wonderful parents, warm, loving, enthusiastic, and always there when they are needed.

TAURUS

BORN BETWEEN: APRIL 21—MAY 20
EARTH SIGN

Taurus, the second sign of the Western astrological year, roughly corresponds to the Chinese month known as the Snake Moon.

If you were born at this time of the year you can either call yourself a Taurean, or you might like to think of yourself as a native of the Locust Bean Tree Moon, which is an alternative name given to this month in the East.

According to the Chinese, this time of year is also broken up into two fortnights, each describing an aspect of the weather, or a feature relevant to the agricultural year. The first fortnight is called Grain Rain and this corresponds to the first two weeks of Taurus. If you were born in the second half of the sign, though, you belong to the second Chinese fortnight, Summer Commences.

But it is, of course, when both your month and your year of birth are combined that the various influences begin to interweave themselves in a way that is essentially unique for you.

In whatever combination, as a practical and creative force, Taurus will bring steadiness and artistic flair to the mix.

EAST WEST FUSION

TAURUS-RAT

EAST
Taurus calms the nervous tendencies
of the Oriental Rat

WEST
The Rat brings energy to the
normally placid Bull

Add the stubborn, slow-burning determination of the Bull to the sharply-honed intellect of the Rat and the combination produces a formidable personality. There is no doubt about it, Taurus-Rats have their heads firmly screwed on. Plodding and methodical they may appear on the surface, but their razor-sharp minds never miss a trick. Whether in business or in personal relationships, these masterful individuals never lose sight of their ultimate goals. Traditionalists at heart, accumulating wealth is a major need which fuels their drive. And, given their tenacity and strength of purpose, Taurus-Rats usually achieve everything they set out to accomplish.

KEY CHARACTERISTICS
- tenacious
- cautious
- down-to-earth
- materialistic

YOUR COMPATIBLE SIGNS
Virgo-Monkey
Capricorn-Dragon

OBSERVATIONS

*Though few and far between,
a Taurus-Rat's bouts of temper
can be volcanic*

*Taurus-Rats love the
sweet things in life.*

THE ESSENTIAL YOU

*When motivated, Taurus-Rats
can be fast on their feet.*

WORK, HEALTH, HOBBIES

Taurus-Rats are not only persistent and determined workers, but they are also extremely clever, so no matter what occupation they take up, they will stick with it until they make a success of their work. They have an excellent eye for spotting gaps in the market, and are able to handle tasks practically and with common sense. They are not afraid of rolling up their sleeves and getting involved. Members of this sign are linguistically gifted and many gravitate toward a career in the media.

LOVES, LIKES, DISLIKES

There is no getting away from the fact that Taurus-Rats like and need money. For them, this is one of the top priorities in life, not because they are especially avaricious, but because to them money provides the second biggest need in their lives—security. Stylewise, the Taurus-Rat will usually go for the classical look because they like things to last. And this goes for their relationships too. Once they have given their hearts, they will be faithful and constant companions, and they expect fidelity and constancy from their partners in return.

CHILDREN AND PARENTS

Youngsters belonging to this dual sign show early promise in reading and writing skills. With the proper encouragement, they should do well in all literary subjects and foreign languages. Ideally, they love to see their pocket money growing in a savings account, but if they do spend, it could be on candies and cakes because Taurus-Rats are ferociously sweet-toothed! As parents, Taurus-Rats are loving and caring, but also sticklers for rules.

TAURUS-OX

Considering that Taurus is the Bull of Western astrology and the Ox is its equivalent in the East, these two combined will intensify the bovine characteristics of each. Immovable and implacable, the Taurus-Ox could never, by any stretch of the imagination, be described as impulsive and hot-headed. Taurus-Oxen are perhaps the steadiest and, in their way, the most laid-back of the whole Ox tribe. Stubbornness and dogged persistence are perhaps their overriding character traits. Diligent and methodical, they get what—and whom!—they want in the end, simply through their sheer tenacity. Taurus-Oxen are supremely sensual beings with a strong sex drive and a fondness for their creature comforts.

KEY CHARACTERISTICS

- strong-willed
- stubborn
- decisive
- thorough

YOUR COMPATIBLE SIGNS
Capricorn-Snake
Virgo-Rooster

Even to the children of this dual sign, details matter—they can spend hours on hobbies that require a steady hand and an eye for intricacies.

EAST WEST FUSION

EAST
The Western Bull strengthens the Oriental Ox's determination

WEST
The Ox of the East reinforces the steely grit of the Bull of the West

OBSERVATIONS

When they have a mind to, Taurus-Ox can be downright mean and cruel

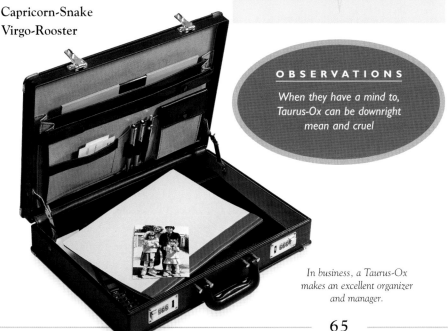

In business, a Taurus-Ox makes an excellent organizer and manager.

WORK, HEALTH, HOBBIES
With their formidable drive and determination, Taurus-Oxen are prepared to labor long and hard to achieve the targets they set for themselves. They are excellent at organizing their time and resources, and like to work in a methodical fashion at their own pace. Blessed with a strong underlying constitution, they plow their energies into their work and can keep going long after those around them have dropped out. With their painstaking eye for detail, they make fine researchers, art restorers, editors, indeed anything that requires minute precision and meticulous persistence.

LOVES, LIKES, DISLIKES
Members of this sign are not renowned for taking risks, since security and routine are essential to their well-being. They are arch pragmatists and many are prepared to marry for wealth and material possessions. In fairness, though, once they have found the mate who satisfies their needs, the Taurus-Ox will develop a deep and profound love for that person and will remain stubbornly faithful to him or her for life.

CHILDREN AND PARENTS
In class, children of this sign like to do things in their own time. Rushing them to finish a task, or forcing them to do something against their will, are likely to result in an almighty tantrum. Art, handicrafts, and design will take their fancy, where they excel in meticulous execution of skill rather than originality or imagination. As parents, Taurus-Oxen are disciplinarians and favor the no-nonsense approach to childrearing.

TAURUS-TIGER

Steadier and more down-to-earth than the average Tiger, those born under the Taurean influence can apply themselves in a practical way to all tasks they undertake. The Tiger energizes the normally placid bovine nature of Taurus, while the Bull brings a stabilizing influence to the Oriental sign. Together, these two produce individuals who can sustain the pace and who are able to keep their shoulders to the grindstone long enough to bring their dreams to reality. Moreover, because Taurus-Tigers do not suffer from restlessness quite as much, their lifestyle and relationships tend to be more stable— without, however, losing a single ounce of that famous Tiger passion!

EAST WEST FUSION

EAST
Taurus brings stability to the impetuous Tiger

WEST
The Tiger brings good fortune to the Bull

KEY CHARACTERISTICS
- observant
- friendly
- protective
- curious

YOUR COMPATIBLE SIGNS
Virgo-Horse
Capricorn-Dog

Taurus-Tigers do it all with ease and panache: they'll think nothing of cooking a three-course, cordon bleu meal after an eight-hour day at the office.

OBSERVATIONS

When they think they are right, little will influence Taurus-Tigers to change their minds

THE ESSENTIAL YOU

WORK, HEALTH, HOBBIES
Not much passes the eagle-eyed Taurus-Tiger, which means that members of this dual sign are able to pick up skills at a glance. Being quick on the uptake coupled with the ability to be flexible means that these people can fit into a wide range of careers. No matter what job they choose, they will carry out their tasks enthusiastically and stick with them until they achieve results. Fairly resilient and always individualistic, whatever they take on, Taurus-Tigers must be left to do it their own way.

LOVES, LIKES, DISLIKES
Easy to get along with, Taurus-Tigers are socially-minded individuals who enjoy being in the company of others. They love travel, too, but members of this duality like to avoid the usual tourist routes, preferring instead to get to the essence of a foreign country and its natives. To their friends, they are loyal and generous, and to their lovers they are passionate and all-giving. Their partners they put on a pedestal.

All things foreign attract the cosmopolitan nature of the Taurus-Tiger.

CHILDREN AND PARENTS
Even from a young age, children of this dual sign have very definite ideas of their own. They work hard at school and especially so in the creative subjects that they particularly enjoy. Popular with their classmates, they get along well with everyone and, more often than not, end up as leaders of the gang. Taurus-Tiger parents bring up their children with a fairly firm hand.

TAURUS: **APRIL 21–MAY 20**
YEARS OF THE RABBIT: 1903 ✳ 1915 ✳ 1927 ✳ 1939 ✳ 1951 ✳ 1963 ✳ 1975 ✳ 1987 ✳ 1999 ✳ 2011
HOUR OF THE RABBIT: 5AM – 6.59AM

TAURUS-RABBIT

Two sensual signs each characterized by a strong acquisitive streak, when joined together will produce natives whose top-of-the-list requirement in life is to obtain as many creature comforts as they possibly can. Next on the agenda comes security which, for the Taurus-Rabbit, means a healthy bank account. Aside from money, members of this sign really do need to live and work in a gracious and refined environment. A comfortable home, pleasant office, nice car, and designer clothes are all important to the happiness and well-being of the Taurus-Rabbit. Moreover, this industrious Rabbit is prepared to work hard to meet these material needs.

KEY CHARACTERISTICS

- discriminative
- placid
- indulgent
- polished

YOUR COMPATIBLE SIGNS
Capricorn-Sheep
Virgo-Pig

Despite a frail appearance, Taurus-Rabbits are actually blessed with a robust and resilient constitution.

OBSERVATIONS
A tendency to self-centeredness is a Taurus-Rabbits weakness

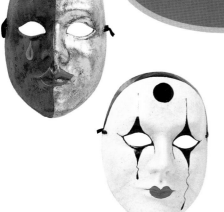

Taurus-Rabbits are drawn to sophisticated entertainment.

EAST WEST FUSION

EAST
The Bull fortifies the Rabbit's fragility

WEST
The gentle Rabbit refines the Bull's character and tastes

WORK, HEALTH, HOBBIES
Multitalented, Taurus-Rabbits are blessed not only with a prodigious imagination, but also with the practical ability to put their ideas into material form. Interior design is a passion, whether as a career or spare-time pursuit. Artistic fields of all sorts are a draw and many find fame as singers, dancers, and performers of the stage and screen. The world of fashion and glamor, too, are often populated with members of this sign.

LOVES, LIKES, DISLIKES
Prime sensualists, Taurus-Rabbits adore being pampered. And, fortunately for them, members of this duality do find people who are prepared to indulge them. These are home-lovers who use their immense creative talents to embellish their nests, and, of course, to turn their homes into the most luxurious environment money can buy. Taurus-Rabbits have exclusive tastes—both materially and when it comes to people. They cannot abide anything that remotely smacks of the low-life.

CHILDREN AND PARENTS
Youngsters belonging to this sign excel in the artistic subjects at school and show early promise in art and music. Any such leanings should be encouraged from an early age since many go on to find their fame and fortune in these fields. These children are definitely not the rough-and-tumble sort and, though they may appear frail on the surface, they are fairly wiry of constitution. They can be moody or sullen if they don't get their own way. Taurus-Rabbit parents instil genteel manners into their children and expect them to grow up into highly cultured individuals.

TAURUS: **APRIL 21–MAY 20**
YEARS OF THE DRAGON: 1904 ✳ 1916 ✳ 1928 ✳ 1940 ✳ 1952 ✳ 1964 ✳ 1976 ✳ 1988 ✳ 2000 ✳ 2012
HOUR OF THE DRAGON: 7AM – 8.59AM

TAURUS-DRAGON

OBSERVATIONS

An arrogant, self-important attitude is a definite Taurus-Dragon turn-off

Taurus steadies the Dragon's over-the-top personality and brings the members of this dual sign down to earth. In its turn, the Dragon contributes a frisson of excitement and adds verve and sparkle to the normally placid Taurean. Here then, in the Taurus-Dragon, is an individual with strength of purpose, tenacious enough to stick with a task until it reaches fruition, yet not so bogged down that he or she is not able to enjoy the lighter side of life. Taurus-Dragons are prepared to work both hard and consistently in order to acquire the material comforts and the high standards of living that are deemed so essential to the well-being of the natives of this sign.

KEY CHARACTERISTICS

- 🐉 ingenious
- 🐉 formidable
- 🐉 strong
- 🐉 achievement-motivated

YOUR COMPATIBLE SIGNS

Virgo-Rat
Capricorn-Monkey

EAST WEST FUSION

EAST
The Bull teaches the Dragon to keep his feet on the ground

WEST
The Dragon peps up the Bull with Oriental spice

Taurus-Dragons use their imaginations and constructive abilities at work and at play.

THE ESSENTIAL YOU

WORK, HEALTH, HOBBIES
Taurus-Dragons are so versatile they can adapt their talents to suit any job description offered to them. Blessed with extraordinary powers of imagination as well as constructive abilities, members of this dual sign have a genius for invention and many become distinguished in their fields. Bright, vigorous, and determined, once they set their mind on a course of action, they will find a way around all difficulties and refuse to let anything stand in the way of success.

❤ ❤ ❤

LOVES, LIKES, DISLIKES
Because Taurus-Dragons are powerful, pushy people who steamroller their way through life, they tend to make few bosom-buddies along the way. They admire strong, focused people and are themselves respected by those with whom they come into contact. In love, however, they tend to be romantic souls, even soppy at times. Those they hold dear, they love deeply and, having found the partner of his or her dreams, the Taurus-Dragon is likely to remain constant for life.

🐉 🐉 🐉

CHILDREN AND PARENTS
Bright sparks, lively and intelligent, young Taurus-Dragons are born with precocious personalities with talents that need to be directed and honed in order to bring out the best of their potential. Even at an early age, these youngsters are performers par excellence and rarely miss an opportunity to display their talents. Assertive and up front, they're never afraid to take the lead and revel in positions of authority such as class prefect. Taurus-Dragon parents take great pride in their beloved offspring and their achievements.

Taurus-Dragons play to win, and love to display their many trophies.

TAURUS-SNAKE

For Taurus-Snakes, status symbols are important reflectors of their wealth and success.

Both Taureans and those born in the Year of the Snake are tenacious, both have very long memories, and both hate to be hurried. Perhaps members of this dual sign are not the most physically active or energetic people in the world, but behind those languid eyes the Taurus-Snake possesses one of the keenest and most incisive minds around. So it pays never to underestimate a Taurus-Snake. Those who belong to this group are eminently sensible and pragmatic. Security is uppermost in their minds, both of the emotional and material variety. So essential to their well-being are love, comfort, and wealth, that they will contrive throughout their lives to make sure they get all three.

EAST WEST FUSION

EAST
Taurus strengthens the physical constitution of the Snake

WEST
The Oriental Snake brings intuitive understanding to the Bull

KEY CHARACTERISTICS
- connoisseur
- confident
- strong-minded
- tenacious

YOUR COMPATIBLE SIGNS
Capricorn-Rooster
Virgo-Ox

OBSERVATIONS
For the Taurus-Snake a tendency to resort to stimulants ever lurks just beneath the surface

THE ESSENTIAL YOU

WORK, HEALTH, HOBBIES
Art and music are passions in the life of the Taurus-Snake, and in some way or other one or both will feature prominently in their lives—be it as a hobby or career. Because they are highly intelligent people, Taurus-Snakes are likely to gravitate toward high-brow or professional careers. In addition, members of this sign have expensive tastes so they will want a lucrative income in order to support their designer lifestyles. They could marry all these needs and become a museum director, art gallery owner, opera singer, lawyer, doctor, designer, or even a media mogul.

LOVES, LIKES, DISLIKES
Taurus-Snakes are mad about beauty. Firstly, they are usually lovely creatures themselves, and secondly, they like to surround themselves with beautiful things. These people know a piece of art when they see one and they will buy as many paintings, porcelain, and exquisite objets d'art as they can afford. Beautiful people, too, are important to members of this sign and the partner of their choice is as gorgeous as a movie star. Taurus-Snakes don't like soiling their hands and they will not put up with "cheap and cheerful" things. For them, it is quality that counts.

CHILDREN AND PARENTS
Children of this double sign are cute little things and, because of this, they are all too easily spoiled. They have a mature understanding of what is going on around them and an uncanny knack of accurately sizing up people and situations. Wise beyond their years, their opinions are valuable. Taurus-Snake parents care deeply about their offspring but would rather assign the diaper changing to the nanny.

The medical profession can prove a lucrative career choice for members of this dual sign.

TAURUS-HORSE

The common sense and strong practical streak of the Western Bull modifies the notoriously wayward instincts of the Horse and allows those born under this combined sign to take life at a steadier pace. Taureans are more circumspect than Horse-born people, they are security-conscious and driven by a need for creature comforts, so this half of the equation is likely to encourage members of the dual sign to put down roots more readily than the average Horse individual might do. Neither the Taurus nor the Horse are intense signs, but they are both imaginative and each has highly developed creative talents.

KEY CHARACTERISTICS

- stylish
- artistic
- brilliant
- egocentric

YOUR COMPATIBLE SIGNS

Virgo-Dog
Capricorn-Tiger

Whether professionally or in their leisure time, Taurus-Horses make wonderful dancers.

EAST WEST FUSION

EAST
Taurus teaches the Horse to reason with common sense

WEST
The Oriental Horse speeds up the Bull's intellectual processes

OBSERVATIONS
Vanity can be a dampener to an otherwise excellent set of qualities

Once they have found their ideal environment, Taurus-Horses are happy to stay put.

WORK, HEALTH, HOBBIES
If Taurus-Horses can harness their determination to their varied talents, there is no telling what these individuals are capable of achieving. Certainly, many show early promise, for they are, as a group, highly gifted people. But it's in learning to sustain their efforts, and not giving up half-way through that will make all the difference to their careers, happiness, and well-being. At their sparkling best, these people will excel in the worlds of art, public relations, journalism, advertising, and television.

LOVES, LIKES, DISLIKES
Chic and fashion-conscious, Taurus-Horses pay a great deal of attention to the way they present themselves to the world. Music and the arts remain passions throughout their entire lives. In love, they need a supportive partner who will take them out of themselves and who will introduce them to a deeper, more spiritual meaning to life.

CHILDREN AND PARENTS
In lots of ways, young Taurus-Horses are very advanced for their years and, whether it is with some sporting prowess, singing, dancing, playing a musical instrument, or showing dramatic flair, many will develop their talents remarkably early in their lives. The problem they have to face is early burn-out, so wise parents will know how to teach their little sons and daughters to pace themselves. When they are parents in turn, Taurus-Horses will lavish their children with expensive gifts. However, they do insist on obedience in return.

TAURUS-SHEEP

It is no secret that the Taurus-Sheep has expensive tastes! This dual rulership is the product of two signs that match each other at every twist and turn in their respective love of luxury and their dogged pursuit of wealth. In combination, then, this group has a double helping of materialism and a seemingly insatiable desire for all the creature comforts that their lifestyles can afford. To be fair, Taurus-Sheep are not money-grabbing per se, although the Sheep is perhaps slightly more rapacious than the Bull. But to these folk, wealth affords security and Taurus-Sheep put their safety and security right at the top of their list of priorities. To attain true happiness, though, Taurus-Sheep need to be wedded and feather-bedded.

KEY CHARACTERISTICS
- attractive
- orderly
- sentimental
- self-interested

YOUR COMPATIBLE SIGNS
Capricorn-Pig
Virgo-Rabbit

EAST WEST FUSION

EAST
The Bull strengthens the Sheep's resolve

WEST
The Sheep teaches the Bull to be more flexible

OBSERVATIONS
Wishful-thinking counteracts the Taurus-Sheep's forward momentum

Taurus-Sheep aspire to a life of luxury and ease.

THE ESSENTIAL YOU

WORK, HEALTH, HOBBIES
Despite the massive talents that all Taurus-Sheep are blessed with, unless they have a fixed regime, or a person to motivate them, these delicate, creative souls can all too easily fritter their energies and dream their lives away. Routine and regular work, therefore, will keep them on the straight and narrow. Having agents or business partners who allow the Taurus-Sheep scope for his or her imagination, while taking on all the administrative duties themselves, is another solution. Acting, modeling, tour guiding, textile design, and office or reception work are all suitable outlets for the members of this sign.

LOVES, LIKES, DISLIKES
It is a cushy, safe, and easy life that Taurus-Sheep desire and, if they could, they would probably spoil themselves silly. They like quietly pottering about, perhaps arranging flowers, making pretty things, or redecorating the house. What they certainly do not like is having their routine disturbed, their plans messed up, or their feathers ruffled in any way. Happiness for them is being loved, cossetted, and looked after by an adoring mate.

A career in the fashion or beauty industry often attracts the members of this dual sign.

CHILDREN AND PARENTS
Just like the adults, so the children belonging to this dual sign relish the feeling of warm, loving, and protective arms around them. These youngsters are extremely laid-back and rarely in a hurry to exert themselves. They do need firm encouragement to do their homework and to tidy up after themselves, otherwise there is the danger that they will turn into vapid adults. Taurus-Sheep make easy-going, though sometimes neglectful, parents.

TAURUS: **APRIL 21–MAY 20**
YEARS OF THE MONKEY: 1908 ∗ 1920 ∗ 1932 ∗ 1944 ∗ 1956 ∗ 1968 ∗ 1980 ∗ 1992 ∗ 2004 ∗ 2016
HOUR OF THE MONKEY: 3PM – 4.59PM

EAST WEST FUSION

TAURUS-MONKEY

A dual sign whose component parts act beneficially on each other, the Taurus-Monkey is a well-adjusted individual. Taurus, solid and down-to-earth, steadies the Monkey's jitters while, in turn, the simian high spirits enliven the stolidity of the Bull. Taurus-Monkeys have a penchant for luxury and an eye for beauty—talents which draw many of them to careers in the fashion trade and beauty industry. In love, part of the Taurus-Monkey wants a steady life and a stable relationship but another part longs for freedom and autonomy. With an understanding partner, who knows how to provide a loving environment while allowing his or her Monkey partner enough space to maneuver, these people can achieve a long-term relationship that is both happy and settled.

KEY CHARACTERISTICS

- realistic
- resilient
- well-balanced
- streetwise

YOUR COMPATIBLE SIGNS

Virgo-Dragon
Capricorn-Rat

EAST
Taurus endows the Monkey
with maturity

WEST
The Chinese Monkey shows the
stolid Bull how to be agile

OBSERVATIONS

A pull between conservative needs and liberal desires can cause conflict in the life of the Taurus-Monkey

Young Taurus-Monkeys have a passion for life and are fascinated by everything in it.

Taurus-Monkeys like a steady relationship with plenty of room for maneuver.

THE ESSENTIAL YOU

WORK, HEALTH, HOBBIES

Taurus-Monkeys are excellent in business and able to wheel and deal with the best of them. Highly socially skilled, members of this sign are well suited to dealing with the public. But they are also self-motivated and so equally happy working on their own. Clever and energetic, their interests are far-ranging, and they are able to make a success of whatever activity or career takes their fancy. Taurus-Monkeys are as able in the Humanities as they are in the softer sciences. However, they are especially happy when commanding a very good income!

♥ ♥ ♥

LOVES, LIKES, DISLIKES

Taurus-Monkeys are not the most sentimental of people and do not appreciate gooey shows of emotion. They are realists and like to keep their feet firmly on the ground. Fiercely protective of their independence, they admire those who, like themselves, can fend for themselves. A lively, intelligent partner with a sparkling sense of humor would make a suitable soulmate.

CHILDREN AND PARENTS

Young Taurus-Monkeys are curious about their world. They like to experiment and to know something about everything. They'll try and tackle tie-dying, playing the violin, or singing in the choir. They will try archery lessons, collecting bugs, or studying Japanese. Life is one big adventure for them and they love reading about exciting exploits. As parents, Taurus-Monkeys retain their sense of wonder and enjoy imparting their knowledge to their sons and daughters.

TAURUS: **APRIL 21–MAY 20**
YEARS OF THE ROOSTER: 1909 ∗ 1921 ∗ 1933 ∗ 1945 ∗ 1957 ∗ 1969 ∗ 1981 ∗ 1993 ∗ 2005 ∗ 2017
HOUR OF THE ROOSTER: 5PM – 6.59PM

THE ESSENTIAL YOU

TAURUS-ROOSTER

The Bull of the West meeting the Cockerel of the East produces a group of sober-minded individuals who are industrious to the point of becoming workaholics. Both are signs of dogged persistence, neither prepared to let up once they have set their mind on a course of action. And both are achievement-oriented. Neither Taurus nor Rooster respects a shirker, and they are not afraid to make these feelings known. Taurus-Roosters are robust. Letting their hair down now and again would help to lighten their serious outlook. A fun-loving partner would help by putting some sparkle into these sterling characters.

KEY CHARACTERISTICS

- industrious
- robust
- cautious
- wry

YOUR COMPATIBLE SIGNS

Capricorn-Ox
Virgo-Snake

Dedicated to their careers, Taurus-Roosters all too often bring their work home with them.

EAST WEST FUSION

EAST
Taurus softens the Rooster's asceticism

WEST
The Rooster energizes the languorous Bull

OBSERVATIONS
Taurus-Roosters have a tendency to be lugubrious

WORK, HEALTH, HOBBIES

Members of this sign are robust and feisty individuals who carry responsibility well. They work best on their own, where they can go at their own pace, call the shots, and absorb themselves in their activities undisturbed. They put a lot of energy into making a success of their careers, for these people are some of life's top achievers. Taurus-Roosters make exceptional archivists, researchers, and scholars.

LOVES, LIKES, DISLIKES

Not the most tender nor the most romantic of the double signs, Taurus-Rooster folk like plain-speaking. They have a strong aversion to shirkers and respect those who pull their weight. Despite their acerbic exterior, these people do have the proverbial heart of gold. They like to help others and feel no sacrifice is ever too great when assisting friends and family in need.

CHILDREN AND PARENTS

Youngsters belonging to this group tend to be serious and solemn little things, who get on with their class-work dutifully and hand in immaculately presented homework. Even when they are very young, they come across as mature and responsible and don't seem as prone to the silly antics of other children of their age. Taurus-Rooster parents are deeply caring, good providers, especially where the larder is concerned. They are, however, sticklers for tidiness and discipline.

No matter how busy they may be, Taurus-Roosters should not neglect the need to follow a sensible diet.

TAURUS-DOG

Both the Western sign of the Bull and the Oriental sign of the Dog have a reputation for conservative beliefs and traditional values. Both produce dedicated, hard-working individuals who are always prepared to roll up their sleeves and pitch in when required, no matter how dirty the job may be. Stability and security are always paramount to those born under this dual rulership, and they will work hard to provide a safe and comfortable haven for the ones they love. To a relationship these people bring affection, devotion, fidelity, and stability. Taurus-Dogs are solid individuals, towers of strength, and pillars of the community. Sensible and down-to-earth, others feel comfortable and reassured in their presence. But Taurus-Dogs are stubborn and they like things done their way.

KEY CHARACTERISTICS

- considerate
- accommodating
- level-headed
- dignified

YOUR COMPATIBLE SIGNS

Virgo-Tiger
Capricorn-Horse

OBSERVATIONS

A tendency to bemoan their fate can depress the spirits of the Taurus-Dog

EAST WEST FUSION

EAST
The Bull teaches the Dog to appreciate comfort and beauty

WEST
The Dog shows the Bull how to be more altruistic

With their infinite patience, Taurus-Dogs make excellent teachers.

THE ESSENTIAL YOU

WORK, HEALTH, HOBBIES

Taurus-Dogs don't mind working in the back room, nor do they mind getting their hands dirty when necessary. For these are diligent and industrious people whose aim is to do a fair day's work for a fair day's pay. With a strong constitution, they hang on in there and their attitude is that if a job's worth doing, it is worth doing well. Since they like to help and to please, they make good nurses, government officials, counselors, and politicians.

Taurus-Dogs have great compassion and don't let dirty work bother them; nursing is a good career choice.

LOVES, LIKES, DISLIKES

A warm, cozy domestic environment, where the family comes together at mealtimes, makes the Taurus-Dog happy. Members of this dual sign devote themselves to their loved ones. These are serious people, not given to displays of frivolity and their inherent reticence means they don't usually make the first move in forming personal relationships. Therefore, a partner who is outgoing, good at giving compliments and able to kiss the blues goodbye would be worth his or her weight in gold.

CHILDREN AND PARENTS

Preferring to be one of the crowd, Taurus-Dog children don't actively seek the spotlight. They are intrinsically timid and they do what they are told. Excellent little helpers, they look after their younger siblings most responsibly. As parents, the Taurus-Dog likes to run a very tight ship.

TAURUS-PIG

OBSERVATIONS

Middle-age spread is often a result of the Taurus-Pig's prodigious appetite

Being born under the signs of the Western Bull and the Eastern Pig gives its natives a double helping of sensuality and buckets and buckets of charm. Members of both signs relish their security, and neither is happy unless surrounded by as many creature comforts as money can buy. Taurus-Pigs adore luxury and, if they can, they travel first class all the way. But Taurus-Pigs are also realists and they have a good head for money. They are no strangers to hard work and, although they have an eye for the good things in life, they also have their feet firmly planted on the ground.

EAST WEST FUSION

EAST
Taurus endows the Pig with staying power

WEST
The Chinese Pig brings a lightness of heart to the Western Bull

Among members of this dual sign, homely comforts are a girl's best friend.

KEY CHARACTERISTICS

✿ good-humored
✿ sociable
✿ cooperative
✿ easy-going

YOUR COMPATIBLE SIGNS

Capricorn-Rabbit
Virgo-Sheep

A love of flowers can take the Taurus-Pig into a career in floristry or horticulture.

THE ESSENTIAL YOU

WORK, HEALTH, HOBBIES
Best working as part of a team, Taurus-Pigs make cheerful and amenable workers who are always ready to meet their colleagues halfway. Creatively gifted and conscientious, these people do well in an artistic setting, such as the theater, design studio, or art gallery. Since they are constitutionally robust, they also fare well in the hotel business or catering trade, both of which are physically as well as imaginatively demanding. Floristry, market gardening, and landscape design are also suitable avenues for their talents.

♥ ♥ ♥

LOVES, LIKES, DISLIKES
Healthy appetites mean that Taurus-Pigs adore good food and drink. They also delight in lovemaking. These people are open, generous souls who are made for partying. No Taurus-Pig can abide dirty, dingy surroundings and none worth his or her salt would be seen in drab, downmarket gear. A life of opulence, luxury, comfort, and material pleasures is what their hearts desire. No other sign will be as sensual, as giving, and as tender in love as this one.

✿ ✿ ✿

CHILDREN AND PARENTS
So creative are Taurus-Pig youngsters that they never seem to be far away from paper and colored pens. Or else they are playing a musical instrument, or singing and dancing to their favorite pop tunes. Children of this dual sign are fun-loving and easy-going. They chuckle with glee and love having their friends over to play. Taurus-Pigs make loving parents, who encourage and applaud their children's talents.

GEMINI

BORN BETWEEN: MAY 21—JUNE 20
AIR SIGN

Gemini, the third sign of the Western astrological year, roughly corresponds to the Chinese month known as the Horse Moon.

If you were born at this time of the year you can either call yourself a Gemini, or you might say you are a native of the Pomegranate Moon, which is a much prettier alternative name for this month in the East.

According to the Chinese, this time of year is also broken up into two fortnights, each describing an aspect of the weather, or a feature relevant to the agricultural year. The first fortnight is called Grain Sprouting and this corresponds to the first two weeks of Gemini. If you were born in the second half of the sign, though, you belong to the second Chinese fortnight, Grain in Ear.

But it is, of course, when both your month and your year of birth are combined that the various influences begin to interweave themselves in a way that is essentially unique for you.

Whatever the combination, Gemini as the sign of adaptability and mental dexterity, will add the power of communication to the mix.

GEMINI: **MAY 21–JUNE 20**
YEARS OF THE RAT: 1900 ∗ 1912 ∗ 1924 ∗ 1936 ∗ 1948 ∗ 1960 ∗ 1972 ∗ 1984 ∗ 1996 ∗ 2008
HOUR OF THE RAT: 11AM – 12.59AM

THE ESSENTIAL YOU

GEMINI-RAT

Silver-tongued and mercurial of mind, Gemini-Rats are blessed with the gift of the gab. Many excel in the literary world, information technology careers, or the media. In fact, the combined influences of the articulate Gemini and the perceptive Rat produces writers or directors of distinction. Quick to grasp ideas, clever, but easily distracted, Gemini-Rats therefore thrive on change and variety. For these lively characters are interested in everything and everybody and are at their happiest when they have their fingers in a myriad of pies. However, the Gemini-Rat's low boredom threshold and their more than occasional indecisiveness can hamper their chances of success.

Here, there, and everywhere, Gemini-Rats lead busy lives.

EAST WEST FUSION

EAST
The Heavenly Twins augment the Rat's versatility

WEST
The Chinese Rat endows Gemini with charisma

Witty and sociable, the party-loving Gemini-Rat is great fun to have around.

KEY CHARACTERISTICS
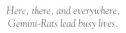 sociable
 active
 amusing
 inquisitive

YOUR COMPATIBLE SIGNS
Libra-Monkey
Aquarius-Dragon

OBSERVATIONS
Gemini-Rats can be whimsical, blowing hither and thither as the mood takes them

WORK, HEALTH, HOBBIES
Where the communication business is concerned, Gemini-Rats come top. Talking and expressing ideas is their special gift. So the worlds of journalism and broadcasting are tailor-made for these lively minds. Presentation work, courier work, and sales jobs would also suit. Given their inexhaustible fund of energy, the more variety they can pack into their working day, the happier they are.

❤ ❤ ❤

LOVES, LIKES, DISLIKES
An insatiable curiosity characterizes all who are born under this dual rulership. So Gemini-Rats like to be here, there, and everywhere. They adore get-togethers, parties, shopping, and endless conversations. Blessed with a razor-sharp wit, these people like being entertained. They especially enjoy listening to amusing stories and are great at telling jokes. Gemini-Rats have bulging address books and seem to know everyone. Settling down to one activity, one idea, or to one person in life is difficult for them. When they do find a soulmate, it must be someone who is very independent.

CHILDREN AND PARENTS
Intelligent, lively, and social, youngsters born under this duality are bright sparks, full of chatter and questions. Because they are into everything, they succeed at keeping their parents on their toes. At school they excel at literature and languages, and at home, if they're not surfing the net, they'll be on the phone to their friends. Gemini-Rat parents are amusing and life is full of fun and games when they're around. But these are busy, busy, busy people and probably out a good deal.

GEMINI-OX

EAST
Gemini speeds up the thinking
processes of the Ox

WEST
The Ox from the East calms the
restlessness of the Twins

Together, these two form a beneficial combination, with Gemini's influence bringing a good deal more spirit and a wider vision to the basically steadfast Oxen character. In turn, the Ox's methodical approach will moderate the Gemini's erratic tendencies and raises the boredom threshold. Consequently, Gemini-Oxen are focused people, with enough tenacity and strength of purpose to complete whatever task it is they have undertaken. Additionally, Gemini-Oxen tend to have outgoing natures and are not averse to the company of others. Witty and sociable, these people excel in business and other commercial ventures. They do particularly well in positions of authority, preferring to run the whole enterprise themselves than work as underlings.

OBSERVATIONS

Gemini-Oxen can give the impression that they are devoid of feelings

A career in clinical research attracts the medically minded Gemini-Ox.

KEY CHARACTERISTICS

- detached
- demanding
- raconteur
- inscrutable

YOUR COMPATIBLE SIGNS

Aquarius-Snake
Libra-Rooster

Reading is a favorite pastime of the Gemini-Ox.

THE ESSENTIAL YOU

WORK, HEALTH, HOBBIES

Beneath the ponderous exterior of the Gemini-Ox lies a brilliant intellect and a mind that can work at the speed of light. Members of this sign are rational beings, who take an analytical view on life. They are unsentimental thinkers and shrewd negotiators. As such, they do well in business and finance, wheeling and dealing with the best of them. Given their logical bent, Gemini-Oxen are also drawn toward the sciences, and particularly to clinical research and development. In addition, they make fine storytellers with strong critical talents, they have a genius for literature.

LOVES, LIKES, DISLIKES

In affairs of the heart, Gemini-Oxen may come across as rather cool and distant. That is because these people have the ability to rationalize their feelings. They tend not to be overwhelmed by emotions, whether they be their own or those of other people. Unmoveable, unflappable, and unshakeable, Gemini-Oxen hardly ever overreact to situations. These people have a way of compartmentalizing the different aspects of their lives. Work is one thing, play is another, love is something else, and sex quite separate altogether. According to the Gemini-Ox, none of these need encroach on the other.

CHILDREN AND PARENTS

Young Gemini-Oxen are fairly quiet and self-contained creatures. They like nothing better than to watch, take stock, and silently make up their own minds about what is going on. Gemini-Oxen should never be underestimated. Though they may not be contributing actively, be assured that nothing passes them by. Just as they are fascinated by the human condition, as parents, Gemini-Oxen are fascinated by their child's development. This parent can spend hours relating memories and telling stories to their youngsters.

GEMINI-TIGER

Those people belonging to the Gemini-Tiger dual sign like to be on the move. This band constantly hungers for new places to go and new faces to meet. Variety is the keyword and, for them, that is what provides the spice of life. Intelligent and witty, Gemini-Tigers are the life and soul of every party, never short of sparkling stories to recount, or of risqué jokes, which even female Gemini-Tigers can tell with aplomb. Members of this sign do have a low boredom threshold, however, which can mean that the Gemini-Tiger individual goes from one relationship to another at a brisk dip. Being tied to one place, one job, or even to one person for the rest of one's life is the worst scenario a Gemini-Tiger could possibly imagine.

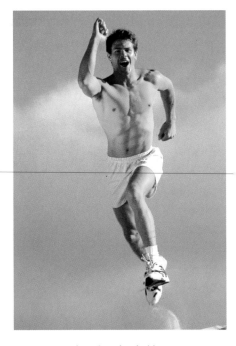

Fleet of mind and of foot, Gemini-Tigers know how to outpace their rivals.

EAST WEST FUSION

EAST
Gemini adds inspired thinking to the speedy Tiger

WEST
The Tiger gladdens the Twins with joyful exuberance

KEY CHARACTERISTICS
- restless
- alert
- versatile
- stimulating

YOUR COMPATIBLE SIGNS
Libra-Horse
Aquarius-Dog

OBSERVATIONS
Inconsistency undermines the Gemini-Tiger's potential for achievement

---

THE ESSENTIAL YOU

WORK, HEALTH, HOBBIES
Too fast, too soon, too much, too suddenly, Gemini-Tigers are unable to pace themselves. With their enthusiasm for life, these people are dazzling. However, they are often too impulsive for their own good, taking on far more than they can handle. They do learn fast, however, and they can mold themselves to suit any role or occupation that grabs their interest. As long as these people can work a varied routine, choose their own hours, and have the opportunity to meet lots of people along the way, they will be in their element. Sales jobs appeal to them, so too does anything to do with communication, travel, and trouble-shooting of all kinds.

LOVES, LIKES, DISLIKES
Members of this duality like a bold statement. These are colorful people who like to present a dramatic image. They know a little about a lot of things, because what they want in life is to experience as much as possible, dipping their toes into as many ponds as they can find. It's the same with relationships. Gemini-Tigers can't bear to be tied down to the same person forever. These people seek variety so are unlikely to remain faithful for long.

CHILDREN AND PARENTS
Gemini-Tiger children can be exhausting, but hugely entertaining. They are forever on the go and, if allowed, breeze through tasks so fast that one game or household chore is hardly finished before another is started. Gemini-Tigers must learn early on to follow tasks through to the end. Learning the value of concentration and the need for discipline is paramount, for, with their intelligence and vivacity, they could shine at whatever they take on. Gemini-Tiger parents are youthful and fun-loving.

Young Gemini-Tigers like to keep at least three activities on the go at once.

GEMINI: **MAY 21–JUNE 20**
YEARS OF THE RABBIT: 1903 ✳ 1915 ✳ 1927 ✳ 1939 ✳ 1951 ✳ 1963 ✳ 1975 ✳ 1987 ✳ 1999 ✳ 2011
HOUR OF THE RABBIT: 5AM – 6.59AM

THE ESSENTIAL YOU

GEMINI-RABBIT

A low boredom threshold means that Gemini-Rabbits need constant stimulation. Chatty and sociable, they are excellent communicators, rarely short of something to say. It is no wonder, therefore, that they are popular members of their set. People go out of their way to invite the Gemini-Rabbit to make up the numbers at their dinner party, for they are guaranteed to be entertaining, witty, and highly amusing. Their place is to be at the center of a crowd. Like all Gemini, they relish a good gossip, but the Rabbit influence means they can also be the soul of discretion. With such a lively mind, only an intelligent, articulate partner would make these people a good match.

Gemini-Rabbits are popular people and often invited to parties.

KEY CHARACTERISTICS

- clever
- resourceful
- gossipy
- changeable

YOUR COMPATIBLE SIGNS

Aquarius-Sheep
Libra-Pig

Working in partnership brings out the best in the Gemini-Rabbit.

OBSERVATIONS

Making hasty decisions for the sake of a quiet life can lead to unwanted consequences

EAST WEST FUSION

EAST

Gemini rewards the Rabbit with mercurial powers

WEST

The Chinese Rabbit teaches Gemini the value of discretion

WORK, HEALTH, HOBBIES

Creative intellectuals, it is the world of ideas that attracts these people. Advertising is a suitable avenue for their talents, and so is publishing. Gemini-Rabbits are not happy running the show, however, since they are not the best organizers in the world and they tend to fatigue easily. But, as long as they are allowed to generate the ideas while a colleague pays attention to the nitty-gritty of business life, these people will be happy at work. Consequently, members of this double sign work better in a partnership than they do on their own.

♥ ♥ ♥

LOVES, LIKES, DISLIKES

Heaven, for Gemini-Rabbits, is a tranquil afternoon spent reading a pleasant book, watching an old black-and-white movie on television, or else listening to a play on the radio while embroidering a cushion cover. Members of this sign like a peaceful life. Home is important to them too, and they enjoy collecting beautiful pictures, porcelain, and other artifacts with which to adorn their environment. Balance, harmony, and symmetry are what these people look for in life as well as in love. Discord and strife cuts them to the very quick.

CHILDREN AND PARENTS

Gemini-Rabbit children like to talk and talk. However, they are equally happy alone with their toys inventing imaginary friends. They tire easily, so perhaps are better suited to creative or academic subjects rather than sports. A stable and calm environment is essential to their well-being. Gemini-Rabbit parents are sedate and refined. There will be plenty of discussion around the dinner table but raised voices will be strongly discouraged.

GEMINI: **MAY 21–JUNE 20**
YEARS OF THE DRAGON: 1904 ∗ 1916 ∗ 1928 ∗ 1940 ∗ 1952 ∗ 1964 ∗ 1976 ∗ 1988 ∗ 2000 ∗ 2012
HOUR OF THE DRAGON: 7AM – 8.59AM

GEMINI-DRAGON

If talking and flirting were Olympic sports, the Gemini-Dragon would scoop a handful of gold medals standing on his or her head. Easy. In fact there would be no contest. For these people are life's performers, relishing the company of others and at their best when they are center stage. Gemini-Dragons are proficient jugglers. They can perform several tasks all at the same time, conduct four conversations without ever losing the gist of one, and work at two jobs without anyone ever being the wiser. Gemini-Dragons are successful at this balancing act, for most of the time, they are just skimming the surface. Undertaking anything in depth is not in the Gemini-Dragon's remit.

KEY CHARACTERISTICS

- courageous
- meteoric
- breezy
- superficial

YOUR COMPATIBLE SIGNS
Libra-Rat
Aquarius-Monkey

OBSERVATIONS

Though absolutely heartfelt at the time, Gemini-Dragons make far more promises than they are ever able to keep

With their radiant smiles, Gemini-Dragons conjure up good cheer wherever they go.

EAST WEST FUSION

EAST
Gemini graces the Dragon with quick intelligence

WEST
The Chinese Dragon brings dynamic courage to the Western Twins

Curious about people, Gemini-Dragons make wonderful gossip columnists.

THE ESSENTIAL YOU

WORK, HEALTH, HOBBIES
Like mini whirlwinds, Gemini-Dragons breeze through their work. They can get through a prodigious number of tasks in the course of a day. But they can't sustain their efforts over a long period of time. Members of this sign are born with the twin blessings of a brilliant mind and a charismatic personality. Areas befitting their talents include the entertainment business, leisure industry, hotel and catering, teaching and lecturing, writing, journalism, and music. If they can learn to pace themselves, Gemini-Dragons are well equipped to reach dazzling heights of success. Otherwise, early burnout is a distinct possibility.

♥ ♥ ♥

LOVES, LIKES, DISLIKES
Living life in the fast lane is the preference of the Gemini-Dragon. These people paint the world with bright colors, and they bring magic and spread good cheer wherever they go. They simply get a kick out of making people happy. But they do like to be in the spotlight and they need people to praise and admire them. Gemini-Dragons who have no one to love them wilt like flowers deprived of sunshine. As lovers, they know how to give their partners a good time. They need to be cherished, warts and all, in return.

🌹 🌹 🌹

CHILDREN AND PARENTS
Sunny and bright, little Gemini-Dragons are full of chatty cheer. They are charming and enthusiastic and popular with teachers and classmates alike. However, teachers despair about their lack of concentration on their work, their minds always flitting from one subject to another. These youngsters have an opinion on anything and everything and can contribute to discussions on any subject. Truth to tell, they are show-offs, fueled by their need and desire for attention. They also crave love and affection. Adult Gemini-Dragons are always the boss in their household. Consequently any offspring they have will have to respect and abide by their wishes.

GEMINI-SNAKE

Gemini-Snakes can be dastardly clever. They can slip and slither their way out of the most difficult and awkward situations imaginable. After all, Gemini are mercurial and Snakes have such insight that they can see right to the heart of a matter and know instinctively what makes a person tick. But it is these very qualities, too, combined with their charm and sociability, that enables the Gemini-Snake to captivate the minds and hearts of others with his or her truly sparkling personality. Chatty, breezy, and witty, these people are well-read and highly skilled at social interaction. They are never short of an instant quip or an amusing story to tell. Indeed, no party or social gathering should ever be without a Gemini-Snake in its midst.

EAST WEST FUSION

EAST
Gemini enlivens the mind of the Oriental Snake

WEST
The Snake brings Gemini a profound wisdom

KEY CHARACTERISTICS
- intuitive
- indolent
- complex
- seductive

YOUR COMPATIBLE SIGNS
Aquarius-Rooster
Libra-Ox

Gemini-Snakes like nothing better than spending an afternoon reading a good book.

OBSERVATIONS

The devil has ways of finding work for the idle hands of the Gemini-Snake

Verbally dexterous, Gemini-Snakes also enjoy word games in their spare time.

WORK, HEALTH, HOBBIES
The brilliant mind and sparkling repartee of the Gemini-Snake are coupled to an underlying physical slothfulness. Essentially, Gemini-Snakes are intellectual giants and have a genius with words. As writers, philosophers, and psychologists, their powers are impressive. Their articulate skills, too, attract them to the legal profession, and to positions where they are required to mediate, arbitrate, and negotiate. However, to find true success, they must sustain their impetus and not let their enthusiasm, or their energies, flag before they reach their goal.

♥ ♥ ♥

LOVES, LIKES, DISLIKES
Members of this sign have profound insight and they take pleasure in analyzing people's behavior and motivation. Reading is a passion and these people are inveterate bookworms. Quizzes on television, too, are favorites and these bright souls invariably get most of the answers right. Physical work is not for them, however. Getting up late and then lounging around is much more up their street. Gemini-Snakes are gorgeous creatures who attract admirers like moths to a candle. Fidelity is not found in their vocabulary at all.

CHILDREN AND PARENTS
Even as toddlers, Gemini-Snakes are intelligent and understand what is going on. They are easy to teach because their minds love to absorb knowledge. These youngsters will prefer word or boardgames to running around a pitch. But best of all, they adore reading in bed. As parents, Gemini-Snakes can be cold and aloof. They must fight a streak of selfishness in order to get closer to their offspring.

GEMINI-HORSE

Like a sprinter, Gemini-Horses work much better in short bursts.

Gemini-Horses are like greased lightning—fast and mercurial, they are original rolling stones that gather no moss. Clever and astute, persuasive talkers, and sparklingly witty, those born under this dual sign love being in the limelight. Neither Gemini nor the Horse bring qualities that might be described as particularly deep, for the Gemini-Horse prefers to know a little about a number of subjects. In terms of a race, Gemini-Horses would be the sprinters: they can put in a lot of effort over the short distance, but if it came to a marathon, they simple would not possess the stamina to run the course. With their charms, outrageous flirtatiousness, and youthful good looks, Gemini-Horses will tend to take center stage. Emotionally, they are immature and need a solid partner to keep them on a steady path.

OBSERVATIONS

An exceedingly low boredom threshold means the Gemini-Horse is highly-strung and often restless

KEY CHARACTERISTICS
- mercurial
- persuasive
- volatile
- freedom-loving

YOUR COMPATIBLE SIGN
Libra-Dog
Aquarius-Tiger

High-spirited and ever-youthful, Gemini-Horses never tire of having fun.

EAST WEST FUSION

EAST
Gemini enhances the Horse's quick wits

WEST
The Horse doubles Gemini's talents

THE ESSENTIAL YOU

WORK, HEALTH, HOBBIES
Endowed with mental acuity and physical agility, Gemini-Horses have the potential to achieve great things. The problem is they lack depth and staying power. They have a genius for analyzing people and picking up skills. Jobs which offer instant satisfaction, which require flashes of inspiration, or which depend on short bursts of intense activity would therefore suit these characters best. Working in the media would make an ideal career.

LOVES, LIKES, DISLIKES
Gemini-Horses are life's Peter Pans, maintaining youthful good looks, high spirits, and a childlike wonder throughout their lives. Perhaps what keeps them young is their sense of fun, or the fact that they have so many interests and so many friends and acquaintances to keep their minds sharp and alive. What Gemini-Horses cannot bear is being tied down, so long-term fidelity will be difficult unless they manage to find a soulmate clever enough to keep them on their toes.

CHILDREN AND PARENTS
Young Gemini-Horses are lively, spirited little things who just love having fun. Games are more preferable to maths, drama far more enjoyable than physics. And they shine at languages and literature. But keeping their concentration on one task is a huge challenge. Since they are so young at heart, Gemini-Horse parents have little problem with the generation gap. Parents and offspring tend to be more like brothers and sisters.

GEMINI-SHEEP

Many Gemini-Sheep are drawn to a career in show business.

THE ESSENTIAL YOU

WORK, HEALTH, HOBBIES

As long as Gemini-Sheep have someone to set the agenda, they will be happy work-fellows. These people have many talents but they lack self-motivation, so it is essential that they have a boss, an agent, or strict deadlines to keep them on the mark. Once given their marching orders, they can turn in some pretty impressive creative work. They make excellent entrepreneurs as long as they have support. Their natural talent for foreign languages would indicate success in a career as an interpreter. Manual work does not suit Gemini-Sheep. Being rather more cerebrally minded, they are adept at the well-timed one-liner.

♥ ♥ ♥

LOVES, LIKES, DISLIKES

Gemini-Sheep need the contact of other people. For all their talk of independence, they are actually very attached to their

home and family. Giving intimate dinner parties, chatting to a pal over coffee, and generally being surrounded by their loved ones are what Gemini-Sheep enjoy best. For members of this sign, then, coupledom is important and they are best with a partner at their side, preferably a strong partner who will steer and encourage them to develop their talents. Despite this, infidelity is not totally out of the question since they hate being left alone, even for an hour.

CHILDREN AND PARENTS

Young Gemini-Sheep are sweet, pretty children, loving, and irresistibly cute. Their easy-going nature tends to make them rather malleable, prone to taking the line of least resistance. Any activity where they can get involved using their hands—cookery, pottery, cutting-and-pasting—will grab their interest. They excel linguistically. Gemini-Sheep are happy homemakers and devoted parents.

Gemini-Sheep delight in a long chat over a cup of coffee with a friend.

C hatty, witty, and sociable, all members of this twin sign are brilliant dilettantes. The mercurial element of the Twins sharpens the intellectual faculties of the Sheep, lending speed of thought and a retentive memory. Gemini-Sheep are skilled communicators, being both amusing and irresistibly charming. They are adept at putting other people at ease. Many among this group find their forte in the world of entertainment. Friends are important to the Gemini-Sheep and their address books are invariably full to overflowing. Indeed, the Gemini-Sheep spends a good deal of time chatting on the phone and enjoys nothing better than cozy soirées or dinner parties surrounded by friends and family.

KEY CHARACTERISTICS

- talkative
- elegant
- charming
- artistic

YOUR COMPATIBLE SIGNS

Aquarius-Pig
Libra-Rabbit

EAST WEST FUSION

EAST

Gemini's lively spirits dispel the Sheep's characteristic mawkishness

WEST

The Chinese Sheep graces the Heavenly Twins with gentility

GEMINI-MONKEY

OBSERVATIONS

Jack and Jill of all trades and master and mistress of none is a foible of the Gemini-Monkey

Full of high jinks, the Gemini-Monkey's love of life is contagious.

EAST WEST FUSION

EAST
Gemini enhances the Monkey's spontaneous wit

WEST
The Monkey increases Gemini's dexterity

KEY CHARACTERISTICS
- ingenious
- easily-distracted
- proud
- hyperactive

YOUR COMPATIBLE SIGNS
Libra-Dragon
Aquarius-Rabbit

Young Gemini-Monkeys like to be entertained.

THE ESSENTIAL YOU

Gemini-Monkeys want to know everything that is going on around them. Both Gemini and the Monkey, independently, are renowned for their intelligence, versatility, high-speed chatter, and volatile brains. Therefore, fused together, members of this twin rulership are doubly silver-tongued and able to process any information at the speed of light. Gemini-Monkeys are whizz-kids, expert communicators, agile prevaricators, inventors, and magicians extraordinaire. Some might call them hyperactive. Whatever, these people possess such dynamic energy and verve that they race through life like whirling dervishes. Emotionally, Gemini-Monkeys are miserable without an adoring partner at their side.

WORK, HEALTH, HOBBIES

If Gemini-Monkeys succeed in focusing their considerable physical and mental energies, the sky is the limit. These people are blessed with a super-abundance of talents and, chameleonlike, they can adapt to any occupation that takes their fancy. Their linguistic skills can take them into any number of literary occupations, from compiling crosswords to writing best-selling thrillers. Their sparkling wit finds an appreciative audience in television work or on the after-dinner circuit. As lecturers or politicians, as lawyers or therapists, as information officers or sales personnel, the Gemini-Monkey has the ability to make his or her mark.

LOVES, LIKES, DISLIKES

Company and conversation are two Gemini-Monkey passions. They like people and parties. Terrific mimics, amusing raconteurs, and wonderful hosts, they can keep their guests enthralled for hours. Gemini-Monkeys enjoy theater and cinema and all manner of grand spectacles. Members of this duality do not like being hemmed in or confined to one place, so travel is extremely important and many Gemini-Monkeys invest in second homes in order to get a sense of the cosmopolitan. In love, they are generous, adventurous, and highly entertaining.

CHILDREN AND PARENTS

Gemini-Monkey children are full of japes and high jinks. They are on the go from dawn until dusk, and even then have energy left over to keep their parents awake at night. They want to be played with; they want to be amused. They are busy little beavers with a thousand and one questions to ask. Bright as buttons but naughty little things, they are intelligent mischief-makers. Gemini-Monkey parents have a lot of time for their offspring; they enjoy devising intricate games for them.

GEMINI-ROOSTER

Gemini-Roosters can run rings around almost anyone. They know a lot, or so it seems. And there is little a Gemini-Rooster likes better than a good old-fashioned debate. People born under the influence of this combination are athletic—mentally, physically, and emotionally. Restless and impulsive, Gemini-Roosters are full of brilliant schemes and ideas. Their talents lie in organization and many are highly computer literate. Engineering is a field in which these people can excel. Gemini-Roosters admire strength and intelligence in other people. Friends are important to them, for this group needs to maintain a high profile in a wide social network.

KEY CHARACTERISTICS

- precise
- hot-headed
- quick-thinking
- self-centered

YOUR COMPATIBLE SIGNS

Aquarius-Ox
Libra-Snake

Organized and forward-thinking, Gemini-Roosters like to be prepared.

EAST WEST FUSION

EAST
Gemini diffuses the Rooster's priggishness

WEST
The Rooster's exactness keeps Gemini's shoulder to the grindstone

Logical and articulate, Gemini-Roosters enjoy a good debate.

OBSERVATIONS

Gemini-Roosters can be mightily bossy

THE ESSENTIAL YOU

WORK, HEALTH, HOBBIES
Gemini-Roosters are sharpshooters. They are robust creatures who mean business and don't fool around. Members of this squad can march into an ailing company, size up the problem, and turn it around in two weeks. For these people are terrific organizers, focusing in on what is required in an instant. They excel in managerial positions, and can efficiently head up a new business. They are good at delegating, arbitrating, negotiating, and manipulating, until everything they see around them is ship-shape, watertight, and going full steam ahead.

♥ ♥ ♥

LOVES, LIKES, DISLIKES
Gemini-Roosters like organizing things. They clean up, straighten pictures, sort through problems, and arrange parties. Generally, they dominate in relationships and consequently don't like being told what to do. When it comes to love, Gemini-Roosters need someone strong-willed and capable of standing up for themselves. They certainly cannot respect a weakling. Therefore, someone who gives as good as he or she gets will win the approval of a Gemini-Rooster.

🐓 🐓 🐓

CHILDREN AND PARENTS
Sports are great for these robust young things. Gemini-Rooster children won't be afraid of stepping forward and being counted. Inventing stories and characters, dressing up, and putting on shows for an audience will especially delight them. But they will insist on producing, directing, and taking the leading role too! Gemini-Rooster parents are good at planning ahead. The cleaning of shoes, packing of lunches, and finishing up of homework will not be left to the last minute in this household.

GEMINI-DOG

Bright, breezy, and intelligent, Gemini-Dogs could talk the hind leg off a donkey. Full of ideas, flexible and multitalented, people born under this twin sign are far less intimidated by the idea of change than many of the other Dogs in the pack. Indeed, Gemini-Dogs positively enjoy the adventure of new experiences. Moreover, Dogs like to be out and about, and in this they are supported by the Gemini restlessness. Consequently, these natives are always on the go. Affable, companionable, and easily contented, Gemini-Dogs have little trouble when it comes to making and keeping friends. In love, these people are charming, considerate, and some of life's great romantics.

KEY CHARACTERISTICS

- accommodating
- adaptable
- peace-loving
- analytical

YOUR COMPATIBLE SIGNS

Libra-Tiger
Aquarius-Horse

Clever and talented on many levels, Gemini-Dogs are highly accomplished people.

The ability to empathize with others makes Gemini-Dogs excellent counselors or therapists.

EAST WEST FUSION

EAST
Gemini encourages the Dog to be more confident

WEST
The Chinese Dog teaches Gemini the satisfaction of constancy

OBSERVATIONS
Gemini-Dogs can be too trusting for their own good

THE ESSENTIAL YOU

WORK, HEALTH, HOBBIES
Best at second-in-command, Gemini-Dogs feel their role in life is to assist other people. They don't really like to give the orders; they don't want to carry that sort of responsibility. But as a back-up, they are invaluable. So, a position as a secretary, personal assistant or aide-de-camp would suit these people well. Not that they aren't intelligent. Indeed, their minds are as sharp and as slick as quick-silver. In addition, their insight and analytical skills enables them to understand and empathize easily with others. Gemini-Dog natives, therefore, make excellent psychologists, nurses, therapists, and doctors.

LOVES, LIKES, DISLIKES
Gemini-Dogs dislike conflict in any shape or form. What they are after in life is a peaceful existence in comfortable surroundings. They encourage their friends to drop by for visits and will enjoy spending many a convivial hour chatting and exchanging news and views over a cup of coffee or glass of wine. However, Gemini-Dogs can become restless and impatient creatures, so will benefit and appreciate some form of regular physical activity. In matters of the heart, members of this dual sign will search for a stable, somewhat conventional, partner who will be capable of returning the Gemini-Dog's unwaving loyalty without question.

CHILDREN AND PARENTS
Gemini-Dog youngsters don't like to make waves. They like to row in the tranquil waters of harmony and good will. By nature, they are dutiful and hard-working, respectful both of their parents and people in authority. Although these children might appear quiet on the surface, rest assured that their minds are ticking over the whole time. Indeed, the sharp Gemini-Dog child rarely misses a trick. They enjoy group activity and function best as part of a team. Gemini-Dogs make loving, caring, and devoted parents. They are fair-minded in all aspects of the upbringing of their children.

GEMINI-PIG

Wherever there is a Gemini influence, so intelligence, dexterity, astuteness, and a rapier-sharp wit will be in evidence. But there will also be restlessness and a low boredom threshold that demands a life of change and variety to add a certain piquancy. So it is that the Gemini influence will magnify the already sparkling personality of the Pig. Moreover, Gemini-Pigs are hugely sociable creatures, in their element when presiding over a dinner party with an assortment of guests and a table laden with a feast fit for a king. Appearances are so important to members of this dual sign that they are liable to fall in love with someone for all the wrong reasons. Gemini-Pigs would do well to remember not to judge a book by its cover!

KEY CHARACTERISTICS

✼ flexible
✼ cultured
✼ trustworthy
✼ impressive

YOUR COMPATIBLE SIGNS

Aquarius-Rabbit
Libra-Sheep

OBSERVATIONS

The Gemini-Pig's love of food can pile on the weight around middle-age

Gemini-Pigs adore good food and wine.

EAST WEST FUSION

EAST
Gemini puts a spring into the Chinese Pig's step

WEST
The Oriental Pig teaches Gemini to be more decisive

Party-lovers one and all, when they are in good company, Gemini-Pigs are in seventh heaven.

THE ESSENTIAL YOU

WORK, HEALTH, HOBBIES
Gemini-Pigs are wonderfully adaptable people, able to bend and bow according to whose company they are in or the job they are doing. They work as well in a self-employed capacity as they do in a team, and are as productive whether as employer or employee. Their talents, too, are flexible for these people can excel both in business or in a creative occupation. But whatever they do, Gemini-Pigs think big. They have grand ideas and mega schemes, which one way or another seem to come off. Many Gemini-Pigs are drawn to the art world, as collectors or dealers of priceless artifacts. Some go into haute couture. Others gravitate toward the hotel and restaurant business.

♥ ♥ ♥

LOVES, LIKES, DISLIKES
Members of this dual sign are impressed by grandeur. So wherever they live, they will want to feel they are surrounded by opulence—the best quality, the most beautiful, the most spectacular, and the most luxurious environment they can muster. They have a keen eye for art and will invest in paintings—classical pieces will be skillfully mixed with contemporary works—and naturally these will acrue exponentially in value. Partners, too, are quite often chosen for their looks. Gemini-Pigs like to show off their mates, so these must be well-dressed, well-groomed, and well able to keep their Gemini-Pigs amused.

🌹 🌹 🌹

CHILDREN AND PARENTS
Young Gemini-Pigs are bright, bubbling children with plenty to say for themselves. At school they show a flair for the expressive arts fairly early on and will confidently recite a poem in class, or read out a passage in assembly. Their handicrafts, too, will be deemed worthy of display. Gemini-Pig children often have a penchant for chocolate, candies, and cakes. As parents, Gemini-Pigs enjoy family life and take pride in their children's talents and achievements.

CANCER

BORN BETWEEN: **JUNE 21—JULY 22**
WATER SIGN

Cancer, the fourth sign of the Western astrological year, roughly corresponds to the Chinese month known as the Sheep Moon.

If you were born at this time of the year you can either call yourself a Cancerian, or you might like to think of yourself as a native of the Lotus Flower Moon, which is the beautiful name the Chinese give to this month.

According to the Chinese, this time of year is also broken up into two fortnights, each describing an aspect of the weather, or a feature relevant to the agricultural year. The first fortnight is called the Summer Solstice and this corresponds to the first two weeks of Cancer. If you were born in the second half of the sign, though, you belong to the second Chinese fortnight, Lesser Heat.

But it is, of course, when both your month and your year of birth are combined that the various influences begin to interweave themselves in a way that is essentially unique for you.

Whatever the combination, Cancer, as a gentle and caring sign, will bring a nurturing and home-loving element to the mix.

CANCER-RAT

EAST
Cancer makes the Rat
more affectionate

WEST
The Rat emboldens the Crab
and makes him or her less timid

Being somewhat sensitive creatures, Cancer-Rats tend to hide their feelings—a characteristic which can make them unfathomable. They like to retain their individuality and to stand out from the crowd. Having plenty of money and an abundance of material comforts are important to them. Members of this dual sign believe their possessions reflect the image of affluence they like to project. However, at the end of the day, what they value most in life—and everything else comes much further down the list—is a close-knit family with whom they can feel loved, protected, and secure. Tender and emotional, Cancer-Rats make intuitive lovers and partners who are both caring and understanding.

KEY CHARACTERISTICS
- intuitive
- refined
- deeply sensitive
- imaginative

YOUR COMPATIBLE SIGNS
Scorpio-Monkey
Pisces-Dragon

Cancer-Rats love to spoil their friends and family with unexpected little gifts.

OBSERVATIONS
A fundamental sense of insecurity hampers the Cancer-Rat

Cancer-Rats need some private moments every day to pursue their own interests.

THE ESSENTIAL YOU

WORK, HEALTH, HOBBIES
Money, domestic harmony, security, and comfort are the major drives in the life of the anxious Cancer-Rat. A lucrative career, therefore, is important to ensure an income that will give members of this dual sign the lifestyle they desire. Cancer-Rats are deeply intuitive, which can enable them, at work at least, to keep one step ahead of the competition. Intelligent and creative, they do well in occupations requiring linguistic or literary skills.

❤   ❤   ❤

LOVES, LIKES, DISLIKES
Members of this dual sign were born to shop. They love to lavish money on themselves, their loved ones, and on their homes. Indeed, Cancer-Rats devote a great deal of time, money, and attention to their domestic environments making them as beautiful and as luxurious as they possibly can. Secondly, they adore their families and enjoy nothing better than seeing all their loved ones sitting around them at the dinner table. As lovers, Cancer-Rats are romantic and sentimental. They love to surprise their partners with unexpected treats. However, even in the most intimate relationships, Cancer-Rats need their own space and a little time to themselves for their private thoughts.

CHILDREN AND PARENTS
Young Cancer-Rats have fertile imaginations and they spend a good deal of the time living inside their own heads. These are sensitive little things, hugely loving, and needy of cuddles and protection. Happiest at home where they feel secure, the world for them can be a very big, and very threatening, place. As far as their children are concerned, Cancer-Rat parents can be over-protective. They are strong-willed and demand to be respected and obeyed.

CANCER-OX

Talent, tempered by sensitivity and honed by determination, will ensure that the Cancer-Ox will develop his or her creative skills to a high degree. Whether these attributes are employed on a professional basis or simply for leisure pursuits, they will certainly stand the members of this sign in good stead when creating a beautiful home environment for themselves and their loved ones. Even independently, the Cancer and Ox signs are domestically oriented, possessing a great love of hearth and home. In combination, then, the Cancer-Ox duality will produce people for whom the home is the center of the universe, and whose partner and family are fundamental to their happiness and well-being in life.

KEY CHARACTERISTICS

- conservative
- determined
- traditional
- crusty

YOUR COMPATIBLE SIGNS

Pisces-Snake

Scorpio-Rooster

Cancer-Oxen like to feel close to the soil so for them, a garden is a must.

THE ESSENTIAL YOU

EAST WEST FUSION

EAST

The sensitivity of the Crab softens the tough hide of the Ox

WEST

The Ox empowers the Crab with gritty strength

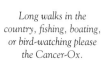

Long walks in the country, fishing, boating, or bird-watching please the Cancer-Ox.

WORK, HEALTH, HOBBIES

Cancer-Oxen are strong characters who have very fixed views and attitudes. They are prodigiously industrious but they are set in their ways. Indeed, they are die-hards who refuse to rock the system, come hell or high water. Serious and sober-minded by nature, they are unlikely to take short-cuts or bend the rules. Because they stubbornly insist on doing their own thing and are impervious to advice, they are better working on their own. Cancer-Oxen are creative innovators, excelling in fields as diverse as craftsman or sculptor, novelist or historian, farmer or marine biologist. What you can be sure of is that they will carry it out with thoroughness and to the very best of their ability.

LOVES, LIKES, DISLIKES

A warm, comfortable home is at the core of the Cancer-Ox's world, for it is here that they find security from the troublesome outside world. They are lovers of Nature, who hate crowds and noisy scenes. They prefer to live in the peace of the country than the hustle and bustle of the town. They dislike their plans being disrupted and can get decidedly grumpy if interrupted when in the middle of a task. Cancer-Oxen may not be particularly romantic and proclaim their feelings from the rooftops, but they are certainly devoted and faithful to the ones they love.

CHILDREN AND PARENTS

Cancer-Ox children build thick, protective walls around themselves. They learn early on the strategies required for protecting their vulnerabilities. These are serious-minded, stolid little things, resourceful and possibly happier working alone than in a group. One-to-one teaching may suit them best. Cancer-Ox parents are caring and accommodating toward their youngsters but they do lay down some rigid guidelines which they expect to be upheld.

CANCER: **JUNE 21–JULY 22**
YEARS OF THE TIGER: 1902 ✱ 1914 ✱ 1926 ✱ 1938 ✱ 1950 ✱ 1962 ✱ 1974 ✱ 1986 ✱ 1998 ✱ 2010
HOUR OF THE TIGER: 3AM – 4.59AM

THE ESSENTIAL YOU

CANCER-TIGER

Couple the sentimental nature of the Crab to the zest for life that Tigers possess and together this dual sign produces a romantic individual who can run through the gamut of emotions in one beat of the heart. By nature, Cancerians are soft-hearted and have a habit of protecting their sensitivities beneath a crusty shell. Tigers, on the other hand, are whimsical and impetuous, boldly going where others might fear to tread. The combined sign, therefore, produces an individual who may roar like a jungle cat, but who is just a tender-hearted old pussycat underneath. Cancer-Tigers are passionate people but, ultimately, it is a secure home and a stable, loving relationship that they really need in life.

KEY CHARACTERISTICS

- fortunate
- emotive
- attractive
- open-minded

YOUR COMPATIBLE SIGNS

Scorpio-Horse
Pisces-Dog

Cancer-Tigers adore their babies and surround them with love, security, and protection.

OBSERVATIONS

A lack of self-discipline is the Cancer-Tiger's major fault

EAST WEST FUSION

EAST
The Crab deepens the Tiger's perception

WEST
The Tiger gives Cancer courage

Carefree Cancer-Tigers need to set themselves firm deadlines if they want to succeed in life.

WORK, HEALTH, HOBBIES

Those Cancer-Tigers who submit to some discipline, order, and routine in their lives will achieve significant success in life. However, members of this sign do tend to buck against any such impositions, preferring to act spontaneously. They feel that working to order dulls their sparks of genius. Yet it is only by taking a consistent approach, or by setting themselves strict deadlines, that Cancer-Tigers will hone their proficiency and become productive. If they don't, they are likely to simply fritter away a lot of time and energy and their undeniable inventive talents will be wasted.

♥ ♥ ♥

LOVES, LIKES, DISLIKES

Like all Cancerians, members of this dual sign love their homes. On the other hand, like all Tigers, these people also need a flexible life full of challenges. Perhaps owning two homes, or taking regular short trips away would satisfy their disparate desires. As lovers, Cancer-Tigers are both tender and ardent. They are romantics who need to be loved yet they also need to be given some space. A den or a study to which they can retreat when they need a little privacy would be appreciated.

CHILDREN AND PARENTS

Youngsters of this double sign are snuggly, cuddly children, apparently intrepid, yet pulling back well before they reach the brink. They may look tough, but they are deeply sensitive with a tendency to hide their wounded feelings. Intuitive and inventive, they often come up with solutions that others have overlooked. As parents, Cancer-Tigers are loving and giving, always prepared to encourage and comfort their little ones.

CANCER-RABBIT

EAST WEST FUSION

EAST
Cancer augments the Rabbit's intuitiveness

WEST
The Rabbit increases Cancer's creative appreciation

Since both Crab and Rabbit are at their happiest around their own hearth, it is no wonder that, for the Cancer-Rabbit, home is definitely where the heart is. These people are strongly attached to their roots and their early conditioning will have a profound effect on them. They form extremely close bonds with their parents, especially so with their mothers. This is an inherently sensitive sign whose natives are soft and sentimental, idealistic, and easily hurt. Cancer-Rabbits are gentle and gravitate toward the caring or nursing professions. Members of this sign have a very traditional attitude toward love and marriage and hold stereotypical views. For true happiness, they need a solid, loving partner who will share their devotion to family and home.

Mothers belonging to the Cancer-Rabbit sign form particularly strong bonds with their babies.

KEY CHARACTERISTICS
- tender
- homely
- devoted
- conformist

YOUR COMPATIBLE SIGNS
Pisces-Sheep
Scorpio-Pig

OBSERVATIONS

Feeling sorry for themselves is a negative characteristic of Cancer-Rabbits

THE ESSENTIAL YOU

WORK, HEALTH, HOBBIES

Working from home is ideal for the members of this dual sign who will find all the stimulation and security they need in their own environment. Or else occupations with a domestic orientation would please, such as cabinetmaking, kitchen design, antique collecting, furniture restoring, and cooking, or perhaps hotel and catering work. Their literary talents would lend themselves to writing novels, romantic film scripts, or contributing to magazines specializing in house-and-garden features. With their love of all things domestic, real estate would be a big draw. Land management or garden design would also suit.

LOVES, LIKES, DISLIKES

Cancer-Rabbits like pretty things. They are blessed with an eye for beauty and quality and can spot an object of value from forty yards away. Their homes will reflect their good taste and everywhere there will be an air of refinement and gentility. Vulgarity of any sort is abhorred.

These people are arch upholders of tradition and nostalgia, and are thoroughly romantic. Cancer-Rabbits need a solid, down-to-earth partner to act as a counterbalance and support.

Wholesome home cooking is a top Cancer-Rabbit occupation; writing cookbooks could be a good career choice.

CHILDREN AND PARENTS

As long as Cancer-Rabbit children feel secure and loved they will shine and grow into confident people. They are not tough cookies, being inclined to quiet games, music, painting, and dancing. Cancer-Rabbit parents will take their children to the theater, museums, and ballet lessons and insist on polish and politeness at all times.

CANCER-DRAGON

EAST
Cancer mellows the egocentric tendencies of the Dragon

WEST
The Dragon lifts Cancer's spirits with optimistic cheer

Creative and artistically gifted, members of the Cancer-Dragon brigade have refined tastes. They are likely to be highly accomplished in one art form or another. Their homes, in particular, reflect this cultured appreciation and act as showcases of their talents with beautiful paintings, musical instruments, or books. A marked sentimentality, courtesy of the Crab, underlays the character of Cancer-Dragons and modifies the otherwise brashness of the Dragon sign. The combination produces a less egotistical Dragon, a more caring and sensitive individual, someone for whom a close relationship and settled homelife are essential to happiness.

Devotion to home and family is an innate characteristic of the Cancer-Dragon.

OBSERVATIONS

Soppy sentimentality can get the better of the Cancer-Dragon

KEY CHARACTERISTICS

- discerning
- proficient
- responsive
- inventive

YOUR COMPATIBLE SIGNS
Scorpio-Rat
Pisces-Monkey

THE ESSENTIAL YOU

WORK, HEALTH, HOBBIES
Blessed with a vibrant personality and formidable intellect Cancer-Dragons are born to go far. They are also sensitive souls and find it easy to empathize with others. It is, therefore, a powerful concoction of traits. Cancer-Dragons have creative minds and a genius for making imaginative breakthroughs where knotty problems are concerned. Yet they are fairly modest individuals, not shouting about their abilities—they know their strengths and quietly get on with the job in hand. Many are drawn, in one capacity or another, toward the media, particularly television. Politics also interests them greatly as do the arts.

LOVES, LIKES, DISLIKES
Like all Dragon influences, this combination comes with an inborn magnet that attracts admirers. The second half of the mix adds kindness and consideration, so that Cancer-Dragons seem dynamic on the outside while being soft and romantic on the inside. They are essentially family-oriented people, fiercely protective of their loved ones and strongly devoted to their partners. Cancer-Dragons are, in the main, equable, though they can also be stubborn. When their patience is tried, however, those in the vicinity would be wise to be on the lookout for the volcanic eruption!

CHILDREN AND PARENTS
Brainier than average, children belonging to this dual sign generally do well at school, with many tending to go onto higher education and beyond. They are blessed with a retentive memory so they learn quickly in class. Young Cancer-Dragons have bags of energy and oodles of charm which makes them popular in school—everyone wants to be their friend.
Adult Cancer-Dragons make fun-loving parents and children find them easy to get along with.

Cancer-Dragons have a genius for picking up unusual or original works of art.

CANCER-SNAKE

Everything around the Cancer-Snake shines and gleams. People born under this twin sign are twinkling stars, attracted to the limelight, to the best environments, and the choicest company available. Cancer-Snakes are not really designed for hard, manual work, nor are they at their best in lowly positions where the job is menial and poorly paid. Instead, Cancer-Snakes are glamorous types, who strive for kudos and prestige. They will, however, work hard to feather their nests with beautiful—sometimes irresistibly gorgeous—possessions. They have excellent taste and aspire to furnish their houses with the best that money can buy. But, when all is said and done, Cancer-Snakes are domestic souls whose hearth and home are sacrosanct.

Cancer-Snakes may be chic and elegant, but they don't let style get in the way of hands-on, loving parenting.

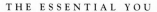

THE ESSENTIAL YOU

WORK, HEALTH, HOBBIES
Cancer-Snakes are not made for manual work. They don't really have the build or the stamina for physical labor, and they certainly don't like to get their hands dirty. Instead, these people succeed in intellectual occupations where they can use their considerable verbal skills and creative talents. The fashion design, beauty business, and luxury trades make excellent careers. Floristry, real estate, and interior design, too, would suit. And so would the legal profession, PR, and advertising.

LOVES, LIKES, DISLIKES
Chic and soigné describe the Cancer-Snake, whose elegant body is always well dressed in the latest, most exclusive fashions. People ruled by this duality have good taste, and expensive taste at that. They like to be seen in the best quality, designer labels and to frequent the latest trendy bar or restaurant. Moreover, these sexy sophisticates only have to snap their fingers and admirers will come in droves. Of course, there will always be so many rich and eager lovers to choose from that, when it comes to potential suitors, Cancer-Snakes are really spoilt for choice.

CHILDREN AND PARENTS
Cancer-Snake children love to be cuddled and cosseted. But they also like to do their own thing in their own space and in their own time. Arguments about untidy rooms are unlikely here since they dislike mess and will look after their possessions meticulously. Nor will they come home spattered in mud since a swim or, at the outside, a leisurely game of tennis will be preferred to contact sports. Reading, chess, and horseriding will feature among their favorite pastimes. Despite all their glamor, adult Cancer-Snakes are tolerant where their children are concerned.

KEY CHARACTERISTICS
- creative
- understanding
- seductive
- well-groomed

YOUR COMPATIBLE SIGNS
Pisces-Rooster
Scorpio-Ox

OBSERVATIONS
A tendency to bend the truth can be a peccadillo of this double sign

Horse-riding is a favorite of young Cancer-Snakes.

EAST WEST FUSION

EAST
Cancer brings loving warmth to kindle the Snake's affections

WEST
The Snake rationalizes the Crab's emotions and lifts his or her moods

CANCER: **JUNE 21–JULY 22**
YEARS OF THE HORSE: 1906 * 1918 * 1930 * 1942 * 1954 * 1966 * 1978 * 1990 * 2002 * 2014
HOUR OF THE HORSE: 11AM – 12.59PM

THE ESSENTIAL YOU

CANCER-HORSE

The Cancer-Horse likes the company of other people. In fact, in character with most Horses who tend to kick up their heels and gallop off into the sunset, the Cancerian influence encourages those born of this twin sign to actively seek the crowd. Cancer-Horses either find the love of their lives when young or go on searching for the rest of their lives. Perhaps this is because members of this duality, with their high standards, are looking for the perfect mate. Finding that paragon, however, would make the Cancer-Horse a very happy partner indeed because this combination sign is big-hearted and has a lot of love to give.

KEY CHARACTERISTICS

- genial
- idealistic
- refined
- whimsical

YOUR COMPATIBLE SIGNS

Scorpio-Dog
Pisces-Tiger

A long chat with a friend is a life-long passion of the Cancer-Horse.

The Crab reins in the frisky Horse, while the Horse rocks the cautious Crab.

EAST WEST FUSION

EAST
Cancer calms the Horse's roaming instincts

WEST
The Horse introduces the Crab to pleasurable sociability

OBSERVATIONS

The Cancer-Horse's idealistic expectations can lead to disappointments in love and in life

WORK, HEALTH, HOBBIES

Best working as part of a team and preferably dealing with the general public, there is no doubt that Cancer-Horses do well around other people. Whether as boss or employee, members of this dual sign are cheerful and cooperative, always prepared to roll up their sleeves and get involved. The hotel and catering trade is an excellent career avenue for Cancer-Horses and so is childcare. The health profession appeals, perhaps in the form of complementary medicine.

♥ ♥ ♥

LOVES, LIKES, DISLIKES

In almost every aspect of life, Cancer-Horses are moderate people. They react with aplomb, are full of presence of mind and dislike anything done to excess. Good taste is important and this will be reflected in their homes and possessions. These are hospitable people who delight in entertaining their friends and family, and who like nothing better than a long chat over a cup of coffee, or catching up on news over the phone with their pals. Where they do lose their poise, however, is in affairs of the heart. For they are idealistic people who spend their lives looking for perfection in love.

CHILDREN AND PARENTS

Youngsters of this dual sign are tender and loving. They work hard at school and excel in the expressive arts. They find working in groups particularly satisfying. Though they are popular among their peers, friendships can be fraught. They tend to get crushes on people and then are disillusioned and suffer greatly when or if they are let down. Cancer-Horses make loving parents who do their best to provide for all their children's needs.

CANCER-SHEEP

Sensitive, gentle, devoted, and kind, with so much love to give and so much need to be loved, it is hardly surprising that Cancer-Sheep are the archetypal family men or women. When young, Cancer-Sheep are warm and affectionate, children who never think of straying too far from home. As they mature, they have an urge to build cozy nests for themselves and their loved ones. They fill them with as many comforts as they can. Ultimately, sentimental ties draw them in and, if they can, they settle close to the neighborhood in which they grew up. People born under this sign tend to be anxiety-ridden. But above all, they worry about loneliness. Living with an extended family helps them sleep more soundly at night.

KEY CHARACTERISTICS

- ❧ kind
- ❧ anxious
- ❧ sensitive
- ❧ insecure

YOUR COMPATIBLE SIGNS

Pisces-Pig
Scorpio-Rabbit

Teaching young children is an ideal occupation for the Cancer-Sheep.

EAST WEST FUSION

EAST
Cancer enhances the Sheep's love of beauty

WEST
The Sheep brings the Crab an inventive mentality

OBSERVATIONS

Lack of confidence can be the Cancer-Sheep's stumbling-block

Cancer-Sheep adore cuddles and are at their happiest when next to the one they love.

THE ESSENTIAL YOU

WORK, HEALTH, HOBBIES

At work, just as at home, Cancer-Sheep like to please, so these people make cheerful and helpful employees. They can be dreamers, so going it alone in business can be a bit risky. Best, then, if they work as part of a team or in a partnership with a more realistic associate. Though Cancer-Sheep are prepared to roll up their sleeves and work very hard, they are not physically very robust. Occupations in the service industries would suit them, as would teaching. A career where they can demonstrate their cultural knowledge, such as working in a museum or art gallery, would particularly appeal.

❤ ❤ ❤

LOVES, LIKES, DISLIKES

Cancer-Sheep love a peaceful life. But they also like their lives to be safe, comfortable, and secure. They are born givers, and looking after their loved ones comes naturally to them. Most

Cancer-Sheep will enjoy keeping house. There will always be plenty on the table because a full pantry at this house goes without question. Cancer-Sheep like traditional decor and style in their homes and their byword is quality. Heaven to Cancer-Sheep is a lovely home, a closely-knit family, and a partner who cherishes them.

❦ ❦ ❦

CHILDREN AND PARENTS

Youngsters belonging to the Cancer-Sheep duality are sweet little things, not unlike hothouse flowers, for they need a lot of tender loving care. They are vulnerable and easily hurt by less sensitive types who have no concept of delicate sensibilities. Homely and kind, they are responsible young people, attached to their families, and loyal to younger siblings and parents alike. When they in turn are parents, Cancer-Sheep are caring, nurturing, and encouraging of their young.

CANCER-MONKEY

Monkeys like to be here, there, and everywhere, their nimble minds racing from one project to the next. And, while they do need a place where they can hang their hats, they don't allow themselves to be bogged down with the drudgery of domestic duties. However, with the Cancerian influence subtly working on the simian sign, the Monkey undergoes a sea change and becomes considerably more home-loving and protective of its family and loved ones. The combination of signs, therefore, produces responsible individuals who make good providers for those they love and hold dear. Money is important to Cancer-Monkeys, so it is just as well that they are wizards when it comes to making investments and earning money. Sexually, Cancer-Monkeys have a very healthy libido and are constantly falling madly in love.

Like quicksilver, Cancer-Monkeys can even outsmart a calculator.

KEY CHARACTERISTICS

- intelligent
- observant
- changeable
- forward-thinking

YOUR COMPATIBLE SIGNS

Scorpio-Dragon
Pisces-Rat

EAST WEST FUSION

EAST
Cancer tames the Oriental Monkey's artful tendencies

WEST
The Monkey brings the Crab self-confidence

THE ESSENTIAL YOU

WORK, HEALTH, HOBBIES

Quick-thinking and clever, Cancer-Monkeys are blessed with keen insight and terrific memories to boot. Indeed, the retentive mental powers of the Cancer-Monkey are legendary. At a college reunion twenty years after graduation, they are the ones who remember everyone's name. Naturally, they are quick learners so will pick up skills in a flash. They are also sharp at spotting gaps in the market, especially where the demand is domestically oriented. Both intellectual and creative, Cancer-Monkeys do equally well in the arts and the sciences, in the media as well as in the financial sector.

LOVES, LIKES, DISLIKES

Cancer-Monkeys have exquisite tastes and they like everything to be just so. As with all Cancer subjects, they love their homes, but the Monkey also enjoys the cut and thrust of the outside world. So Cancer-Monkeys like to mix and socialize. They are highly articulate people and make great hosts. Actually, they do rather enjoy a good gossip. Being popular and desirable to the opposite sex is important. In fact, when it comes to amorous liaisons, these people tend to have more of them than average.

CHILDREN AND PARENTS

At school, young Cancer-Monkeys show a particular aptitude for computer studies and information technology. They excel at bringing inventive and innovative ideas to fruition. Given the right environment, these youngsters should develop their intellectual talents and pursue their interests into further education. Adult Cancer-Monkeys are not doting parents and they tend to relate better to older children than they do to young babies.

Cancer-Monkeys adore dressing up to party.

CANCER-ROOSTER

Although in the farmyard roosters like to have the run of the hen-house, their human equivalents are not especially domesticated. In fact, they are more than happy to leave the house in order to follow their star. Not so the Cancer-Rooster. The Crab's influence on this dual sign makes those born into it strongly family oriented. Indeed, for the Cancer-Rooster, life revolves around the home. The Crab endows the Rooster with tenderness and softens its spiky edges. The Rooster, on the other hand, brings to the partnership an efficiency that will leave the home as clean and shiny as new. The more children, pets, and other relatives who gather around the Cancer-Roosters' feet, the happier and more secure they feel. And, given a loving and caring partner, the Cancer-Rooster will be faithful, supportive, and happy.

EAST WEST FUSION

EAST
The Crab teaches the Rooster to be more sensitive

WEST
The Oriental Rooster encourages the Crab to become more plucky

Cancer-Roosters like to keep a tidy house.

KEY CHARACTERISTICS
- indefatigable
- homely
- defensive
- suspicious

YOUR COMPATIBLE SIGNS
Pisces-Ox
Scorpio-Snake

OBSERVATIONS
A deep, inner disquiet can make the Cancer-Rooster prone to moodiness

THE ESSENTIAL YOU

WORK, HEALTH, HOBBIES
Brilliant at organizing and delegating, Cancer-Roosters work hard to make a good position for themselves in life. They also like to feather their own nests. Members of this dual sign are robust individuals, strong and persistent, with thick skins. They are able to concentrate on fine detail for long periods of time, spotting errors that many other will have overlooked. So, Cancer-Roosters make excellent accountants, tax inspectors, quality control officers, archivists, engineers, editors, and critics. At work, impatience and a somewhat rapacious attitude can sometimes mar their dealings with colleagues.

LOVES, LIKES, DISLIKES
Order is the key word in the Cancer-Rooster dictionary. These people like to run a tight ship. They will not brook mess and slackness is summarily dealt with. At home, members of this double sign certainly like to rule the roost. By turns indulgent and abrasively hypercritical, Cancer-Roosters' moods can be unpredictable. Their intentions, however, are generally pure and, as far as their loved ones are concerned, their affections are warm and kindly.

CHILDREN AND PARENTS
The belief in their own superiority urges young Cancer-Roosters to go for the top and be the best. So at school these youngsters are bound to work hard and will be praised for their neat work and high standards. As parents, Cancer-Roosters are kind-hearted but strict. Rules are to be obeyed and the house is to be kept immaculate.

Neatness is the hallmark of the Cancer-Rooster.

CANCER: **JUNE 21–JULY 22**
YEARS OF THE DOG: 1910 ✱ 1922 ✱ 1934 ✱ 1946 ✱ 1958 ✱ 1970 ✱ 1982 ✱ 1994 ✱ 2006 ✱ 2018
HOUR OF THE DOG: 7PM – 8.59PM

CANCER-DOG

Cancer-Dogs are people of quiet, yet discriminating tastes. Independently, the Crab and the Dog have a strong affinity to the home. The Oriental Dog is the sign of the family and the guardian of the house, while the Western Crab loves nothing better than sitting by his or her own fireside. It follows then, that this combination would produce people who are instinctive homemakers, happiest at their own hearths and surrounded by their families and loved ones. As a rule, Cancer-Dogs are sensitive to people and surroundings. However, they have a tendency to suffer from personal insecurities and need solid, loving partners to provide the support and reassurance to enable them to develop their talents and reach their potential.

Cancer-Dogs will spend hours creating the perfect setting in their homes.

THE ESSENTIAL YOU

WORK, HEALTH, HOBBIES
Cancer-Dogs have the happy knack of coming up with creative solutions to apparently insoluble problems. They have a good eye for line and color and they tend to work instinctively, with their feelings rather than with cold reason. On the whole physically and psychologically unsuited to heavy, manual work, they do however shine in the world of art and design. Whether for leisure or as a career, members of this double sign will be attracted to interior decorating, craftwork, book or magazine illustration, and art collecting.

LOVES, LIKES, DISLIKES
On the one hand, Cancer-Dogs can be practical and down-to-earth. On the other, they can live life with their heads in the clouds. A lot of this dreaminess pays off, however, especially when they translate their imaginative ideas into tangible artifacts. For, with paints and paper, fabrics, and knickknacks, Cancer-Dogs can transform the dreariest hovel into a palatial haven. Using their hands to create something exquisite seemingly from nothing gives them immense pleasure.

CHILDREN AND PARENTS
Young Cancer-Dogs like to make and create. As long as the teacher gives them crayons and paints, these little souls can keep themselves happy and amused for hours on end. As children, they are quiet and reserved, but invariably the first to offer their services when someone needs a helping hand. Young Cancer-Dogs are emotional creatures and tend to cry easily. Plenty of cuddles and reassurances are necessary if they are to thrive. As family and home are quintessentially important to the Cancer-Dog, members of this sign make devoted mothers and fathers.

Creative children of this sign paint and draw with skill and imagination.

KEY CHARACTERISTICS
- demure
- emotional
- affectionate
- inhibited

YOUR COMPATIBLE SIGNS
Scorpio-Tiger
Pisces-Horse

OBSERVATIONS
Exaggerating their feelings and their problems can make life difficult for the Cancer-Dog

EAST WEST FUSION

EAST
Cancer brings out the Dog's imaginative talents

WEST
The Oriental Dog helps to stabilise the mood swings of the Crab

CANCER: **JUNE 21–JULY 22**
YEARS OF THE PIG: 1911 ✷ 1923 ✷ 1935 ✷ 1947 ✷ 1959 ✷ 1971 ✷ 1983 ✷ 1995 ✷ 2007 ✷ 2019
HOUR OF THE PIG: 9PM – 10.59PM

THE ESSENTIAL YOU

CANCER-PIG

The Western Crab sign sits happily and harmoniously beside the Oriental sign of the Pig. These are both home-loving creatures with finely honed nurturing instincts. Both are idyllically happy sitting by their own hearth. To spend an afternoon cooking or baking, jam making, or transplanting lettuces is heaven to those who are born under this dual sign. Cancer-Pigs are the archetypal family men or women. Moreover, these are enormously generous and big-hearted people, especially so where their loved ones are concerned. Tender, lovable, and creative, they are incorrigibly sensual. With their mega sex drive, it is only inevitable that Cancer-Pigs will enjoy a large family.

Cooking and eating in the company of their loved ones brings Cancer-Pigs enormous pleasure.

KEY CHARACTERISTICS

❀ indulgent
❀ sentimental
❀ pleasure-loving
❀ passive

YOUR COMPATIBLE SIGNS

Pisces-Rabbit
Scorpio-Sheep

OBSERVATIONS

Wasting energy and resources can limit the Cancer-Pig's chances of success

EAST WEST FUSION

EAST
Cancer moderates the Oriental Pig's excesses

WEST
The Chinese Pig fills the Crab with cultural appreciation

Cancer-Pig children do love their toys but are also willing to share them with their siblings.

WORK, HEALTH, HOBBIES

Cancer-Pigs like to work in a team. But they also like to be in charge of the team. So whatever occupation these people choose to follow, it won't take them long to find their way to the top. Either that, or members of this double sign are best setting up and running their own businesses from the outset. Though there is a temptation to be laid-back, they are also capable of working very hard indeed. If they can maintain their impetus, Cancer-Pigs have the ability to do extremely well in whatever profession they choose. However, to be truly rich and successful a career with a creative slant would be best.

♥ ♥ ♥

LOVES, LIKES, DISLIKES

Going without makes Cancer-Pigs absolutely miserable. Perhaps that is why collecting, or hoarding (simply different degrees of the same activity), is a passion of the Cancer-Pig. For these people are materialistic and they like the feeling of security that they derive from "counting" their possessions. Often, however, there is a great deal of value among their chattels, since Cancer-Pigs have a superb eye for beauty and a desire for rich-living. These people also have big appetites for all of life's pleasures.

🌹 🌹 🌹

CHILDREN AND PARENTS

Little Cancer-Pigs are very loving and the most generous creatures of any sign. In fact, they are so generous that they would give away their favorite toy to a child less fortunate them themselves. For these are big-hearted youngsters, emotionally easily swayed, sensitive, and impressionable. At school, art is perhaps their best subject. Cancer-Pig parents are doting and have a tendency to wrap their youngsters in a cocoon.

LEO

BORN BETWEEN: **JULY 23—AUGUST 22**
FIRE SIGN

Leo, the fifth sign of the Western astrological year, roughly corresponds to the Chinese month known as the Monkey Moon.

If you were born at this time of the year you can either call yourself a Leo, or you might like to say you were born during the Orchid Flower Moon, which is a much more beautiful alternative name given to this month in the East.

According to the Chinese, this time of year is also broken up into two fortnights, each describing an aspect of the weather, or a feature relevant to the agricultural year. The first fortnight is called Greater Heat and this corresponds to the first two weeks of Leo. If you were born in the second half of the sign, though, you belong to the second Chinese fortnight, Autumn Commences.

But it is, of course, when both your month and your year of birth are combined that the various influences begin to interweave themselves in a way that is essentially unique for you.

Whatever the combination, as a warm and passionate force, Leo will add color and drama to the mix.

LEO-RAT

EAST
The Lion instills high principles into the Rat

WEST
The Rat curbs the Lion's tendency to extravagance

If ever there existed a charismatic figure, it has to be the Leo-Rat. People born under this twin sign are dynamic, generous, and responsive. Enthusiasm is one of their key assets and this, coupled with high moral standards and the ability to make wise judgments, guarantees that the Leo-Rat will go far. People respect Leo-Rats and are drawn to their warm and magnetic personalities. At work, members of this combined sign are not afraid to take the initiative. Far-sighted and brilliant as managers, it is rare for these people not to reach the top of their chosen profession.

Warm, friendly, and highly ethical, everyone likes and respects the Leo-Rat.

THE ESSENTIAL YOU

KEY CHARACTERISTICS

- courteous
- daring
- freedom-loving
- charitable

YOUR COMPATIBLE SIGNS

Aries-Dragon
Sagittarius-Monkey

OBSERVATIONS

Because they pitch their expectations very high, Leo-Rats can come across as demanding

Once Leo-Rats pledge their hearts, they remain constant and true.

WORK, HEALTH, HOBBIES

Enthusiastic and constantly on the go, Leo-Rats can get through a prodigious quantity of work in a day. In fact, the busier the schedule, the happier these people will be. Members of this double sign are born to manage and direct, so whatever their chosen occupation, they soon gravitate toward a position of authority and control. Whatever leisure time these vigorous individuals have is usually devoted to cultural pursuits.

LOVES, LIKES, DISLIKES

A close, supportive relationship makes all the difference to the Leo-Rat's self-confidence, since, above all else, members of this team need to be loved and admired. Once they have found the partner of their dreams, they are unlikely to roam. Constant individuals, unfaithfulness and a lack of enthusiasm are their abiding dislikes.

CHILDREN AND PARENTS

Even as youngsters, these people are impressive. With wide-ranging interests, they always have some intelligent contribution to make to a discussion, whatever the subject matter. These are high-profile little individuals who like to be noticed. As parents, people of this dual sign are ambitious for their offspring and will do their utmost to set them up on the right path in life. Consequently, they expect their youngsters to succeed in whatever activity they take part.

LEO: **JULY 23–AUGUST 22**
YEARS OF THE OX: 1901 ✳ 1913 ✳ 1925 ✳ 1937 ✳ 1949 ✳ 1961 ✳ 1973 ✳ 1985 ✳ 1997 ✳ 2009
HOUR OF THE OX: 1AM – 2.59AM

THE ESSENTIAL YOU

LEO-OX

The Leo-Ox duality produces leaders, people who are compelled to take charge and control of every situation in which they are involved. Leo-Oxen take themselves very seriously, throwing their whole being into whatever they undertake—something that applies not only to their professional work, but also to their personal lives as well. Leos are sunny creatures and therefore bring a buoyant influence, adding warmth and lifting the spirits of the usually dour Oxen personality. Generosity is marked in the Leo-Ox. Magnanimous and giving, members of this dual sign are at their happiest with an adoring, loving partner at their side.

KEY CHARACTERISTICS

✵ focused
✵ forceful
✵ obstinate
✵ serious

YOUR COMPATIBLE SIGNS

Sagittarius-Rooster
Aries-Snake

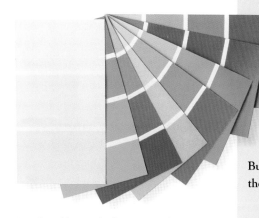

Leo-Oxen like to make the decisions—from whom to employ, down to the choice of decor in their homes.

EAST WEST FUSION

EAST
Leo brings dramatic élan to enliven the erstwhile stolidity of the Ox

WEST
The Ox gives the Lion determination and strength of purpose

WORK, HEALTH, HOBBIES

With their broad, solid shoulders, Leo-Oxen carry responsibility well and invariably rise to positions of power within large corporate organizations where their excellent managerial skills come to the fore. These people are no strangers to hard work since they are achievement-motivated and programed to succeed. In fact they tend to overwork and need to learn to relax and unwind. But with their strength and resilience, they are well able to last the course.

❤ ❤ ❤

LOVES, LIKES, DISLIKES

Leo-Oxen are proud people—proud of their achievements, proud of their families, homes, and partners. They possess extraordinarily high standards and expect themselves and their loved ones to live up to them. They are not great socializers, putting their time and efforts into their work and their homes, so that little energy is left for spare-time pursuits. When they fall in love, they give themselves over body and soul. For the Leo-Ox it is one hundred percent or nothing.

CHILDREN AND PARENTS

Teachers appreciate Leo-Ox children because they plod diligently through their lessons and homework. In the playground, though, they can be bossy and arrogant, taking charge of games and telling their classmates what to do. It is wise to give these youngsters responsibilities and they invariably shine if elected to positions such as class prefect. As parents, members of this sign are big-hearted toward their children but strict. They lay down the rules and insist that their youngsters comply.

A sunny, secure family environment is what Leo-Oxen like best.

OBSERVATIONS

All too often, Leo-Oxen are reluctant to take advice from anyone else because, essentially, they usually think they know best

LEO-TIGER

A dynamic combination, the Leo-Tiger is all feline. Bold, courageous, and fervent, members of this sign are charismatic creatures, powerful of personality and noble of bearing. Born leaders, they command respect in whatever occupation they choose to follow, rising to the top as if ordained according to the divine right of kings. And, in the true spirit of *noblesse oblige*, these majesterial people go about their duties with fervor and magnanimity. Many find satisfaction in working for humanitarian causes, some excel in management, while others find the world of the arts a natural outlet for their considerable creative talents.

KEY CHARACTERISTICS

- positive
- understanding
- successful
- committed

YOUR COMPATIBLE SIGNS

Aries-Dog
Sagittarius-Horse

OBSERVATIONS

Arrogance will lose friends and win enemies for the Leo-Tiger

Leo-Tigers exude strength, power, and burning passion in all that they do.

THE ESSENTIAL YOU

WORK, HEALTH, HOBBIES

There is little that truly daunts this fiery combination of big cats. They don't allow obstacles to stand in their way and, if ever struck down by ill-health or adversity, they simply pick themselves up, dust themselves off, and carry on as normal. Single-minded, better off working alone, and quixotic in spirit, there is a good deal of the knight errant among members of this sign. Success comes with reflection and often later, rather than earlier, in life.

LOVES, LIKES, DISLIKES

Neither the trappings of materialism nor the acquisition of the latest fad inspire the Leo-Tiger. These people are strong and can be fierce—they're made for the big chase, and when they growl they respect those who growl back. Only another person, as strong, as resilient, and as prepared to give as he or she gets will win over this formidable heart. Unfortunately, as far as the Leo-Tiger is concerned, very few make the grade.

CHILDREN AND PARENTS

The precocious talent of young Leo-Tigers can all too often make them act in a superior manner toward their peers. The lion, after all, is the king of the jungle, so it is understandable that these youngsters are born with a sense of nobility. But since only a small minority are actually lords and ladies of the manor, children of this sign do need to learn the spirit of cooperation. As parents, Leo-Tigers are completely dedicated to their families and would courageously lay down their lives for the ones that they love.

EAST WEST FUSION

EAST

Leonine grandeur adds a sense of presence to the Tiger's nature

WEST

Tiger luck augments the fortunes of the Lion

Crowns sit easily on the regal heads of the members of this dual sign.

LEO: **JULY 23–AUGUST 22**
YEARS OF THE RABBIT: 1903 ✷ 1915 ✷ 1927 ✷ 1939 ✷ 1951 ✷ 1963 ✷ 1975 ✷ 1987 ✷ 1999 ✷ 2011
HOUR OF THE RABBIT: 5AM – 6.59AM

THE ESSENTIAL YOU

LEO-RABBIT

With the Lion's noble bearing and the Rabbit's finesse, people born under the Leo-Rabbit sign are confident individuals. They are blessed with a charismatic personality, which makes them attractive to others and popular both among friends and fellow workers. Leo-Rabbits are persuasive people who know how to go about getting what they want without ruffling anybody's feathers. Refined and accomplished, they are poised and well-mannered. Both signs have a penchant for the good things in life, so the Leo-Rabbit will not deny him- or herself little luxuries in life. Moreover, they like to live in elegant style surrounded by beautiful things.

KEY CHARACTERISTICS

- careful
- amenable
- gracious
- talkative

YOUR COMPATIBLE SIGNS

Aries-Sheep

Sagittarius-Pig

The Leo-Rabbit's refined elegance shines through.

WORK, HEALTH, HOBBIES

Leo-Rabbits enjoy many pleasures and devote a great deal of their time to their private interests. Many find ways of turning a hobby into a lucrative living, or else they follow occupations akin to their own favorite pastimes. Whatever the case, there are few Leo-Rabbits who would claim their jobs were not agreeable. Popular with bosses, colleagues, and employees, members ruled by this duality have a gentle and caring disposition and do well in media and design, or else in teaching or complementary medicine.

♥ ♥ ♥

LOVES, LIKES, DISLIKES

Refinement is what the Leo-Rabbit seeks in life. Quality rather than quantity is essential and this will be evident in the home and working environment of all those ruled by this dual sign. These people spend a long time getting everything just so and they do not appreciate their neat and tidy world being cluttered up. This applies as much to physical mess as it does to emotional embroilment. Consequently, when it comes to the choice of a mate in life, Leo-Rabbits will be highly selective.

CHILDREN AND PARENTS

Clean, neat, and well-dressed, Leo-Rabbit youngsters are rarely boisterous tearabouts. They are more likely to be drawn to musical or artistic subjects than they are to sports or manual work. A Leo-Rabbit parent will expect his or her offspring to be respectful to adults and to appreciate their homes and possessions.

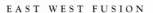

EAST WEST FUSION

EAST
Leo imbues the Rabbit
with courage

WEST
The Rabbit teaches the Lion
to be prudent

Whether as a career choice or for soothing relaxation, aromatherapy suits these people well.

OBSERVATIONS

Whether literally or metaphorically, Leo-Rabbits don't like soiling their hands

LEO: **JULY 23–AUGUST 22**
YEARS OF THE DRAGON: 1904 ∗ 1916 ∗ 1928 ∗ 1940 ∗ 1952 ∗ 1964 ∗ 1976 ∗ 1988 ∗ 2000 ∗ 2012
HOUR OF THE DRAGON: 7AM – 8.59AM

THE ESSENTIAL YOU

LEO-DRAGON

As well as being the king of the jungle, the Lion enjoys the reputation of king of the Zodiac in the West. In Oriental astrology, the Dragon too is the sign of the emperor, the ruler of the dynasty. Each is an emblem of royalty, and married together they generate people who possess an innate sense of nobility, born leaders who naturally gravitate to the top of their professions. They are flamboyant people and, albeit consumate show-offs, they are nevertheless the luckiest and most charismatic of the Dragon clan. Moreover, it is the warmth and joie de vivre of this sign that makes its members irresistibly attractive.

KEY CHARACTERISTICS

- regal
- chivalrous
- magnanimous
- fortunate

YOUR COMPATIBLE SIGNS

Aries-Monkey
Sagittarius-Rat

The King of the Jungle and the Emperor of the East unite in a formidable alliance.

OBSERVATIONS

With so much combined fire, passion and color, the Leo-Dragon can sometimes go over the top

The expensive tastes of the Leo-Dragon are reflected in everything they possess.

EAST WEST FUSION

EAST
The Lion ensures the Dragon conducts him or herself with probity

WEST
The Dragon extends the Lion's physical resources

WORK, HEALTH, HOBBIES

Leo-Dragons put so much effort into everything they do that there is no question they will succeed in whatever occupation they follow. However, menial jobs are not for these people, because their charismatic presence automatically pitches them on to a higher echelon from the outset. These people seem to have it all—they exude good health, they are lucky, they get noticed, and their talents are usually rewarded. For Leo-Dragons, the world is their oyster. All they have to do is put out a hand and take it.

♥ ♥ ♥

LOVES, LIKES, DISLIKES

There is only room for one star player in a Leo-Dragon relationship—and that has to be the Leo-Dragon. Anyone else must be prepared to take a subordinate role. So only a partner who is happy to give support from the wings, without ambition to steal any of the limelight will do for a member of this sign. Beautiful and expensive possessions are a passion for Leo-Dragons. Being thwarted in their aims is a definite downer.

CHILDREN AND PARENTS

When Leo-Dragon children smile it is with such radiance that one might suppose the sun has just come out from behind a cloud. This happy disposition, together with their talents and self-confidence, ensures that the youngsters of this dual sign stand head and shoulders above everyone else. They are certainly unmissable. As parents, Leo-Dragons are extremely loving people and encourage their children to grow into confident and resourceful human beings.

EAST WEST FUSION

LEO-SNAKE

Snakes born under the influence of Leo are proud individuals with a strong self-image and almost overbearing confidence in themselves and in their abilities. Leo-Snakes believe in their own infallibility. What's more, they hate deferring to others or coming second in the race. In life, members of this sign should be given just enough encouragement, approval, and admiration to function well, but not so much that it goes to their heads. Getting the balance just right, especially when these people are still youngsters,

will ensure that the Leo-Snake develops into a well-adjusted individual. They are not the most domesticated or family-oriented of people but they will build the most comfortable and luxurious home they can for themselves and for those that they love.

KEY CHARACTERISTICS

- physically attractive
- intense
- restless
- vain

YOUR COMPATIBLE SIGNS

Aries-Rooster
Sagittarius-Ox

Looking good is essential for all Leo-Snakes.

OBSERVATIONS

Dealing arrogantly with people definitely earns minus points for the Leo-Snake

EAST
The Snake brings savoir faire to the rangy Lion

WEST
Leo adds warmth and approachability to the normally aloof Snake

Behind the gloss of the Leo-Snake there lies a powerful brain.

THE ESSENTIAL YOU

WORK, HEALTH, HOBBIES

Seductive charms coupled with drop-dead good looks single these people out for a career in the glamor business. Modeling, acting, or singing are appropriate avenues for them and would ensure they could earn the quantities of money they require in life. Hard, physical work is out of the question, for Leo-Snakes simply don't have the stamina or vitality for a heavy, manual job. They are intelligent and will use their brain to get the most returns for the least effort.

LOVES, LIKES, DISLIKES

The combination of beauty and brains ensures that Leo-Snakes are never short of admirers who are ever ready to shower them with gifts and adulation. This is just as well, because members of this sign like to be pampered and adore expensive trinkets. However, they can be fickle when it comes to affairs of the heart, and an inner restlessness can mean that these people have a succession of lovers and tend to drift from one relationship to another throughout their lives.

CHILDREN AND PARENTS

Leo-Snake youngsters have got life sussed. They are not the most robust children of the Zodiac and so they learn from an early age to get what they want in subtle ways. This may be through academic achievement or through knowledge that makes them streetwise and admired by their peers. Certainly, they're clever enough to get others to do the dirty work for them. Leo-Snakes are not natural earth mothers or fathers and many prefer not having children at all.

LEO-HORSE

Leo combines with the Horse to form a resplendent individual, who dispenses sunshine upon all those with whom he or she comes into contact. Leo-Horses are dynamic, high-profile people of regal poise and noble bearing. Members of this group have bags of innate self-confidence and get to the top of their chosen profession simply because they believe they can. Passionate and strong-willed, once members of this dual sign have set their minds on a course of action, nothing will deflect them from their goal. This applies equally to their worldly ambitions as it does to their sexual desires. Moreover, whenever Leo-Horses fall in love, they are totally blind to reason.

OBSERVATIONS
A lack of patience and clarity of thought can sometimes limit the Leo-Horse's chances of success

In love with love—Leo-Horses are forever seeking the ideal.

KEY CHARACTERISTICS

- impulsive
- extravagant
- altruistic
- impatient

YOUR COMPATIBLE SIGNS
Sagittarius-Dog
Aries-Tiger

Elegant and chic, Leo-Horses are born with an innate sense of style.

THE ESSENTIAL YOU

WORK, HEALTH, HOBBIES
Travel is a passion for members of this clan and, if they can combine it with a career, they will be in seventh heaven. They make excellent roving reporters, foreign correspondents, sales representatives, or import and export merchants—anything, in fact, that requires having an up-to-date passport and a suitcase ready by the door. Leo-Horses are unlikely to stay in the same job for long. But with plentiful energy at their disposal, they make a success of each job they take on before moving on to the next.

LOVES, LIKES, DISLIKES
Image is important to the Leo-Horse. That's why they are so fashion-conscious and always dressed beautifully. They do have a sizeable amount of egocentricity in their nature and they can be skittish in affairs of the heart. Love is big for the Leo-Horse, all-encompassing and all-embracing. When they fall in love—which they tend to do many times in their lifetimes—they completely lose their power of reasoning.

CHILDREN AND PARENTS
Leo-Horse children are delightfully sunny and happy little individuals, spontaneously loving and affectionate. They are a joy in the classroom because they are so enthusiastic about everything and they launch themselves with boundless energy into sports, art, music, mathematics or whatever subject is on the agenda. It can be difficult for others to keep up with a young Leo-Horse! Equally as parents, Leo-Horses have plenty of love and masses of energy to share with their beloved offspring.

LEO-SHEEP

Leo-Sheep are kind and dignified creatures. The Lion's influence invigorates the Sheep, contributing a greater sense of independence and a certain spunkiness to the normally placid sign. Leo is fair and just and honorable, always generous and magnanimous, and endows the Sheep with a noble presence and lofty ideals. With the Lion's influence, these Sheep are passionate and possess a rather romantic and courtly notion of love. But they also have an eye for luxury and are never backward when it comes to seeking out the good things in life. Leo-Sheep certainly know how to have a good time. In their books, five-star pampered luxury is the only way to live.

Leo-Sheep combine fashion and creativity to produce a look that is fresh and original.

KEY CHARACTERISTICS
- discerning
- open
- honorable
- luxury-loving

YOUR COMPATIBLE SIGNS
Aries-Pig
Sagittarius-Rabbit

When Leo-Sheep travel, it has to be first class all the way.

OBSERVATIONS
Leo-Sheep live so much for the present that they tend to blind themselves about their future needs

EAST WEST FUSION

EAST
The Lion endows the timid Lamb with assertiveness

WEST
The Sheep shows the Lion how to do it with style

WORK, HEALTH, HOBBIES
The worlds of film, fashion, and art appeal to Leo-Sheep. These stylish creatures, with masses of imaginative flair, sing and dance and paint the world with beautiful rainbows of light. But they need managers, partners, agents, accountants, and a whole host of other backup assistants both to steer them in the right direction and to take care of the nitty-gritty bits of everyday living. It isn't so much that they are lazy, but that they are dependent types who need constant support and encouragement. That given, the energetic Leo-Sheep will be confident to shine and radiate.

♥ ♥ ♥

LOVES, LIKES, DISLIKES
Leo-Sheep like to have money—lots and lots of it. They have expensive tastes and an eye for the best in everything. But indulgent though they may be, they do like to share their belongings and are at their happiest with a partner by their side—preferably a rich one. With the right mate, these people will be trusting and honest and true.

CHILDREN AND PARENTS
Soft and affectionate, the Leo-Sheep youngster likes to feel protected. So these children will nuzzle up to their parents, sighing happily as they snuggle close. At school they will excel in the gentle arts and are likely to win the starring roles at the end-of-year performance. Leo-Sheep turn into loving parents and, just as they are self-indulgent themselves, so they also like to indulge their little sons and daughters.

LEO: **JULY 23–AUGUST 22**
YEARS OF THE MONKEY: 1908 ✳ 1920 ✳ 1932 ✳ 1944 ✳ 1956 ✳ 1968 ✳ 1980 ✳ 1992 ✳ 2004 ✳ 2016
HOUR OF THE MONKEY: 3PM – 4.59PM

LEO-MONKEY

Born performers, even as children, Leo-Monkeys like to be the star.

Leo-Monkeys have to be the biggest show-offs in the whole of the cosmos! Wherever there is a spotlight, there will be a Leo-Monkey smack bang in the middle of it. Both the Lion native and the Monkey are terrific attention-seekers in their own right, essentially because each has an overwhelming need to be loved and reassured. They are show-men and women and, because they are beautiful as well as talented, they are also showstoppers to boot. With their fine features, noble deportment, and huge expressive eyes, Leo-Monkeys turn heads wherever they go. In love, they become adoring partners, hard-working, passionate, and true.

KEY CHARACTERISTICS

- intelligent
- witty
- curious
- subtly manipulative

YOUR COMPATIBLE SIGNS

Aries-Rat
Sagittarius-Dragon

EAST WEST FUSION

EAST
The Lion inspires the Monkey with integrity

WEST
The Monkey brings humor into the Lion's soul

Leo's confidence coupled with the intelligence of the Monkey often leads to high academic achievement.

OBSERVATIONS

Any ruction between Leo-Monkeys and their partners is likely to be about their untidiness around the house

---

THE ESSENTIAL YOU

WORK, HEALTH, HOBBIES
Bright, clever, and adaptable, Leo-Monkeys can turn their hands to almost any profession one cares to name. They can be as successful on their own as they can in company, their lively chatter and sense of humor amusing all and sundry. Equally, they work as well at the bottom of the ladder as they do at the top as long as the job doesn't entail mopping up after other people. But members of this sign are intelligent sparks for whom academic life is a positive draw.

LOVES, LIKES, DISLIKES
Leo-Monkeys will happily lose themselves for hours when engaged in philosophical debate with their colleagues or simply discussing the price of bread with their friends. It matters little what the subject of the conversation is—it is the chatting in convivial company that is important. In love, Leo-Monkeys need partners who give them lots of room to maneuver. However, they themselves can be possessive and demand that their partners never stray.

CHILDREN AND PARENTS
A Leo-Monkey is never really what one might call a child. Even as babies, one look into their eyes will reveal a little adult, already equipped with an understanding of life. Perhaps this is what gives them that perspicacity and psychological edge which enables them to manipulate others so subtly and deftly. As parents, the impish sense of fun of the Leo-Monkey goes down well with their offspring.

LEO-ROOSTER

OBSERVATIONS

A bossy nature can undermine some of the Leo-Rooster's more worthy qualities

Here, under this dual rulership, are two signs which can each match the other in terms of color, drama, and flamboyance. Each can fill a whole room with his or her mega-personality alone. Fused together in this way results in a character who can appear larger than life, someone who enjoys overtly displaying his or her fine feathers, and someone who, like the strutting rooster among the hens, has an undisguised belief in his or her own superiority. But, although Leo-Roosters are proud individuals, they are sincere. Loving and passionate, with a devoted partner to help keep their feet on the ground, the Leo-Rooster will not stray.

KEY CHARACTERISTICS
- faithful
- honest
- orderly
- moody

YOUR COMPATIBLE SIGNS
Aries-Ox
Sagittarius-Snake

Outgoing and flamboyant, Leo-Roosters like to stand out from the crowd.

EAST WEST FUSION

EAST
The Lion's magnanimous heart wins over the Rooster's priggishness

WEST
The Rooster brings style to gloss the Lion's mane

The very latest in fashion attracts the Leo-Rooster like a magnet.

THE ESSENTIAL YOU

WORK, HEALTH, HOBBIES
New ideas, the latest in fashions and technology grab the Leo-Rooster's imagination. An unfortunate superior attitude can sometimes mar their working relationships and, given that they do like to be in control of both their agenda and environment, perhaps they are better off working alone. For one reason or another, the Leo-Rooster's early career can be fraught with difficulties, some of his or her own making, others perhaps due to a delicate constitution. Whatever, it is later on in life that Leo-Roosters come into their own and truly make their mark.

♥ ♥ ♥

LOVES, LIKES, DISLIKES
Leo-Roosters are prone to mood swings, one day high as a kite, and the very next day down in the deepest dumps. A loving and understanding partner who can provide time to listen, a broad shoulder to cry on, and a ready smile to cheer, can make all the difference to these people's lives. In return, Leo-Roosters will offer faithfulness, constancy, and devotion.

CHILDREN AND PARENTS
Leo-Roosters are precocious young things who really do work hard to achieve and who take great pleasure in making their parents proud of them. They have plenty of talent right across the board and will make a good contribution to every subject in class. Leo-Roosters make solid and sensible parents who do their utmost to provide for the ones they love.

LEO: **JULY 23–AUGUST 22**
YEARS OF THE DOG: 1910 * 1922 * 1934 * 1946 * 1958 * 1970 * 1982 * 1994 * 2006 * 2018
HOUR OF THE DOG: 7PM – 8.59PM

LEO-DOG

Proud, confident, and dignified, Leo-Dogs come across as worldly-wise and self-assured. None but those truly close to a native of this sign, however, would suspect that the Leo-Dog is tortured by inner doubts and in need of constant encouragement to bolster his or her fragile ego. Yet members of this sign are some of the most genuine and caring individuals a person is ever likely to meet. Courteous, noble-minded, faithful, and loyal, people born under the aegis of this dual sign are warm and loving. In personal relationships, the Leo-Dog needs a supportive partner, someone on hand who can help to boost his or her morale.

Compassionate and understanding, Leo-Dogs are always ready to offer a word of advice.

KEY CHARACTERISTICS
- modest
- analytical
- moral
- trusting

YOUR COMPATIBLE SIGNS
Sagittarius-Tiger
Aries-Horse

OBSERVATIONS
Self-doubt and a lack of confidence can hinder the Leo-Dog's progress through life.

EAST WEST FUSION

EAST
The Lion warms the cockles of the Dog's heart

WEST
The Dog keeps the Lion's paws firmly on the ground

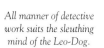

All manner of detective work suits the sleuthing mind of the Leo-Dog.

WORK, HEALTH, HOBBIES
Disturbed by the injustices of the world, Leo-Dogs make excellent detectives, skilled at working through clues and painstakingly tracking down miscreants. Medical research, too, appeals to their love of detail, their analytical mentalities, and their desire to do good in the world. These people are not especially high-profile types and don't fare particularly well under pressure. Instead, they prefer to work away quietly and methodically on their own, earning an honest wage for an honest day's work. These upright, uncomplaining souls form the backbone of industry everywhere.

♥ ♥ ♥

LOVES, LIKES, DISLIKES
Leo-Dogs do not have expensive tastes. These are honest, hard-working, and unpretentious people, whose lifestyles reflect their virtues. But they are solid citizens who like to be useful and to help others less well off than themselves. Members of this sign do best with a kindly and supportive partner who will shore up their insecurities.

CHILDREN AND PARENTS
Youngsters of this double sign are often found on the sidelines, rarely under the glare of the spotlight. They don't as a rule push themselves forward and need time to acclimatize to situations. Like the adults of the sign, they too need a lot of encouragement to build up their confidence and to learn to value their talents. Leo-Dog parents are dutiful people and utterly committed to their offspring.

LEO-PIG

Passionate, voluble, colorful, and theatrical, Leo-Pigs may be described fairly accurately as characters who are larger than life. People born under this twin rulership put one hundred percent into everything they do, whether this be work, play, homelife, relationships, or even sex. Perhaps the most open and generous of the Pigs, they can let their appetites get the better of them. But they are equally benevolent and big-hearted and they give freely to those they love. Full of sincerity and childlike wonder, Leo-Pigs are blessed with high spirits that are at once infectious and irrepressible.

Leo-Pigs find life's little pleasures irresistible.

Generous and sociable, Leo-Pigs will bring gifts galore and the sunny glow of their exuberant personalities to any party.

KEY CHARACTERISTICS
- friendly
- talented
- sensual
- unselfish

YOUR COMPATIBLE SIGNS
Sagittarius-Sheep
Aries-Rabbit

EAST WEST FUSION

EAST
Leo presents the Pig with dignity

WEST
Pigs touch the Lion's heart with their openness and sincerity

OBSERVATIONS

A patent lack of humility works against the Leo-Pig's interests in life

THE ESSENTIAL YOU

WORK, HEALTH, HOBBIES

Leo-Pigs take on a lot. They are multi-talented creatures who can turn their hands to a variety of jobs and more often than not veer toward artistic occupations. Their taste for an expensive lifestyle drives them into highly paid occupations. Healthwise, a tendency to indulge in the best and the finest has a nasty habit of piling on the inches around the Leo-Pig's midriff in later life! For all sorts of reasons, members of this sign really do need to learn to say "No" more often.

LOVES, LIKES, DISLIKES

Generous to a fault, Leo-Pigs like to share with those they love. They will share their property, money, food, and in fact, all they possess. This is the way that they show their love, and all that they ask is to be loved in return. Leo-Pigs make wonderfully warm and faithful partners. Unkindness and disloyalty, though, firstly will break their hearts, and then will turn them bitter.

CHILDREN AND PARENTS

Leo-Pigs are driven to seek the best from a very young age and, even when they are children, members of this sign strive for excellence. At school, if they don't achieve the results they desire, there's a tendency to sit back and watch the world go by. Encouraging them to keep on trying is a valuable lesson for these youngsters. As parents, Leo-Pigs are protective and loyal to their offspring, but also realistic and practical in the way they bring them up.

VIRGO

Virgo, the sixth sign of the Western astrological year, roughly corresponds to the Chinese month known as the Rooster Moon.

If you were born at this time of the year you can either call yourself a Virgo, or you might like to think of yourself as a native of the Cinnamon Moon, which is the poetic name the Chinese give to this month.

According to the Chinese, this time of year is also broken up into two fortnights, each describing an aspect of the weather, or a feature relevant to the agricultural year. The first fortnight is called End of Heat and this corresponds to the first two weeks of Virgo. If you were born in the second half of the sign, though, you belong to the second Chinese fortnight, White Dews.

But it is, of course, when both your month and your year of birth are combined that the various influences begin to interweave themselves in a way that is essentially unique for you.

Whatever the combination, Virgo as a logical and methodical force, will instill caution and endow the powers of analysis to the mix.

VIRGO: **AUGUST 23–SEPTEMBER 22**
YEARS OF THE RAT: 1900 ✳ 1912 ✳ 1924 ✳ 1936 ✳ 1948 ✳ 1960 ✳ 1972 ✳ 1984 ✳ 1996 ✳ 2008
HOUR OF THE RAT: 11PM – 12.59AM

VIRGO-RAT

When it comes to research and analysis, Virgo-Rats can knock the rest of the Animal signs into a cocked hat. With their exquisite eye for detail and ability to make minute assessments, these hard-working individuals will find their deepest satisfaction in any occupation where critical faculties and painstaking investigation are required. The Virgo-Rat's mission statement is to love and to serve. They will thrive in the caring professions, such as nursing and charity work, yet equally they will excel in the fields of scientific research or investigative work. There is something charmingly naive and idealistic about Virgo-Rats and all too often lame ducks are attracted to them. They care desperately about other people and would give the shirt off their backs to anyone in need.

KEY CHARACTERISTICS

- neat
- analytical
- industrious
- idealistic

YOUR COMPATIBLE SIGNS
Taurus-Monkey
Capricorn-Dragon

Fierce analytical powers and a cool head make Virgo-Rats forceful protagonists in the workplace.

OBSERVATIONS
A tendency to disclose their personal secrets too readily can render the Virgo-Rat vulnerable to predators

EAST WEST FUSION

EAST
Virgo teaches the Rat to be punctilious

WEST
The Chinese Rat puts a cheering sparkle into Virgo's eyes

Virgo-Rats excel in scientific or mathematical occupations.

WORK, HEALTH, HOBBIES
With their feet firmly planted on the ground, these industrious individuals excel in organizational skills and are meticulous in their affairs. Thorough and efficient, they make valued employees and trusted colleagues. Jobs that offer glamor and pizzazz are not especially attractive to Virgo-Rats. Instead, members of this sign tend to go for the sort of career that helps humanity or that oils the mechanics of day-to-day living. So they make fine medical researchers, cashiers, bankers, accountants, and solicitors.

❤ ❤ ❤

LOVES, LIKES, DISLIKES
Virgo-Rats are very good with money and many take an interest in the stock market—perhaps not so much as a vehicle for investment, but purely out of curiosity. They do like a neat and tidy environment because mess upsets their sense of order. In love, Virgo-Rats tend to wear their hearts on their sleeves and they will put their beloved on a pedestal. Their openness and their naivety can often work against them in a relationship.

CHILDREN AND PARENTS
A Virgo-Rat child is sweet and a model of good behavior. In class, youngsters of this dual sign are quiet and polite and get on with their work. They especially enjoy mathematics and science, and turn in work that is neat and precise. Virgo-Rat adults take their childrearing duties very seriously and make good, loving, and fair-minded parents.

VIRGO: **AUGUST 23–SEPTEMBER 22**
YEARS OF THE OX: 1901 ✳ 1913 ✳ 1925 ✳ 1937 ✳ 1949 ✳ 1961 ✳ 1973 ✳ 1985 ✳ 1997 ✳ 2009
HOUR OF THE OX: 1AM – 2.59AM

VIRGO-OX

Virgos have a notoriously critical eye, while Oxen have a reputation for taking a pedantic approach to life. Therefore, when these two signs merge, they produce individuals who are both practical and meticulous, but whose skills in dealing with the fine minutiae of life can perhaps all too easily develop into a tendency to fuss. Morally upright, few others can match Virgo-Oxen's honesty, integrity, and ethical correctness. Moreover, Virgo-Oxen respond well to responsibility. They become respected pillars of society, people who, once they have given it, will keep their word come hell or high water. It could not be said that these are the most romantic or flamboyant people in the world but, if they are able to find the right partner, they will certainly stay faithful and true.

EAST WEST FUSION

EAST
Virgo teaches the Ox the niceties of social behavior

WEST
The Chinese Ox will strengthen the sinews of the Maiden

KEY CHARACTERISTICS
- sincere
- selective
- reserved
- methodical

YOUR COMPATIBLE SIGNS
Capricorn-Snake
Taurus-Rooster

Meticulous Virgo-Oxen keep their houses in order and always have the right tools for the job.

THE ESSENTIAL YOU

WORK, HEALTH, HOBBIES
Quiet, ponderous, and determined, people born under the rulership of the Virgo-Ox sign possess enduring strength, enabling them to concentrate on a specific task for long periods at a stretch. At work, they impose high standards of excellence on themselves and expect others to do the same. These are responsible people who work well in positions of authority, although they like to work on their own and preferably undisturbed. Their love of peace and their instinctive rapport with Nature make them ideal horticulturalists, farmers, vets, geologists, scientists, tree surgeons, and environmental engineers.

LOVES, LIKES, DISLIKES
Ideally, Virgo-Oxen like an undramatic sort of life, one that enables them to pursue their interests in a peaceful setting. Gardening, reading, hiking, and long-distance running are all suitable pastimes for members of this sign. In love, they are not given to romantic overtures and, though good-hearted underneath, their critical nitpicking can put off potential suitors. With an honest, unpretentious, and hard-working partner by their side, these people will never err.

CHILDREN AND PARENTS
Virgo-Oxen youngsters like to learn, so choosing the right school environment for each one of these children is vital. They have plenty of muscle and staying power and do well on the sportsfield. Their determination can turn into stubbornness and confrontations with them are best avoided. As parents, Virgo-Oxen are staunch disciplinarians—what they say, goes, no fooling around.

Plants thrive under the tender loving care of the Virgo-Ox.

VIRGO: **AUGUST 23–SEPTEMBER 22**
YEARS OF THE TIGER: 1902 ∗ 1914 ∗ 1926 ∗ 1938 ∗ 1950 ∗ 1962 ∗ 1974 ∗ 1986 ∗ 1998 ∗ 2010
HOUR OF THE TIGER: 3AM – 4.59AM

THE ESSENTIAL YOU

VIRGO-TIGER

The natural Virgo caution acts as a brake to the feline impetuosity making the Virgo-Tiger stop and think before taking any of those irrevocable steps the pure Tiger is so prone to doing. Tigers are not usually famed for their love of the minutiae so would not ordinarily be found in occupations where strict precision is a requisite. With the Maiden's influence, however, the Virgo-Tiger can become a stickler for the finer points and will excel in any profession where an eye for detail is a must. Practical and hard-working, the high expectations that are so characteristic among Virgos mean that Virgo-Tigers tend to be mightily selective when it comes to choosing someone with whom to share their lives.

Virgo-Tigers are famous for putting the final individualistic details to their work themselves.

EAST WEST FUSION

EAST
Virgo teaches the meaning of restraint to the Oriental Tiger

WEST
The Tiger brings dash and daring to the Maiden

KEY CHARACTERISTICS
- sociable
- perceptive
- choosy
- independent

YOUR COMPATIBLE SIGNS
Taurus-Horse
Capricorn-Dog

OBSERVATIONS
Virgo-Tigers are too independent to ask for help when they need it

Virgo-Tigers are happy doing their own thing in their own time.

WORK, HEALTH, HOBBIES
Virgo-Tigers know where they are heading. Moreover, they know in precise detail what achieving their ambition entails. Undaunted, they go for it. But they understand that getting to the top will require dedication and hard work, and they balk at neither. In their work, these people couple a methodical eye with a daring hand and produce work of great flair. But they will suffer if they don't pace themselves and must learn not to leave everything to the last minute. Fashion and design are particular favorites among members of this dual sign.

♥ ♥ ♥

LOVES, LIKES, DISLIKES
Virgo joined with the Tiger produces an outwardly modest individual with inward fire and passion. Like all Virgo mergers, this group is highly selective when choosing a partner, since imperfections in people and situations disappoint them deeply. So, for their happiness and well-being, it is imperative they find someone they can admire and look up to. With the right soulmate by their sides, Virgo-Tigers like to busy themselves practically and creatively around the house.

🐾 🐾 🐾

CHILDREN AND PARENTS
Young Virgo-Tigers are energetic little souls who pack their days with activity. On the whole they are willing and loving, but they can be fussy about their rooms, their clothes, and their possessions. They like things the way they like them and so develop a strong streak of independence which they take with them throughout their lives. As adults, Virgo-Tigers make good parents, and are solicitous and caring of their young.

VIRGO-RABBIT

OBSERVATIONS

A lack of focus can reduce a Virgo-Rabbit's chances of success

The combination of the Virgo and Rabbit signs produces practical and capable individuals who can turn their hands to almost anything. In addition, because both are punctilious types in their own right, together they sometimes verge on the downright fussy. In their homelife, they like everything to be just so and at work they painstakingly dot every i and cross every t. Neat and orderly, they approach everything they do in a thorough manner, with efficiency and organization. The caring influence is present in both signs, so when the two merge, it is natural that Virgo-Rabbits should gravitate toward the medical or therapeutic professions. In their personal relationships, however, Virgo-Rabbits can be a little too self-sacrificing for their own good.

KEY CHARACTERISTICS

- cautious
- fastidious
- caring
- exacting

YOUR COMPATIBLE SIGNS

Capricorn-Sheep

Taurus-Pig

Virgo-Rabbits are careful about their diets—pure ingredients and organic produce are preferred.

EAST WEST FUSION

EAST

Virgo endows the Eastern sign of the Rabbit with an analytical mind

WEST

The Oriental Rabbit brings the Maiden cultured refinement

A quiet, slow-paced occupation suits the Virgo-Rabbit very well.

THE ESSENTIAL YOU

WORK, HEALTH, HOBBIES

Neither the glare of the spotlight nor the cut and thrust of big business will, in general, attract members of this sign. For Virgo-Rabbits like to work on the sidelines and, if they could choose, on their own in peace and quiet. What they do tend to go for is a secure job, with a good, regular salary and a guaranteed decent pension on retirement. They are, on the whole, wiry people but a bit wimpish when it comes to their health, so they probably won't want a job that overtaxes their energies.

LOVES, LIKES, DISLIKES

Virgo-Rabbits are careful about all sorts of things. They are genteel people who like their routine and who get discomfited by sudden changes to their plans. They are fussy about their clothes and their homes, meticulously ironing each frill and straightening the pictures on the wall. They watch their health and their diet, many following the latest diet fad. They are happiest with a partner who will provide them with a secure and comfortable home life.

CHILDREN AND PARENTS

Youngsters of the Virgo-Rabbit tribe are not given to the rough-and-tumble life. They much prefer more sedate games where they are unlikely to get their hands dirty or their clothes rumpled. Above all, they hate bad feelings and tension and suffer miserably if they argue with a friend. Virgo-Rabbit parents will teach their offspring to be polite and well-mannered. They will also encourage them to take an interest in art and culture—be it theater, dance, or music.

VIRGO-DRAGON

OBSERVATIONS

A lack of sensitivity and understanding can mar a Virgo-Dragon's relationships with others

Status matters a great deal to the Virgo-Dragon. With dogged determination, people of this dual sign will work hard to reach both the station and the standard of living to which they aspire. Wherever there is a Virgo presence there will inevitably be a substrata of organization and efficiency at work. With these people, occupational matters, social life, relationships, and domestic matters are carefully planned and nothing is left to chance. Thus it is that the erratic tendencies of the Dragon are quelled and the Virgo-Dragon combination influences a steadier, more practical approach to life which ultimately reaps rewards.

Virgo-Dragons drive themselves hard to achieve the success they desire.

KEY CHARACTERISTICS

- confident
- abrasive
- precise
- ambitious

YOUR COMPATIBLE SIGNS

Taurus-Rat
Capricorn-Monkey

EAST WEST FUSION

EAST
Virgo's reserve dilutes the Dragon's bravado

WEST
The Dragon flies the sedate Maiden to dizzy heights

THE ESSENTIAL YOU

WORK, HEALTH, HOBBIES
Blessed with intelligence and agile minds, members of this dual sign know how to maximize their talents to best effect. Virgo-Dragons have big ideas and ambition to match. Their indomitable energy, coupled with a genius for meticulous planning, means they know exactly how to structure their progress through life in order to get to the pinnacle of their chosen careers. The legal profession, high finance, and politics will all provide them with a slow but sure track to success.

LOVES, LIKES, DISLIKES
For Virgo-Dragons, reaching their goals is so all-important that they are prepared to put considerable efforts into their interests and appearance in order to be ready when opportunities arise. To give them their due, they are not shirkers or slackers and they are very unforgiving of failure, which is abhorrent to them. Partners of these demanding and tough cookies must inevitably possess a thick skin, and also be prepared to do much of the running around in the relationship.

CHILDREN AND PARENTS
Young Virgo-Dragons like to come top in class so it is a sure bet that they will work hard to get the marks they desire. At home, youngsters belonging to this dual sign must be taught the importance of taking other people's feelings into consideration. In general, Virgo-Dragon parents are more suited to older rather than younger children.

The Virgo-Dragon's insensitivity can be carelessly destructive of others' feelings.

THE ESSENTIAL YOU

VIRGO-SNAKE

Highly ambitious and bossy to boot, Virgo-Snakes like to be in charge, both of their working environment and of their relationships. Virgo is a busy, hard-working sign and brings to the Snake an ability to apply him- or herself industriously. With cool efficiency and superb organizational powers, Virgo-Snakes can accomplish a good deal more in one week than many of their other compatriots do in one month. Driven intellectually more than emotionally, members of this dual sign are not especially demonstrative in love, but they are responsible and dedicated homemakers, tirelessly giving of themselves and their energies to improve their status and position in life.

KEY CHARACTERISTICS
- perceptive
- logical
- aloof
- unemotional

YOUR COMPATIBLE SIGNS
Capricorn-Rooster
Taurus-Ox

Cool, calm, and collected, Virgo-Snakes detach themselves from cloying sentimentality.

EAST WEST FUSION

EAST
Virgo curbs the Snake's excesses

WEST
The Oriental Snake brings a keenly incisive mind to the clever Maiden

Model-making satisfies the constructive talents of the children of this sign.

WORK, HEALTH, HOBBIES
Details enthrall Virgo-Snakes. They can handle fine precision, intricate designs, and minute measurements with confidence and aplomb. That is why many are skilled draftsmen and women, or are drawn to careers in civil engineering. Sedentary jobs please them because they are intrinsically lethargic people. But they must make time for a little daily exercise to ensure they keep fit.

♥ ♥ ♥

LOVES, LIKES, DISLIKES
Cool and distant, Virgo-Snakes do not go in for overt showy behavior. Nor do they like too much physical contact. These are remarkably unsentimental people, able to rationalize their feelings. They are essentially independent types and prefer to be detached from emotions—especially complex or sloppy ones. Virgo-Snakes are happy to spend time curled up with a good book, or to indulge their passion for travel. But they do like comfort and good food wherever they go.

CHILDREN AND PARENTS
Children of this duality will show technical talents from a very young age. They are inherently intelligent and wizards at modelmaking. All forms of constructional toys will please them and keep them amused for hours. Not the most cuddly of youngsters, they simply don't like to be made a fuss of. As adults, Virgo-Snakes make indulgent parents to their offspring.

OBSERVATIONS
There is no getting away from the fact that Virgo-Snakes can be downright catty

VIRGO-HORSE

If a comparison with the other Horse combinations had to be made, it would be fair to say that people belonging to the Virgo-Horse sign are more sensible, more practical, and more hard-working than the others. The Virgo influence steadies the erratic tendencies of the Horse and calms the emotional make-up. Consequently, Virgo-Horses think twice before kicking up their heels and galloping off through the meadows. But though more composed, they lose none of that frisson of excitement that is an integral part of the Horse sign. Nor, for that matter, do they lose any of their sex appeal either. It is simply that, with both feet firmly on the ground, Virgo-Horses take a mature and responsible attitude to their commitments and love affairs.

KEY CHARACTERISTICS

- capable
- alert
- helpful
- attractive

YOUR COMPATIBLE SIGNS

Taurus-Dog
Capricorn-Tiger

Virgo circumspection brings maturity to the handsome Horse—especially in affairs of the heart.

THE ESSENTIAL YOU

WORK, HEALTH, HOBBIES
Virgo-Horses are articulate and usually well-read. They do well in any occupation that deals with the spoken or written word. Members of this sign make fine television presenters, reporters, or writers. They are not averse to the limelight and come across well to the general public. A career, too, in business often draws these clever people. But no matter what career they choose, laziness is not part of their vocabulary. Virgo-Horses are prepared to put in whatever time it takes to hone their bodies and their minds to gain the success they believe they deserve.

LOVES, LIKES, DISLIKES
Virgo-Horses ooze animal magnetism and tend to be highly attractive to members of the opposite sex. Self-image is high on these people's agendas and they will spend considerable time and money dressing and grooming themselves impeccably. People ruled by this dual sign do have expensive tastes, something which is reflected in their homes and the cars they drive. They are fairly flirty but generally sensible in love.

CHILDREN AND PARENTS
Popular youngsters, Virgo-Horse children are socially competent and appeal to teachers and adults alike. Their many talents are in evidence from an early age and they are happy to entertain any appreciative audience. Music lessons, dance, and elocution classes, debating societies and amateur dramatics make suitable extracurricular activities for these little charmers. Virgo-Horse parents tend to be glamorous and want their children to grow up to become stylish people too.

EAST WEST FUSION

EAST
The Maiden sits astride the Horse and calms its nerves

WEST
The beautiful Chinese Horse quickens the Maiden's pulse

OBSERVATIONS

Virgo-Horses are beautiful creatures and the problem is that they know it

Dancing lessons teach poise to young Virgo-Horses.

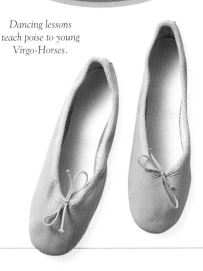

VIRGO-SHEEP

Those born under this dual sign have exceptionally high standards of excellence and they often find that people and situations simply fail to meet their expectations. Virgos have a naturally critical eye and people who are born in Sheep years can be overly fussy. This can mean that Virgo-Sheep, with their nitpicking ways, fail to see the wood for the trees. Although there are many situations in which such finesse is a definite plus factor, this can work to the Virgo-Sheep's disadvantage in matters of the heart. For the Virgo-Sheep desperately wants a loving and fulfilling relationship, but their selection methods tend to be rather too rigorous. Learning to accept people, warts and all, would make life altogether simpler for the Virgo-Sheep.

Virgo-Sheep love the stage and screen. Careerwise they could make trenchant critics.

KEY CHARACTERISTICS

- esthetic
- perfectionist
- carping
- intense

YOUR COMPATIBLE SIGNS

Capricorn-Pig
Taurus-Rabbit

EAST WEST FUSION

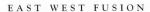

EAST
Virgo teaches the Sheep
to be practical

WEST
The Sheep bedecks the Maiden
with elegance

THE ESSENTIAL YOU

WORK, HEALTH, HOBBIES
Virgo-Sheep have a built-in ability to make fun of contemporary life. This mordant wit can be put to good—and lucrative—use as a writer of biting documentaries for television or sitcoms with a bittersweet edge or maybe as a newspaper critic or even a wry stand-up comedian. Healthwise, Virgo-Sheep are not the strongest of the combination signs and they tend to tire easily.

♥ ♥ ♥

LOVES, LIKES, DISLIKES
Things are never quite good enough, it seems, for the critical eye of the Virgo-Sheep. Their ideal partner is one who is able to recognize that this is the Virgo-Sheep's attempt to mask his or her own feelings of insecurity and inadequacy. But it can be exasperating and often downright hurtful. It is this unfortunate trait that risks spoiling many beautiful friendships.

CHILDREN AND PARENTS
Poetry appeals to Virgo-Sheep youngsters, who need to be encouraged from a young age to speak from the heart. Being taken to the movies, theater, and musicals would delight them too. Active sports are not really their cup of tea at all, since their energies tend to flag rather quickly. As parents, Virgo-Sheep have an offbeat sense of humor which children find irresistible.

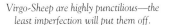

Virgo-Sheep are highly punctilious—the least imperfection will put them off.

VIRGO: **AUGUST 23–SEPTEMBER 22**
YEARS OF THE MONKEY: 1908 * 1920 * 1932 * 1944 * 1956 * 1968 * 1980 * 1992 * 2004 * 2016
HOUR OF THE MONKEY: 3PM – 4.59PM

THE ESSENTIAL YOU

VIRGO-MONKEY

Detail pleases the Virgo-Monkey who can happily lose him or herself in intricate minutiae for hours on end. Virgos are the perfectionists of the Western Zodiac, while Monkeys are quick as lightning, having the ability to pick up a skill at a glance. Together, then, this duo produces intelligent individuals with razor-sharp perception and so acutely alert that they never miss a trick. Indeed, it is virtually impossible to get anything past a Virgo-Monkey without their noticing. With this kind of mentality, Virgo-Monkeys make outstanding organizers and formidable businessmen and women. Wherever an analytical mind is required, the clever Virgo-Monkey is sure to fit the bill perfectly.

EAST WEST FUSION

EAST
The Western Maiden teaches the Oriental Monkey to stick to his tasks

WEST
The Monkey makes Virgo shrewd and streetwise

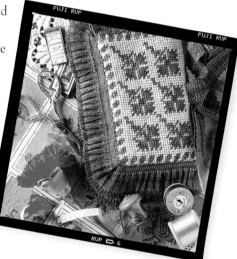

KEY CHARACTERISTICS
- clever
- curious
- dextrous
- insecure

YOUR COMPATIBLE SIGNS
Taurus-Dragon
Capricorn-Rat

The intricacies of needlepoint suit the Virgo-Monkey's nimble fingers and love of precision.

OBSERVATIONS

Self-consciousness can all too often be a draw back for the Virgo-Monkey

Chess, the game of strategy, organization, and a lightning mind is ideal for Virgo-Monkeys.

WORK, HEALTH, HOBBIES
Precision work is the Virgo-Monkey's forte. Not only do these people have needlesharp minds, but they also have nimble fingers and steady hands that can take them into any occupation where delicate hand-eye coordination is called for. From needlecraft through to surgery, to the delicate plucking of the strings on a mandolin, the Virgo-Monkey's deftness and articulacy will reap rewards. Moreover, these are energetic and clever people who can do extremely well academically. Many Virgo-Monkeys are drawn to teaching and to the world of science.

LOVES, LIKES, DISLIKES
Word puzzles help to keep the Virgo-Monkey's mind sharp. Construction games, too, are favorite interests. But, in fact, these people like any pursuit that keeps their hands busy. So they will enjoy all manner of craftwork, home renovation, needlepoint, mosaic-making, painting miniatures, or repairing engines. In relationships, Virgo-Monkeys will look for intelligent partners. To their loved one they will give one hundred percent devotion and loyalty. But they demand total fidelity in return.

CHILDREN AND PARENTS
Virgo-Monkey youngsters have terrific curiosity and want to know about everything that is going on. They are fidgets who can't keep their hands still. It is wise to keep the minds and bodies of these bright little things busy and amused. Virgo-Monkey children are happy to learn and usually do very well at school. As parents, members of this dual sign have a wealth of knowledge to teach their offspring.

VIRGO-ROOSTER

Possibly more practical and down-to-earth than most other Roosters, people born under the influence of Virgo excel in those tasks that require a logical and linear mentality. Virgo-Roosters are born perfectionists. They home in on detail and are apt to drive partners to distraction with their exacting standards. Nitpicking, some would call it, but it is hardly surprising since both the Virgo-born individual and the Rooster native have a habit of pouring over minutiae. Moreover, each can be as abrasive as the other in the manner in which they deliver their criticism. Partners and colleagues, who know that below the surface the Virgo-Rooster really does mean well, will nevertheless need the protection of a thick skin.

KEY CHARACTERISTICS

- knowledgeable
- fastidious
- rational
- earthy

YOUR COMPATIBLE SIGNS

Capricorn-Ox
Taurus-Snake

Virgo-Roosters don't hold back when delivering their opinions on people's shortcomings.

EAST WEST FUSION

EAST
The Maiden enhances the Rooster's sense of service

WEST
The feisty Rooster makes Virgo resilient

Brain-teasers and mind-bending puzzles intrigue the analytical minds of the members of this sign.

THE ESSENTIAL YOU

WORK, HEALTH, HOBBIES

Virgo-Roosters adore working out problems—the knottier, the better—and pride themselves on coming up with solutions. Robust in health, they are also blessed with minds that can absorb facts as easily as sponges soak up water. They have beady eyes that can absorb details with breathtaking speed and accuracy. So members of this dual sign make excellent quality controllers or editors who can spot grammatical errors and spelling mistakes that a hundred other pairs of eyes have missed. Excellent with figures, they can become successful accountants and statisticians, terrific administrators and are a boon to any office.

LOVES, LIKES, DISLIKES

Members of this duality like a mental challenge and enjoy all kinds of intellectual activities. They don't like disruption and disturbance, they don't want to be countermanded, and they certainly don't care for their opinions being crossed. In love, they like to do all the running, and they need to feel they are the ones who rule the roost.

CHILDREN AND PARENTS

A classical education will best suit the youngsters of this double sign. In fact, of all children, these will actually enjoy the Classics and all manner of learning by rote. Although unquestionably they work hard, most have little trouble passing exams because they have an almost photographic memory and a talent for remembering a prodigious amount of facts and figures. Virgo-Rooster parents can always be relied on for knowing the answers to their offspring's homework.

EAST WEST FUSION

VIRGO-DOG

In both Western and Oriental astrology, the Virgo and the Dog signs stand for the carers of humanity. People born under either of these two signs are dutiful and responsible. Both work hard and totally dedicate themselves to those they love. Steady, quiet, and utterly trustworthy, these people carry out whatever task they are given efficiently and without any fuss. So, careerwise, Virgo-Dogs do best in vocational work or in the medical profession. However Virgo-Dogs do take life terribly seriously. They are born worriers, so a partner who can soothe their furrowed brow and get them to laugh now and again would make an ideal mate.

A career in the nursing profession is ideal for caring, trustworthy, dedicated Virgo-Dogs.

EAST
Virgo gives the Dog depth of understanding

WEST
The Chinese Dog brings Virgo the gift of kindness

KEY CHARACTERISTICS
- earnest
- kindly
- dutiful
- steady

YOUR COMPATIBLE SIGNS
Taurus-Tiger
Capricorn-Horse

OBSERVATIONS

A certain naivety in the Virgo-Dog's make-up means that he or she can all too easily be duped

THE ESSENTIAL YOU

WORK, HEALTH, HOBBIES
Very few of the other 143 combined signs can match this one for hard work, honesty, and reliability in the workplace. Employers can rest easy in their beds when they leave a Virgo-Dog in charge. Their talents and interests lend themselves naturally to the service industries, and to the care and welfare of children and the sick. At home, these are very busy people, bustling about their domestic duties, looking after their families, making jams, feeding the hens, and tending to the garden. Stress gets to them and their fretful, nervous disposition can undermine their health.

LOVES, LIKES, DISLIKES
Virgo-Dogs like being useful. They do not like taking risks nor are they given to dishonesty. That is why they are so terribly hurt if they discover someone has deceived them or taken advantage of their good nature. Perhaps that is also why they are reluctant to give their hearts—they are so fearful of being hurt and let down. When they do find their life's soulmate, however, and they decide to settle, they make wonderfully loving and giving partners, totally devoted and faithful.

CHILDREN AND PARENTS
Old heads on young shoulders well describes youngsters of this dual sign who are born with a sense of responsibility emblazoned on their souls. Whether they are male or female, eldest or youngest, they will always be "mother's little helpers," happy to run errands, take care of their siblings, and organize the family pets. Adult Virgo-Dogs make some of the most loving and dedicated parents a child could hope for.

Making their own delicious jam is one of many of the Virgo-Dogs' domestic virtues.

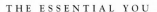

VIRGO-PIG

People born under the twin sign of Virgo-Pig are loyal, faithful, and unwaveringly dedicated to those they love. Despite the Pig's reputation for self-indulgence, those who are born under the influence of Virgo know how to tighten their belts in times of crisis. Indeed, should their families be in need, the Virgo-Pig mother or father would be the first to go without and sacrifice him- or herself for the good of the family. However, should the Virgo-Pigs ever find that those very same people for whom they have given their all have let them down, then hell hath no fury like the Virgo-Pig betrayed.

Virgo teaches the Pig self-control when confronted with rich foods.

KEY CHARACTERISTICS

- sensitive
- reliable
- idealistic
- naive

YOUR COMPATIBLE SIGNS

Capricorn-Rabbit
Taurus-Sheep

OBSERVATIONS

Despite their placid exterior, Virgo-Pigs are prone to some pretty volcanic bouts of temper.

EAST WEST FUSION

EAST

The Maiden brings discipline and self-control to the Chinese Pig

WEST

The Oriental Pig softens Virgo austerity with a touch of sensuality

Virgo-Pigs put their children first in everything.

WORK, HEALTH, HOBBIES

Virgo-Pigs blend practicality with creativity to produce functional yet beautiful objects. They like to make and create so are likely to gravitate toward occupations that require manual skills but where there is also scope for them to use and apply their considerable imagination. As employees, they are honest, amenable, and ready to lend a hand to colleagues in need. As employers, they are fair and not too proud to work alongside their staff. If uncontrolled, overindulgence can lead to weight gain and associated health problems.

♥ ♥ ♥

LOVES, LIKES, DISLIKES

Luxury, softness, and comfort are the Virgo-Pigs' favorite delights. According to their code of morality, disloyalty and unfaithfulness are the two most heinous crimes that anyone could ever perpetrate. The Virgo-Pig's word is his or her bond and he or she naturally assumes that others will live honorably too. This they expect by right in their intimate relationships since, once members of this dual sign have committed themselves, they are unlikely ever to stray.

CHILDREN AND PARENTS

In class, Virgo-Pig children tend to come top in drawing. Anything involving color and design will attract them and they will spend many happy hours coloring in their coloring books, carefully concentrating so as not to go over the lines. But these youngsters are also imaginative and clever do well when it comes to writing essay as well. Encouragement to read when they are still toddlers will stand them in good stead. As parents, Virgo-Pigs are by turn indulgent and strict, but always deeply loving.

LIBRA

BORN BETWEEN: **SEPTEMBER 23—OCTOBER 22**
AIR SIGN

Libra, the seventh sign of the Western astrological year, roughly corresponds to the Chinese month known as the Dog Moon.

If you were born at this time of the year you can either call yourself a Libran, or a native of the Chrysanthemum Moon, which is a much more evocative alternative Chinese name for this month.

According to the Chinese, this time of year is also broken up into two fortnights, each describing an aspect of the weather, or a feature relevant to the agricultural year. The first fortnight is called the Autumn Equinox and this corresponds to the first two weeks of Libra. If you were born in the second half of the sign, though, you belong to the second Chinese fortnight, Cold Dews.

But it is, of course, when both your month and your year of birth are combined that the various influences begin to interweave themselves in a way that is essentially unique for you.

Whatever the combination, Libra as the sign of equilibrium, will lend the ability to take a well-balanced view to the mix.

EAST WEST FUSION

LIBRA-RAT

EAST
Libra refines the tastes and manners
of the Chinese Rat

WEST
The Oriental Rat teaches Libra
financial prudence

Since Librans are the charmers of the Western Zodiac and the Rat is the sign of charm in the East, this double helping of charisma makes the Libra-Rat a very smooth operator indeed. Elegant and refined, these people are sophisticated in every way. Highly cultured and urbane, they are drawn to music and the arts, many making their livelihoods running a gallery, working in the media, or in niches such as a theater critic. Pleasant in speech and manner, Libra-Rats excel in all forms of communication, the diplomatic corps, advertising, and public relations. Emotionally, they fall in love with love. In partnerships, their eye for beauty demands nothing short of a Venus or an Adonis by their side.

OBSERVATIONS

*Libra-Rats will avoid
confrontation at any cost*

*A charming personality helps
the Libra-Rat to smooth a path
to the top.*

KEY CHARACTERISTICS

- charming
- selective
- seductive
- elegant

YOUR COMPATIBLE SIGNS

Gemini-Monkey
Aquarius-Dragon

*An elegant masked
ball makes an ideal
soirée for any
Libra-Rat.*

THE ESSENTIAL YOU

WORK, HEALTH, HOBBIES

Gifted speakers and exceptionally skilled in human relations, Libra-Rats excel in occupations involving the general public. When it comes to business, few can beat these people's sales patter. In terms of career, then, the commercial world would provide a rich seam for the Libra-Rat to mine. But members of this duality also make excellent communicators, mediators, and negotiators, and they would therefore shine in any occupation where such talents are required. Advertising, public relations, hotel and catering, law, and diplomacy would all be suitable careers for the Libra-Rat to pursue.

LOVES, LIKES, DISLIKES

Libra-Rats are hot on esthetics, so good looks are important to them, whether this means living in beautiful surroundings, being well-dressed, or in the company of handsome people. In common with all Libran combinations, the Libra-Rat dislikes unpleasantness of any sort and will agree with others more often than not simply to keep the peace. These are great upholders of customs and traditions, so when it comes to special occasions—particularly birthdays and New Year—Libra-Rats love to pull out all the stops. Whether in love or in friendship, Libra-Rats are one of the best companions one could wish to have.

CHILDREN AND PARENTS

"Talks too much in class" will be a common remark in school reports. Still, youngsters of this dual sign are such amusing and vivacious little things that their ebullience alone will take them far. They will particularly excel in all expressive or linguistic subjects. Libra-Rat parents are very loving, proud, and supportive of their young.

LIBRA: **SEPTEMBER 23–OCTOBER 22**
YEARS OF THE OX: 1901 ✱ 1913 ✱ 1925 ✱ 1937 ✱ 1949 ✱ 1961 ✱ 1973 ✱ 1985 ✱ 1997 ✱ 2009
HOUR OF THE OX: 1AM – 2.59AM

THE ESSENTIAL YOU

LIBRA-OX

Blessed with a good deal more charm and endowed with better social skills than the average Ox, Libra's influence softens the intransigent qualities of the Ox nature. As a result, Libra-Oxen easily make friends and are popular with their peers. Unlike the thoroughbred Ox, the Libra-Ox is able and willing to compromise and makes both a cooperative employer and employee. These are amiable people, eminently peace-loving and never prone to rocking the boat. However, they do tend to attract partners who rock the boat for them! Libra-Oxen are born idealists, constantly looking for perfection in life as well as in love.

KEY CHARACTERISTICS

- principled
- polite
- meticulous
- balanced

YOUR COMPATIBLE SIGNS

Aquarius-Snake
Gemini-Rooster

*Wherever they live,
Libra-Oxen strive to create a
pleasing environment.*

EAST WEST FUSION

EAST
The Ox brings strength and
staying power to the sign

WEST
Libra encourages the Oriental
Ox to be more flexible

OBSERVATIONS

*Expecting perfection at every turn can
lead to unnecessary disappointment
for the Libra-Ox*

*Antiques appeal to the Libra-Ox:
beautiful, refined, tasteful, and
invariably valuable too.*

WORK, HEALTH, HOBBIES

Strong and highly motivated, Libra-Oxen put one hundred percent into everything they undertake and expect others to do the same. Routine appeals to them, since members of this duality do best when working in a logical and methodical manner. On the whole, Libra-Oxen are fair-minded types and, whether employer or employee, are staunch upholders of people's rights. Academically, the history of art offers never-ending fascination to them, as do law and international affairs. With their love of period furniture, many make excellent antique dealers.

❤ ❤ ❤

LOVES, LIKES, DISLIKES

Libra-Oxen have high principles and even higher standards. Messy environments displease them, as do coarse manners and behavior. These are essentially home- and family-oriented people, preferring life in the country to the busy metropolis. Here, they will tend to their gardens, which are usually of a formal style and well-kept. In fact, everything about the Libra-Ox reflects a classical taste. Relationships, too, are likely to be based on stereotypical roles. In love, members of this dual sign are courteous and conciliatory, but they do like things their own way.

🐂 🐂 🐂

CHILDREN AND PARENTS

Youngsters of this dual sign may not look strong but they are robust and resilient. They tend to be steady workers at school, putting consistent effort into their studies, which attracts praise and good marks. Working in a team is preferred to solitary work. As parents, Libra-Oxen give their children a good deal of love and security. House rules, however, must be obeyed.

LIBRA: **SEPTEMBER 23–OCTOBER 22**
YEARS OF THE TIGER: 1902 * 1914 * 1926 * 1938 * 1950 * 1962 * 1974 * 1986 * 1998 * 2010
HOUR OF THE TIGER: 3AM – 4.59AM

LIBRA-TIGER

The Tiger is fierce in the defense of Libran justice and fair play.

The Libra-Tiger lives by justice and fair play. Professionally, these cool, calm characters make good judges, arbitrators, diplomats, or politicians. However, while they are gifted mediators where other people are concerned, in their own personal lives Libra-Tigers have a notorious reputation for dithering. They just have the most enormous trouble making up their minds! People are important to the Libra-Tiger, whose address book bulges with names of friends and contacts. With their affable nature, their charm, and their classic good looks, members of this dual sign are bound to have an army of potential suitors buzzing around them all the time.

OBSERVATIONS

Libra-Tigers all too often commit themselves before fully considering the consequences of their actions

KEY CHARACTERISTICS
- fair-minded
- charismatic
- liberal
- individualistic

YOUR COMPATIBLE SIGNS
Gemini-Horse
Aquarius-Dog

EAST WEST FUSION

EAST
Libra gives the Tiger poise and good breeding

WEST
The Tiger brings courage to embolden Libra's heart

THE ESSENTIAL YOU

WORK, HEALTH, HOBBIES
Libra-Tigers are energetic, intelligent, and gifted. They have brilliant flashes of inspiration and come up with ingenious solutions to problems and intriguing ideas. Such talents are especially valuable in think-tank meetings, strategic planning sessions, or in situations where negotiations have reached a deadlock. Finding the way forward that satisfies all concerned parties is the Libra-Tiger's particular forte. Politics, therefore, is an excellent avenue for these people to explore. So too are careers in counseling or arbitration. Given their fashion sense and keen eye for spotting trends ahead of time, these people would also do well as dress designers.

LOVES, LIKES, DISLIKES
Distinguished men and women, Libra-Tigers possess a powerful presence and a taste for beauty. Vulgarity appals members of this double sign. For these people need to live surrounded by splendor. They are attracted to unusual homes and lovely artifacts—paintings, sculptures, and objects d'art. The grander and the more palatial the residence, the better. And, of course, they can't help but be attracted to beautiful people. When they set their eyes on a potential partner, Libra-Tigers will use all their powers in order to win the object of their desires.

CHILDREN AND PARENTS
Children of this double sign are invariably popular young people, who have a huge following of friends. Often leaders of the gang, they are nevertheless loyal and fair. When it comes to their pocket-money, they are either generous or foolhardy—whichever, they seem to be liberal with their cash. The charming and enduring naivety that Libra-Tigers take with them into adulthood means that, as parents, they find it easy to be on the same wavelength as their children.

Designing fashion accessories appeals to the Libra-Tiger.

LIBRA: **SEPTEMBER 23–OCTOBER 22**
YEARS OF THE RABBIT: 1903 ✸ 1915 ✸ 1927 ✸ 1939 ✸ 1951 ✸ 1963 ✸ 1975 ✸ 1987 ✸ 1999 ✸ 2011
HOUR OF THE RABBIT: 5AM – 6.59AM

THE ESSENTIAL YOU

LIBRA-RABBIT

Two signs renowned for their suave sophistication are fused together in the Libra-Rabbit to produce a polished individual, someone with exquisite taste who is, above all else, fond of gracious living. Charming and cultured, those born under the influence of this dual sign are wonderful social butterflies, with beautiful wings and manners that are delicate and refined. Corporations would be lucky to employ a Libra-Rabbit as a spokesperson. They are not suited to manual occupations, which involve getting their hands dirty. Instead, they prefer to populate the worlds of music, literature, and the arts. Many make excellent designers, artists, and writers. Libra-Rabbits believe in the best of all possible worlds and they go through life in love with love itself.

KEY CHARACTERISTICS
- agreeable
- sentimental
- considerate
- sophisticated

YOUR COMPATIBLE SIGNS
Aquarius-Sheep
Gemini-Pig

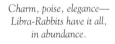

Charm, poise, elegance—
Libra-Rabbits have it all,
in abundance.

EAST WEST FUSION

EAST
Libra enhances the
Rabbit's charm

WEST
The Oriental Rabbit augments
Libra's savoir faire

OBSERVATIONS

*Libra-Rabbits are too ready
to compromise simply to
keep the peace*

Libra-Rabbits collect exquisite
and expensive jewelry
throughout their lives.

WORK, HEALTH, HOBBIES
A harmonious working environment is of fundamental importance to the Libra-Rabbit. The merest whiff of discord, the least bit of unpleasantness, or the faintest hint of aggression and the Libra-Rabbit will take to his or her bed with a cold compress and a couple of aspirin. Yet despite this apparently delicate constitution, members of this duality can actually be as tough as old boots. Careerwise they do best in cultured or literary occupations, attending parties or functions which will get them noticed. Connoisseurs of artworks, they excel as collectors, or as experts in jewelry or antiquarian books.

♥ ♥ ♥

LOVES, LIKES, DISLIKES
Libra-Rabbits cannot live in disagreeable circumstances, and coarseness of any sort fundamentally disturbs them. In truth, a life of elegance, comfort, and ease is every Libra-Rabbit's desire. For these people, quality matters. And that also applies to their intimate relationships. As long as the freshness, magic, and romance can be sustained, Libra-Rabbit lovers are in their element. However, the minute the enchantment begins to fade, so too, alas, does the Libra-Rabbit's interest.

CHILDREN AND PARENTS
Young Libra-Rabbits enjoy painting, music, and all the gentle arts. These tender children do not fare well under stressful conditions. They need a tranquil environment in which to thrive with as much exposure to cultural life as possible. As parents, Libra-Rabbits are happy to read their youngsters stories at bedtime, but they need stronger partners who are prepared to take over the actual nitty-gritty part of childrearing.

EAST WEST FUSION

LIBRA-DRAGON

EAST
Libra restrains the Dragon
from going too far

WEST
The Dragon fires Libra with
enthusiasm and drive

All Librans have a highly developed sense of esthetics. Add to this the Dragon's élan, and what is created is a highly stylish creature, cultured of manners and refined of taste. Charm is the Libra-Dragon's greatest asset, which acts as a magnet drawing people to them like flies to honey. But Librans are normally laid-back people, not given to making rash decisions on the spur of the moment. However, not so the Dragon, whose impulsiveness will all too often land him or her in a good deal of difficulty. Libra stays the hand of the Dragon, who in turn empowers the Libra and energizes the more indolent aspects of that sign. Libra-Dragons are champions of the people, who believe in fair play and the need to help others.

OBSERVATIONS
Libra-Dragons can be somewhat bumptious at times

KEY CHARACTERISTICS
- charming
- conciliatory
- attractive
- distinguished

YOUR COMPATIBLE SIGNS
Gemini-Rat
Aquarius-Monkey

The exotic Dragon inspires Libra to travel far in search of beautiful objects.

According to Libra-Dragons manners maketh man.

THE ESSENTIAL YOU

WORK, HEALTH, HOBBIES
Energetic and enthusiastic, Libra-Dragons throw themselves body and soul into their work. The stage and screen are natural vehicles for their dramatic and musical talents, and many are bound to tread the boards. Glamorous occupations of all kinds attract these creative people. From style consultants to window dressers, Libra-Dragons know how to take the banal and transform it into something quite heavenly.

❤ ❤ ❤

LOVES, LIKES, DISLIKES
No dinner party in town is complete without a dashing and soigné Libra-Dragon as one of the guests. For these people are true showmen and women. They are entertaining speakers, ever armed with marvelous and amusing tales to tell about their exotic trips, or anecdotes about the glamorous movie stars they were talking to the other day.

For Libra-Dragons like to be in the right places at the right times, to be in the thick of things, and to move in rarefied circles. Being popular is important for these people who despise mediocrity. They like to be in the full glare of the spotlight and, in their relationships, desire to be placed on a pedestal.

CHILDREN AND PARENTS
Confident and self-expressive, children of this sign communicate well with young and old alike, and invariably have lots of friends. With their exuberance and precocious talents, these youngsters are bursting with questions, full of interests, and full of life. This can make living with them exhausting, but always richly amusing and rewarding. There is never a dull moment when a little Libra-Dragon is around. Adults belonging to this dual sign are very busy people, so large families are probably unusual here.

LIBRA: **SEPTEMBER 23–OCTOBER 22**
YEARS OF THE SNAKE: 1905 ✳ 1917 ✳ 1929 ✳ 1941 ✳ 1953 ✳ 1965 ✳ 1977 ✳ 1989 ✳ 2001 ✳ 2013
HOUR OF THE SNAKE: 9AM – 10.59AM

LIBRA-SNAKE

Members of the Libra-Snake fraternity make some of the most attractive people of the Snake clan: recherché, cultured, and full of savoir faire. The Libran influence endows the Snake with a more outgoing personality than is usual, making members of this dual sign genial and friendly. Moreover, given their easy manner, social graces, and persuasive charm, Libra-Snakes are decided assets at any gathering. Whether host or guest, they are gracious and considerate, affable, and witty to boot. It is hardly surprising, then, that the Libra-Snake is never short of an invitation to a party. In love, Libra-Snakes are life's romantics. They are in love with the notion of love and typically idealistic when it comes to actually finding a partner.

EAST WEST FUSION

EAST
Libra teaches the Snake to be more sociable

WEST
The Snake brings compassion for others to the Scales

KEY CHARACTERISTICS
- 🐍 peace-loving
- 🐍 soigné
- 🐍 understanding
- 🐍 indolent

YOUR COMPATIBLE SIGNS
Aquarius-Rooster
Gemini-Ox

Magnetic Libra-Snakes often inspire love at first sight.

THE ESSENTIAL YOU

WORK, HEALTH, HOBBIES
In everyday life as well as at work, subtlety and seductiveness are the Libra-Snake's strongest suits. These people are able to curry favor to get what they want simply by smiling at the right people. They don't storm or rant or rave. They don't need to shout or plead or cajole to move mountains. It is their mere presence, attractiveness, and captivating personalities that will do the job for them. Silky and sinuous, those who look for the glamorous life can find it on the catwalk. Otherwise, a deep humanitarian instinct will take many of these people into charity or philanthropic work. Healthwise, Libra-Snakes are prone to suffer from allergies.

LOVES, LIKES, DISLIKES
Physical pleasure and the Libra-Snake go hand in hand. For these people love their creature comforts and, if they can, they will spend hours pampering and preening themselves to their heart's delight. But they don't like to shout about their wealth or their indulgences from the rooftops. Rather, they would prefer it if others thought them modest in their tastes. There is something truly magnetic and beguiling about these creatures. Not only are they exquisite to look but, with such a dry wit, Libra-Snakes can also be extremely amusing people to have around.

Gorgeous and agreeable, Libra-Snakes are always elegant and well dressed from top to toe.

CHILDREN AND PARENTS
Caring and philosophical, the Libra-Snake child is born with a mature head on young shoulders. Watching television or playing boardgames are usually preferred to active sports. As these are endearingly sweet little individuals, there is always the temptation to overindulge them. Libra-Snake parents have a tendency to smother and be overprotective toward their children.

LIBRA: **SEPTEMBER 23–OCTOBER 22**
YEARS OF THE HORSE: 1906 * 1918 * 1930 * 1942 * 1954 * 1966 * 1978 * 1990 * 2002 * 2014
HOUR OF THE HORSE: 11AM – 12.59PM

THE ESSENTIAL YOU

LIBRA-HORSE

WORK, HEALTH, HOBBIES

Libra-Horses like to mingle with amusing company, and over time build up a wide network of friends and acquaintances, many of whom will be influential contacts. Members of this duality are blessed with an abundance of creative talent and verbal skill. Energetic, smart, and well-groomed, they excel in people-oriented occupations. To support the Libra-Horse's expensive tastes, their career must be well-paid. Jobs such as television anchorman, chat-show host, journalist, or novelist would all fit the bill.

❤   ❤   ❤

LOVES, LIKES, DISLIKES

Libra-Horses know what they want. Moreover, they know how to get it. It is the life of stylish elegance that they crave—the coarse and the tawdry are to be eschewed at all costs. Because projecting a good image is of paramount importance to these people, a good address in the right part of town is essential. Their homes will be chic and furnished with flair and, since Libra-Horses put such store by appearances, large mirrors will be in evidence everywhere.

CHILDREN AND PARENTS

Young Libra-Horses are popular individuals and like to have a large crowd of friends. Whether male or female, they adore dressing up, so a trunk full of hats and scarves and the odd theatrical costume will keep them busy for hours. Highly independent and very expressive, at school these youngsters will excel at writing essays. It is an open secret that Libra-Horses can be rather self-centered, so tending to the demands of young babies can be difficult for these people. Consequently, they make better parents as their children get older.

EAST WEST FUSION

EAST
Libra controls the Horse's selfishness

WEST
The Horse ensures Libra maintains a lively and youthful outlook

OBSERVATIONS
Libra-Horses can sometimes miss opportunities through carelessness

Like magnets, flirtatious Libra-Horses find it easy to attract the opposite sex.

Friendship plays a very important part in the lives of the Libra-Horses. Their charming nature, light-hearted banter and their effervescent personalities make people of this combined sign popular members of their group and highly in demand at all social occasions. Libra-Horses have more flair and panache in their little fingers than most people have in their entire bodies. All Horses are gorgeous to look at, but the Libran addition makes people born under this dual sign blatantly sexy! What's more, they are inveterate flirts. Indeed, if flirting were an Olympic sport, the Libra-Horse would run away with the gold medal! Passionate and sensual, elegant and refined, the Libra-Horse does everything in style!

KEY CHARACTERISTICS
- persuasive
- magnetic
- agreeable
- vain

YOUR COMPATIBLE SIGNS
Gemini-Dog
Aquarius-Tiger

Appearances matter to the Libra-Horse.

LIBRA-SHEEP

Intelligent and refined, suave and elegant, Libra-Sheep are the epitome of cultured sophistication. These highly accomplished individuals undertake everything they do with style and ingenuity. Indeed art is synonymous with this dual sign, for creativity and the Libra-Sheep go hand in hand. Cool, gentle, and graceful, Libra-Sheep excel in the beaux arts, many gravitating to the artworld for a career. And it is here that their mega talents in this area will reward them well.

Design, especially of clothes or interiors, is their special forte, for the Libra-Sheep has particular flair for line and color. Even more important financially, however, is the Libra-Sheep's intuitiveness when it comes to predicting trends and fashions. For the Libra-Sheep designer will be streets ahead of any competitor.

OBSERVATIONS

Relying on others to make important decisions in their lives can slow the Libra-Sheep's progress in life

Libra-Sheep make discerning writers, and stylish tools help the ideas to flow.

EAST WEST FUSION

EAST
Libra extends the Sheep's verbal powers

WEST
The Sheep adds inventive imagination to the Libra's creative mind

KEY CHARACTERISTICS
- intuitive
- graceful
- soigné
- fastidious

YOUR COMPATIBLE SIGNS
Aquarius-Pig
Gemini-Rabbit

THE ESSENTIAL YOU

WORK, HEALTH, HOBBIES

Libra-Sheep are graced with personal charm. Glamorous and well-dressed, they present a chic and polished image to the world. Indeed, these individuals need to work in sophisticated careers. With their expertise, they would make fine art auctioneers, musicians, writers, painters, and illustrators. Or they might gravitate to the worlds of ballet and opera, or even to photography or fashion design. Pacing themselves at work is important, because though resilient, they are not physically tough and their nerves will suffer when under pressure.

LOVES, LIKES, DISLIKES

Details are important to the fastidious Libra-Sheep. Everything must be just right. And style is the key. Members of this dual sign are highly cultured beings and their homes will be showcases of their passion for art and literature. Antiquarian, first-edition books, fine porcelain, and beautiful paintings adorn their interiors, all carefully selected over the years and placed with a critical and careful eye. Libra-Sheep are born romantics and, whether physically or metaphorically, they will fill their world with roses and old lace. It is not in the their make-up to live alone. In addition, they find it difficult to make decisions. Therefore, a close intimate relationship with a supportive, encouraging and adoring partner is absolutely essential to the Libra-Sheep's well-being.

CHILDREN AND PARENTS

Pretty and tender, young Libra-Sheep are born with the looks and manners of a child model. At school they will especially enjoy reading and writing, painting, and music. Dancing lessons or learning to play an instrument would be to their advantage. Libra-Sheep parents need quiet, accomplished, and well-behaved children. The noisy, rough-and-tumble sort, leave these parents nonplussed.

Libran style is timeless and Sheep know that everything is in the detail.

LIBRA-MONKEY

Charm is perhaps the Libra-Monkey's most outstanding asset. These people are superb psychologists. Libra-Monkeys know how to flatter, sweet-talk, and cajole. They know instinctively how to turn a situation to their own advantage. Libra-Monkeys are subtle in their ways. They are smooth operators, so slick that it is nigh on impossible to see the sleight of hand. People of this twin sign have a way with words and thus they make expert mediators. Professionally, they excel in the world of negotiation, and many Libra-Monkeys tend to gravitate toward the diplomatic corps. Advertising and public relations, too, are highly suitable outlets for their agile minds.

KEY CHARACTERISTICS
- eloquent
- clever
- charm
- manipulative

YOUR COMPATIBLE SIGNS
Gemini-Dragon
Aquarius-Rat

OBSERVATIONS

A lack of inner confidence can sometimes throw the Libra-Monkey off his or her stride

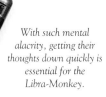

With such mental alacrity, getting their thoughts down quickly is essential for the Libra-Monkey.

Libra-Monkeys weigh their words with care.

EAST WEST FUSION

EAST
Libra teaches the Monkey a sense of justice and fair-play

WEST
The Monkey introduces Libra to a hint of foxy cunning

THE ESSENTIAL YOU

WORK, HEALTH, HOBBIES
Persuasive and silver-tongued, Libra-Monkeys have the gift of the gab and do well in any occupation where linguistic skills are required. Their copywriting skills are unrivaled, and they could come up with at least a dozen slogans every day—each one a winning formula. These people live on nervous energy and need change and variety at work to achieve the best results. A career in foreign affairs would suit their talents, for members of this sign would make fine ambassadors or foreign correspondents for newspapers or television.

LOVES, LIKES, DISLIKES
Libra-Monkeys enjoy dabbling with computers and surfing the net. Getting their message across to other people is a passion, so Libra-Monkeys will write, phone, or gossip until the cows come home. These are entertaining people, excellent raconteurs, but who also like to be amused. They dislike a humdrum existence and so will engage in many intellectual or cultural pursuits. Crosswords, word games, and competitions are favorite pastimes. A close personal relationship is important for them. In love, they are generous and they treat their partners as equals.

CHILDREN AND PARENTS
Youngsters belonging to this duality will be as bright as a button. Nothing much passes them by—their fingers are on the pulse of life. They are active and restless children who learn quickly and know how to get their own way. These children have a low boredom threshold, and love thinking up new pranks to play on adults. These exuberant children seem to have an answer for everything. Libra-Monkey parents are young at heart. They are brilliant storytellers, so it is unlikely that there will be tears at bedtime in this household.

LIBRA: **SEPTEMBER 23–OCTOBER 22**
YEARS OF THE ROOSTER: 1909 ∗ 1921 ∗ 1933 ∗ 1945 ∗ 1957 ∗ 1969 ∗ 1981 ∗ 1993 ∗ 2005 ∗ 2017
HOUR OF THE ROOSTER: 5PM – 6.59PM

LIBRA-ROOSTER

People born under this combined sign do not like getting their hands dirty. Libra-Roosters have been described as snobs. They do not fare well in a down-market environment because mess or unpleasantness of any sort disturbs their sensitivities. And that applies as much to physical clutter and untidiness as it does to emotional embroilment. Nothing will bring down the mood of a Libra-Rooster faster than being forced to live in uncongenial surroundings or among people whom they consider uncouth. Cool and refined, Libra-Roosters take an intellectual rather than practical approach to life. More charming and affable than most other Roosters, people of this combination enjoy lots of friends and happy companionship.

KEY CHARACTERISTICS

- correct
- outspoken
- cool
- finicky

YOUR COMPATIBLE SIGNS

Aquarius-Ox
Gemini-Snake

EAST WEST FUSION

EAST
Libra mellows the Rooster's direct and robust manner

WEST
The Chinese Rooster encourages Libra to be more daring

Flowcharts, lists, agendas, schedules, rotas: the Libra-Rooster loves them all.

Photography is an attractive career option for the techno-minded Libra-Rooster.

OBSERVATIONS

Inner anxiety and self-doubt will prey on the mind of the Libra-Rooster

WORK, HEALTH, HOBBIES

Libra-Roosters have a reputation for acting with honor and impartiality. Unusual people with original talents, sooner or later the work of the Libra-Rooster gets noticed. They are intelligent individuals who prefer to carve out their own path in life and, whether they follow a career in the arts or the sciences, they will usually take a creative approach, coming up with off-beat solutions that get results. Active yet sensitive, a job which marries imagination with technical know-how would suit these people well. They would make fine sculptors, composers, photographers, or landscape architects. Correct dress code is important to them, so any job that requires a uniform or the donning of robes would interest them.

LOVES, LIKES, DISLIKES

Libra-Roosters can be towers of strength. They can also be a study in correctness. Upholders of traditional values, their tastes tend toward the classical. They are affable people, possessing a kind of old-school charm. They are poised and well-mannered and appreciate the same in others. Their word is their bond. Once they have found the partner of their dreams and pledged their love, they are likely to remain faithful and true for life.

CHILDREN AND PARENTS

Youngsters belonging to this dual sign tend to be studious. Many have green fingers or a natural rapport with flora and fauna, so pets and gardens will be instrumental to their development. They also do well in the expressive arts and will enjoy going to concerts and the theater. Libra-Roosters like to live inside their own heads and are not, as a rule, the doting parent type.

LIBRA-DOG

Libra-Dogs are perhaps the most charming of all the Dog fraternity. But they are also very sincere. Members of this dual sign are genuinely concerned about their fellow people. Fair-minded and equitable, they are drawn toward work for the underprivileged in society. At work, they are true egalitarians and believe in fair play for all. But in love, they tend to find it difficult to make up their minds and time and time again relationships fail to make it past first base. What makes matters worse is their idealistic view of love so that all too often partners fail to come up to the Libra-Dog's high expectations. Consequently, these people are not likely to settle down until later on in life.

KEY CHARACTERISTICS

- patient
- honest
- anxious
- willing

YOUR COMPATIBLE SIGNS

Gemini-Tiger
Aquarius-Horse

Ecology, environment, and conservation are important issues to Libra-Dogs.

EAST WEST FUSION

EAST
Libra softens the Oriental Dog's crustiness

WEST
The Chinese Dog gives Libra a strong sense of responsibility

The Dog brings constancy to the flighty Libra. Together they make very caring parents.

THE ESSENTIAL YOU

WORK, HEALTH, HOBBIES

Libra-Dogs like to help. Perhaps that is why so many are drawn to careers in counseling or social work. Psychiatry, too, is another suitable career and many Libra-Dogs make fine psychoanalysts. But they also care about the environment and any job that involves working with plants and animals would equally be of interest to them. These are not people with megalomaniac ambitions. As long as their job brings them satisfaction, and they feel that they are contributing to the good of mankind and the world, Libra-Dogs are happy to toil away until retirement.

♥ ♥ ♥

LOVES, LIKES, DISLIKES

Despite their kindness, altruistic tendencies, and fair-mindedness, there is a great deal the Libra-Dog dislikes. For members of this twin sign are easily disgruntled and tend to find fault easily.

Perhaps this is because they are idealistic, or because they have high standards. Whatever, this insistence on perfection can interfere with their relationships, as many potential partners get dismissed because they don't come up to the Libra-Dog's expectations. Moreover, these people do not have a passionate nature and they don't care for too much body contact. When they do find their match, however, they become giving and constant companions.

CHILDREN AND PARENTS

Libra-Dog children are responsibly-minded little individuals who like to please everybody—parents, teachers, and friends alike. Above all, they are caring youngsters, very happy looking after their younger siblings, and tending unfailingly to their treasured pets. Libra-Dogs make loving parents and even more devoted aunts and uncles.

LIBRA-PIG

OBSERVATIONS

A lack of resolve can undermine many of the Libra-Pig's good intentions

Both signs, whether in the Eastern or Western tradition, take a laid-back attitude to life. For both, beauty, creativity, and refinement are quintessential components in their lives, in their homes, and in their partners. As Libra individuals have a tendency to be indolent, and Pigs are known to have a strong self-indulgent streak, so Libra-Pigs crave a life of ease and comfort, surrounded by the best things that money can buy. Genial, tolerant, and easy-going by nature, these people make sociable and affable companions. The inability to make decisions, however, is the Libra-Pig's greatest foible.

KEY CHARACTERISTICS

- accommodating
- extravagant
- fortunate
- uncomplaining

YOUR COMPATIBLE SIGNS
Aquarius-Rabbit
Gemini-Sheep

Libra-Pigs believe in acquiring the best that money can buy.

THE ESSENTIAL YOU

WORK, HEALTH, HOBBIES
If possible, Libra-Pigs prefer to work from home. Or else, they do well in occupations that are home-oriented. Designing kitchens, for example, interior decorating or architecture are natural avenues for their talents. Catering, too, would suit, and many Libra-Pigs excel in hotel and restaurant work. Some are happy as land or real estate agents, as teachers of home economics, or working in retail. Healthwise, Libra-Pigs have large appetites and are prone to putting on weight in later life.

LOVES, LIKES, DISLIKES
Libra-Pigs love to shop. These are sensual creatures with expensive tastes. But they are also generous to others. Friends and family are wined and dined with the best these people can afford. Libra-Pigs are terrific hosts, with a magical knack for making people feel at home. Comfort is essential to these people who are excellent homemakers, and everywhere luxury prevails.

Housework itself, however, is not a favorite activity, being relegated to someone else or left altogether. In love, Libra-Pigs could be accused of wearing rose-colored spectacles, for these are life's true romantics.

CHILDREN AND PARENTS
Youngsters of this twin sign are loving and affectionate. They are good with their hands and all manner of craftwork pleases them. These children have a notoriously sweet tooth and they are likely to spend their pocket money on confectionery. But they have a generous heart and they will gladly share their booty with their siblings and friends. As parents, Libra-Pigs adore their children and will spoil them rotten.

Libra-Pigs have an eye for stylish accessories.

EAST WEST FUSION

EAST
Libra graces the Oriental Pig with refinement and gentility

WEST
The Chinese Pig brings honesty and sincerity to this combination

SCORPIO

BORN BETWEEN: **OCTOBER 23—NOVEMBER 21**
WATER SIGN

Scorpio, the eighth sign of the Western astrological year, roughly corresponds to the Chinese month known as the Pig Moon.

If you were born at this time of the year you can either call yourself a Scorpio, or you might like to think of yourself as a native of the Plum Tree Moon, which is a far prettier alternative name for this month in the East.

According to the Chinese, this time of year is also broken up into two fortnights, each describing an aspect of the weather, or a feature relevant to the agricultural year. The first fortnight is called Descent of Hoar Frost and this corresponds to the first two weeks of Scorpio. If you were born in the second half of the sign, though, you belong to the second Chinese fortnight, Beginning of Winter.

But it is, of course, when both your month and your year of birth are combined that the various influences begin to interweave themselves in a way that is essentially unique for you.

In whatever combination, Scorpio as a forceful and penetrating sign, will put a powerful emphasis into the mix.

OBSERVATIONS

*Addictions and obsessions
are a weakness of this sign*

SCORPIO-RAT

Scorpio-Rats are the strongest and most intense characters of all the signs. They are driven by their emotions. Few people looking at a member of this twin sign would suspect quite how deep his or her feelings go. Scorpio-Rats carry with them a powerful aura. They are adept at channeling and focusing their energies in a particular direction. In addition, they possess a perspicacity that gets right to the heart of the matter instantly. Scorpio-Rats always play to win, however high or low the stakes. It doesn't matter whether it is a business deal, love affair, or a simple game of gin rummy, they will not be distracted from their goal. Members of this combination sign do not take kindly to being second best, for they are very poor losers indeed.

EAST WEST FUSION

EAST
Scorpio gives the Chinese Rat
a powerful disposition

WEST
The Oriental Rat increases
Scorpio's verbal skills

KEY CHARACTERISTICS
- courageous
- single-minded
- scheming
- seductive

YOUR COMPATIBLE SIGNS
Cancer-Monkey
Pisces-Dragon

*Strong and rugged, Scorpio-Rats
are born with an innate
pioneering spirit.*

THE ESSENTIAL YOU

WORK, HEALTH, HOBBIES
Scorpio-Rats get jobs done. They work with precision and efficiency until they reach their goal. Digging and delving are their forte, so they excel in all manner of investigative work, from historical research to forensic diagnoses. Careers in archaeology, engineering, architecture, or the chemical industry would all suit. Scorpio-Rats like to get their teeth into a project, so challenge and competition are essential. These people perform better when they have the advantage of power, which proves to be a powerful incentive to reach the top. With excellent mental and physical recuperative powers, and inexhaustible energy, Scorpio-Rats have the power to bounce right back after any illness or setback in their lives.

LOVES, LIKES, DISLIKES
The eyes of the Scorpio-Rat are fixed on the present and the future. They don't like to brood on the past. Consequently, members of this dual sign enjoy contemporary tastes rather than classical or period styles—always one step ahead of their peers. As lovers, they are passionate people, intense and demanding. A fairly thick skin is required for those who live with these people since Scorpio-Rats speak their minds. However, because they also relish a challenge, a wise partner will know how to give as good as he or she gets.

*Chemical analysis makes a
suitable occupation for the
Scorpio-Rat.*

CHILDREN AND PARENTS
Young Scorpio-Rats are deeply affectionate children. They watch what goes on and soon learn how to navigate their way through life. Fiercely competitive, they do whatever is required to get to the top of the pile. Scorpio-Rats make strict parents but they are also fair and protective toward their loved ones.

SCORPIO-OX

Being born in this dual sign makes Scorpio-Oxen very focused. They approach life with drive, determination, and cool, calculated logic. Quietly, without fuss, the Scorpio-Ox will strive and toil to attain his or her goals in life. For members of this twin sign want to be the bosses and they do not hesitate to let everyone else know it. And one way or the other, these people get to the top in the end, for they are hungry for power and they set their sights on the very pinnacle of their chosen career. In love, Scorpio-Oxen are passionate and intense, although they hide the seething caldron of their emotions beneath a calm exterior.

EAST WEST FUSION

EAST
Scorpio endows the Ox
with magnetic appeal

WEST
The Chinese Ox enhances
Scorpio's integrity

*Meditation can help release
the Scorpio-Oxen's intensity.*

KEY CHARACTERISTICS

- focused
- tough
- uncompromising
- indomitable

YOUR COMPATIBLE SIGNS

Pisces-Snake
Cancer-Rooster

*Medically minded
Scorpio-Oxen excel as
surgeons.*

THE ESSENTIAL YOU

WORK, HEALTH, HOBBIES

Scorpio-Oxen put everything they have into the work they do. They have indomitable resistance and, once they have a goal in sight, the strength of purpose characteristic of this sign is legendary. Whether they choose to go into medicine, industry, or mining, they will diligently put in the graft and the long hours to become the very best in their profession. For these people like to be expert at what they do. They need the power and they like to rule from high above. Scorpio-Oxen can make their mark as elite surgeons, as commercial artists, and as engineers.

♥ ♥ ♥

LOVES, LIKES, DISLIKES

The intensity of the Scorpio-Oxen nature is reflected in the rich tones, the classical weight, and the deep comfort of the interiors of their homes. As with all Ox signs, they prefer country to city life, and a nice manor or a small baronial estate would do very nicely. Scorpio-Oxen do like to command and dislike being contradicted. In relationships, they insist on having things their own way. For them, giving their word means total commitment and they expect the compliment to be returned.

CHILDREN AND PARENTS

Because young Scorpio-Oxen are deep and intense little children, it is often difficult to know what they are thinking and they need to be encouraged to talk about their feelings. They will work long and hard at the lessons that capture their interest, which usually include science and technology. They are achievement-motivated and will burn the midnight oil night after night to pass their exams with the best grades of the year.

SCORPIO-TIGER

Cats have nine lives, it is said, and no one lives them so intensely as a person born under the dual sign of the Scorpio-Tiger. These people's emotions run deep. Unfathomably deep. Scorpio-Tigers are forceful people, often unaware of the effect their powerful personalities have on other people. Strong-minded and extremely focused in everything they do, they like to put across their point of view and they do not take kindly to being contradicted. Scorpio-Tigers are some of the most sensual people one is ever likely to meet. Their amorous and sultry nature can lead to steamy relationships—these people can positively smoulder with desire. Should they ever be crossed, whether in business or in love, they will seethe with rage until they can take their revenge.

KEY CHARACTERISTICS

- energetic
- strong-willed
- magnetic
- challenging

YOUR COMPATIBLE SIGNS
Cancer-Horse
Pisces-Dog

EAST WEST FUSION

EAST
Concentration is the gift
Scorpio brings to the Tiger

WEST
The fiery Tiger gives power
and energy to Scorpio.

Confrontation does not frighten the Scorpio-Tiger when a moral issue is at stake.

OBSERVATIONS

If they do not agree with a system or a superior, Scorpio-Tigers can be downright uncooperative.

THE ESSENTIAL YOU

WORK, HEALTH, HOBBIES

Scorpio-Tigers like to pack a lot into each day. They possess dynamic energy and can get through a prodigious amount of work in a short time. A career that constantly stretches them both mentally and physically is what they seek because challenge is essential to maintain their interest. These people are excellent organizers and, as troubleshooters, they have the ability to turn an ailing business around in less than a week. But they are ruthless and, if a job requires drastic measures, Scorpio-Tigers will not balk at having to make radical—and sometimes unpopular—decisions. Scorpio-Tigers command a great deal of respect and others will readily follow their lead. A suitable career would be psychology.

LOVES, LIKES, DISLIKES

As far as Scorpio-Tigers are concerned, rules and regulations are made for other people. For these people are a law unto themselves and they like to follow their own code. At home they take the leading role, and they guard their possessions jealously. This applies as much to their loved ones. In relationships, Scorpio-Tigers are honest and faithful, if a little prone to over-possessiveness.

CHILDREN AND PARENTS

Without a strong guiding hand, young Scorpio-Tigers could all too easily go off the rails. For example, if they take a dislike to someone, they can become difficult and obstructive. So, a balance between keeping them busy with plenty of activities, while allowing them enough freedom to pursue their own star, is the key. Encouraging kindness toward others is a worthwhile lesson for these youngsters. Scorpio-Tiger parents teach their children to become strong and independent people.

Scorpio-Tiger cubs are best kept busy with games and toys that intrigue and involve.

SCORPIO-RABBIT

Scorpio-Rabbits are culture connoisseurs, many choosing to work in the antiques business or art world. Or else, with their combination of insight and gravitas, they make excellent therapists. In work as well as in romance, Scorpio-Rabbits play their cards close to their chests. The Scorpio half of this partnership inclines toward the secretive, while the Rabbit presents a facade of cool detachment, which belies the depth of feeling and strength of character that all members of this dual sign possess. Emotionally, these are passionate people, focused, and intense. Scorpio-Rabbits love deeply and possessively. Woe betide anyone who toys with these people's affections. For, beneath that cool, elegant exterior, Scorpio-Rabbits have an unforgiving nature and a deadly sting in their tails!

KEY CHARACTERISTICS
- perceptive
- compassionate
- steady
- discreet

YOUR COMPATIBLE SIGNS
Pisces-Sheep
Cancer-Pig

THE ESSENTIAL YOU

WORK, HEALTH, HOBBIES
Perhaps not the easiest of people to work for, Scorpio-Rabbits are disciplinarians and take a serious approach to their jobs. Physically resilient themselves, they take an interest in health matters and many gravitate toward careers in the medical professions. Work in scientific research and the development of medicines or of health equipment especially appeals. Subjects connected with mind, body, and spirit also draw them and many become excellent alternative practitioners. Landscape architecture and town planning also make suitable careers.

LOVES, LIKES, DISLIKES
Privacy is important to all members of this twin sign who like to keep themselves to themselves. Discretion is the Scorpio-Rabbit's middle name, for they leave few, if any, telltale hints about their private affairs for prying eyes to see. These people like harmony, symmetry, and balance, and they will ensure that their living and working environments are as pleasing and comfortable to their own tastes as

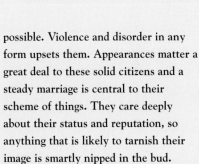

Members of this sign are fascinated by alternative therapies.

possible. Violence and disorder in any form upsets them. Appearances matter a great deal to these solid citizens and a steady marriage is central to their scheme of things. They care deeply about their status and reputation, so anything that is likely to tarnish their image is smartly nipped in the bud.

CHILDREN AND PARENTS
Young Scorpio-Rabbits are self-reliant and happy in their own company. Given building blocks, construction toys, or a chemistry set, these children will keep themselves quietly amused for hours. Scorpio-Rabbit parents bring their youngsters up to be polite and well-behaved individuals.

OBSERVATIONS
Scorpio-Rabbits have a tendency to act condescendingly

Whether in art, fashion, or taste, Scorpio-Rabbits make fine connoisseurs.

EAST WEST FUSION

EAST
Scorpio teaches the Rabbit
to be self-disciplined

WEST
The Rabbit encourages
Scorpio to be compassionate

OBSERVATIONS

The Scorpio-Dragon's belligerence can be off-putting

SCORPIO-DRAGON

With an array of colorful and exotic qualities, Scorpio-Dragons are mighty people, members of a potent sign whose ardor and zeal are legendary. Even when young, they demonstrate powerful personal traits with deep, intense emotions and, as they mature, so they also develop a strong sex drive. There is a compelling, even hypnotic, quality to the members of the Scorpio-Dragon clan, and this attracts potential partners, like moths to a bright light. No matter what they do, the Scorpio-Dragon native will exert in one hundred and ten percent effort. When they love, Scorpio-Dragons love exclusively, even obsessively. What's more, they expect their partners to reciprocate with the same amount of commitment. Otherwise, they will demand to know the reason why.

EAST WEST FUSION

EAST
Scorpio deepens the Dragon's feelings

WEST
The Dragon brings Scorpio a robust constitution

KEY CHARACTERISTICS
- ambitious
- powerful
- excessive
- hypnotic

YOUR COMPATIBLE SIGNS
Cancer-Rat
Pisces-Monkey

Scorpio-Dragons give their love unconditionally to those they hold dear.

THE ESSENTIAL YOU

WORK, HEALTH, HOBBIES
Scorpio-Dragons have big fish to fry. With their mega ambition, these people want to be involved in big schemes—the bigger the better. They are power hungry. Indeed, towering over others from a great height is the preferred position of the Scorpio-Dragon. They are tough taskmasters, believing as they do in their own infallibility. In their hasty progress, Scorpio-Dragons often miscalculate and could go from rags to riches and riches back to rags more than once. But, to give them their due, they will pick themselves up each time and journey upward anew. Scorpio-Dragons are capable of reaching superstardom. Sculpture could be a therapeutic pastime.

LOVES, LIKES, DISLIKES
Recognition and applause make Scorpio-Dragons very happy. Being contradicted, however, is a pet hate. Members of this dual sign are magnetically attractive and they make energetic and charismatic lovers. They rebel if their freedom is restricted, and need to feel they are free agents, able to pick and chose companions as they wish. When it comes to relationships, jealousy—that green-eyed monster—is ever present by the Scorpio-Dragon's side, always ready to rear its ugly head once more.

CHILDREN AND PARENTS
Youngsters born under this twin sign are energetic little children, always eager to take on a dare. Emotionally resilient and buoyant, they will pick themselves up after every tumble, and simply have another go until they succeed. They are popular in the main and aspire to being leaders of the pack. Just as they are ambitious for themselves, so Scorpio-Dragon parents have equally high hopes for their offspring and will encourage their children to succeed.

With their penetrating psychological insight, Scorpio-Dragons would relish writing thrillers.

SCORPIO-SNAKE

Two compulsive and introspective signs are joined here to produce a powerful, enigmatic individual, whose thoughts and feelings are labyrinthine deep. Both Snake and Scorpio play their cards extremely close to their chests, so a person of this combination will be ultra-guarded and secretive and therefore virtually impossible to fathom. Scorpio-Snakes are intensely passionate individuals, as possessive of their property as they are of those they love. Cool, controlled, and streetwise on the exterior, one nevertheless has the impression that deep inside the Scorpio-Snake lie turbulent, even violent, emotions, which, if provoked, could surface and explode. Scorpio-Snakes never forgive or forget, so one only crosses them if one dares!

KEY CHARACTERISTICS
- penetrating
- secretive
- resentful
- suspicious

YOUR COMPATIBLE SIGNS
Pisces-Rooster
Cancer-Ox

OBSERVATIONS
Arrogance can be a negative trait in the Scorpio-Snake's character

EAST WEST FUSION

EAST
Scorpio intensifies the Oriental Snake's perceptive abilities

WEST
The Chinese Snake enhances Scorpio's magnetic qualities

Self-protection is a natural instinct of the Scorpio-Snake.

THE ESSENTIAL YOU

WORK, HEALTH, HOBBIES
Masters and mistresses of psychological penetration, Scorpio-Snakes can pick up at a glance the inflections and nuances of speech and behavior. Not much passes their perceptive gaze without it being instantly registered, analyzed, and processed, which means these people are natural psychotherapists. Acting, too, would suit their formidable talents, for natives of this dual sign can easily get under the skin of a character, and effortlessly assume a role. Hypnotists, clairvoyants, and mediums extraordinaire, with their ability to see into the future, these Scorpio-Snakes will rarely be poor.

LOVES, LIKES, DISLIKES
Scorpio-Snakes like to think. They like to sit and watch human nature at work. Noisy entertainment is not really their

The well-developed sixth sense associated with this sign gives its members psychic talents.

scene and they don't much care to get involved in the hurly-burly of life. Soirées and elegant dinner parties are much more their thing. These are sophisticated people who need to live in a spacious, airy residence which they will have decorated with impeccable style. With their seductive good looks, Scorpio-Snakes have little difficulty attracting admirers. But, when it comes to choosing an intimate partner for themselves, they will be ultra-selective. Beauty, of course, will be important, but a biddable nature will be top of the list.

CHILDREN AND PARENTS
As children, Scorpio-Snakes catch on fast. They are clever youngsters who are artful in many ways. They learn early on about the power they can wield with their personality and they find that swaying others with their charms comes easily to them. Consequently, even when very young, they will not be short of friends and admirers. Scorpio-Snake parents insist on polished manners at all times. They encourage their offspring to concentrate on intellectual pursuits.

EAST WEST FUSION

SCORPIO-HORSE

Intense Scorpio brings focus and concentration to the skittish Horse.

The famous powers of concentration of Scorpio will work to the Horse's advantage, enabling those born under this dual sign to focus on ideas and see projects through to their conclusion. Meanwhile, the zany outlook of the Horse will considerably lighten and brighten Scorpio's mental disposition, lessening the obsessive tendencies and moderating the emotional intensity that is an integral part of the Scorpio nature. Both the West and East signs, independently, have a strong magnetic allure and together produce individuals who are potently seductive and who know how to get the attention of the opposite sex with a simple lift of the eyebrow or toss of the lustrous mane.

EAST
Scorpio brings to the Horse a tenacity of purpose

WEST
The Horse fills Scorpio's heart with fun and laughter

KEY CHARACTERISTICS
- intelligent
- talented
- confident
- independent

YOUR COMPATIBLE SIGNS
Cancer-Dog
Pisces-Tiger

OBSERVATIONS
Once they have made up their minds, little will deflect the Scorpio-Horse from his or her chosen course of action

THE ESSENTIAL YOU

WORK, HEALTH, HOBBIES
While Scorpio-Horses can, and do, concentrate their energies on the task in hand, they tend to find that routine is an irritation that can stifle their spontaneous creativity. A strict nine-to-five occupation, then, is not advisable. Flexible working hours or self-employment are far more suitable for this group. Scorpio-Horses are blessed with essential vitality and, whether professionally or in their spare time, many will plow their energies into any type of sport. Dance, too, is an excellent avenue and will make them feel alive. Those with a scientific bent may consider a career in the mental health services, dentistry, or clinical research.

LOVES, LIKES, DISLIKES
Gifted with creative talents, these people like to make and create. They are skilled at craftwork and relish the prospect of interior decorating and home renovation. They take pride in the fact that their tastes are a little out of the ordinary—indeed the clichéd and the prosaic are shunned—so their homes will always be interesting and different. Image, too, is important, so Scorpio-Horses like to present a stylish appearance. As lovers, Scorpio-Horses are fun and serious by turns: an intriguing combination that adds to their charms.

Scorpio-Horses express their creativity through crafts and home improvement.

CHILDREN AND PARENTS
Young Scorpio-Horses can all too easily bottle up their emotions. Therefore, they should be encouraged, whenever possible, to express and talk about their feelings. Because these children are multitalented, finding a clear direction to follow in life can prove tricky. As a result, these youngsters may try out a wide range of careers in their early days before they discover their true vocation. Scorpio-Horses are devoted parents and enjoy family life to the full.

SCORPIO-SHEEP

Scorpio toughens the sinews of the otherwise placid Sheep and gives those born under this dual rulership a more independent and assertive nature. The Sheep's influence lessens Scorpio's intense nature, making them more emotionally rounded and accepting of others. When joined, Scorpio loses none of the fascination so characteristic of its sign. Indeed, the mixture serves to make these natives magnetically alluring. People will bend over backward to help these delicate flowers who on the surface appear as fragile and as scented as any hothouse lily. However, underneath the façade the Scorpio-Sheep is as tough as old boots!

KEY CHARACTERISTICS
- tantalizing
- moody
- gifted
- selfish

YOUR COMPATIBLE SIGNS
Pisces-Pig
Cancer-Rabbit

OBSERVATIONS

Jealousy of other people's good fortune can be a failing of this sign

Gorgeous, alluring Scorpio-Sheep combine ethereal beauty with a will of iron.

THE ESSENTIAL YOU

WORK, HEALTH, HOBBIES
A lack of self-motivation means that Scorpio-Sheep fare best working in a partnership or as a member of a team. As actors, musicians, or composers, the back-up of an agent, manager, or adviser is essential to ensure these natives direct their talents consistently and productively. Otherwise, regular employment in an office or corporation will keep the Scorpio-Sheep directed. Graphic design, publishing, or archival work are careers that would suit. Wiry and resilient, Scorpio-Sheep are stronger than they look.

♥ ♥ ♥

LOVES, LIKES, DISLIKES
Poverty and loneliness are the two conditions that strike terror into the heart of the Scorpio-Sheep. Being protected in a life of comfort and ease is what they like. Just as well, then, that Scorpio-Sheep know how to attract money. They attract partners too, and make tantalizing lovers. For in love as well as in life, members of this double sign are like beautiful climbing roses that need a pillar or pergola around which to climb. Only with this support will the Scorpio-Sheep, like the rose, be able to reveal his or her full glory.

🦂 🦂 🦂

CHILDREN AND PARENTS
Young Scorpio-Sheep will enjoy all creative subjects. They are cuddly children and need a good deal of affection. It is all too easy to spoil them as toddlers so bowing to their every whim is not advisable. Moreover, teaching them the importance of sticking to a routine from an early age will stand them in good stead later. Scorpio-Sheep parents are soft and tender-hearted but they need a stronger partner to lay down a few ground rules.

EAST WEST FUSION

EAST
Scorpio strengthens the Sheep's emotional disposition

WEST
The passive nature of the Sheep mellows Scorpio's intensity of feeling

The music business is a rewarding career choice for Scorpio-Sheep, but a good agent to manage their efforts is strongly advised.

SCORPIO-MONKEY

Monkeys are fun-loving people and, by and large, amusing companions to have around. But, as with all people, the Monkey also has a negative side, which can be minimized or accentuated according to the sign with which it is combined. With this mixture, Scorpio actually activates some of those skeletons the Monkey might have preferred kept in the closet. Here, the Monkey's ingenuity can turn to guile; inventiveness can flip into mendacity; dexterity into plain craftiness. On a bad day, the Scorpio-Monkey can be downright misbehaved. But Scorpio-Monkeys also have an insight that is awesome in its penetrative ability, and this is a talent they can employ to fathom character and understand the motivation of others. Thus, these people make excellent police investigators, lawyers, psychotherapists, and prison reformers.

KEY CHARACTERISTICS
- accomplished
- astute
- persuasive
- mischievous

YOUR COMPATIBLE SIGNS
Cancer-Dragon
Pisces-Rat

OBSERVATIONS

Scorpio-Monkeys can be downright underhanded in the pursuit of their aims

Scorpio-Monkeys like to maintain an aura of cool mystique.

THE ESSENTIAL YOU

WORK, HEALTH, HOBBIES
The Scorpio-Monkey is an independent agent. At work, natives of this duality prefer to be in charge of their own schedules, and to come and go as they see fit. Tying these people down to a desk and expecting them to maintain rigid hours is the surest and quickest way to alienate them from their managers and ultimately the job itself. As masters and mistresses of their own destinies, however, Scorpio-Monkeys will triumph in whatever tasks they undertake. For these people have an unusual and individualistic creative genius and they must be allowed to carve a niche that is all their own. Deep-thinking, active, and always full of pep, Scorpio-Monkeys excel in occupations where linguistic skills are a prerequisite. They do very well as criminal lawyers, interpreters, foreign correspondents, and all kinds of cloak-and-dagger occupations requiring covert activities.

LOVES, LIKES, DISLIKES
In love, Scorpio-Monkeys are spicy creatures with a positively charged sex drive. They are prepared to be faithful, as long as their partners maintain the right amount of mystique to keep their interests aflame. A doting, fawning, or clinging mate will not do at all. An exotic, fiery, independent individual, on the other hand, will secure this person's affections for life.

CHILDREN AND PARENTS
Young Scorpio-Monkeys are lively, talkative little souls, who amuse everyone with their ready wit. They have wide-ranging abilities and take an interest in everything they see. Indeed, these are curious youngsters, with an urgent need to know. As they mature into parents, Scorpio-Monkeys retain their youthful zest for life and enjoy watching their children grow.

Scorpio-Monkeys bring a steamy intensity to their love partnerships.

SCORPIO-ROOSTER

The word "compromise" simply does not exist in the vocabulary of the Scorpio-Rooster. A strong will and fierce determination mean that when members of this sign set their sights on something or someone, they simply refuse to give up until they achieve their objective—to the very letter. Scorpios have a well-known sinister side to their natures, which thankfully rarely breaks through. However, this darker element gives the Scorpio-Rooster a certain potency, fueling the duo with as yet untapped reserves of energy, which are ready to explode to the surface at any given moment. Emotionally, the Scorpio-Rooster is deep to the point of obsession.

Scorpio-Roosters like their voices to be heard.

EAST
Scorpio brings depth to the Rooster's knowledge

WEST
The Rooster endorses Scorpio's powerful determination

KEY CHARACTERISTICS
- 🦂 uncompromising
- 🦂 driven
- 🦂 disciplined
- 🦂 principled

YOUR COMPATIBLE SIGNS
Pisces-Ox
Cancer-Snake

OBSERVATIONS
Excessive fault-finding can be a negative characteristic of Scorpio-Roosters

---

THE ESSENTIAL YOU

WORK, HEALTH, HOBBIES
Strong in mind and body, Scorpio-Roosters are blessed with indomitable spirits. Members of this dual sign are energetic and clever, sharp and astute, and gifted with many talents. They will master to perfection any skill they care to take up. Scorpio-Roosters can be prickly to work with. In dealings and conversations with their colleagues, they can be somewhat blunt. They don't take kindly to being contradicted, but they do admire those who stand up to them. Many careers are suited to these hard-working, dedicated souls. Some are drawn to the police and security services, as well as to the armed forces. Others do well in the petrochemical business, in the financial sector, and in sports. Taking up a martial art would make an appropriate spare-time activity.

LOVES, LIKES, DISLIKES
Scorpio-Roosters like their routine. They need to be in control and do not appreciate outside disturbance or disruption to their plans. Tidiness, too, is essential and so anyone who clutters the place is given short shrift. At home, cupboards are organized, brasses are buffed, glasses sparkle, and dust is nowhere to be seen. Their relationships, too, have to be squeaky-clean and partners must be models of perfection. Nothing less will do.

CHILDREN AND PARENTS
Sturdy and robust, Scorpio-Rooster children will show sporting prowess from a very young age. Most are gifted academically as well and they are prepared to work hard in order to do well in their studies. They do especially well in science, mathematics, and technology. Young Scorpio-Roosters mature to become diligent and deeply caring parents. They insist on orderliness—with everything in its proper place.

The discipline and control of martial arts appeal greatly to the Scorpio-Rooster.

SCORPIO: **OCTOBER 23–NOVEMBER 21**
YEARS OF THE DOG: 1910 ✳ 1922 ✳ 1934 ✳ 1946 ✳ 1958 ✳ 1970 ✳ 1982 ✳ 1994 ✳ 2006 ✳ 2018
HOUR OF THE DOG: 7PM – 8.59PM

THE ESSENTIAL YOU

SCORPIO-DOG

The notorious Scorpio determination brings passion and strength to all those who are born under this twin sign. Therefore, Scorpio-Dogs are some of the most deeply committed people among the Dog clan. Once they have given their word, it is their bond. Members of this Oriental sign tend toward the unobtrusive and seem to maintain a low profile. Scorpio-Dogs, however, are the exception, for they have powerful personalities and prefer to be the leaders rather than followers of the pack. In their personal relationships they give one hundred percent loyalty to their chosen partner, and demand one hundred percent in return. Hell hath no fury like a Scorpio-Dog betrayed!

KEY CHARACTERISTICS

- serious
- alert
- honest
- analytical

YOUR COMPATIBLE SIGNS

Cancer-Tiger
Pisces-Horse

EAST WEST FUSION

EAST
Scorpio sharpens the Dog's
penetrative abilities

WEST
The Chinese Dog raises
Scorpio's social awareness

*Deep-thinking, passionate, and
intense, self-analysis appeals
to the Scorpio-Dog.*

OBSERVATIONS

*Prejudice and small-mindedness
can be failings in this double sign*

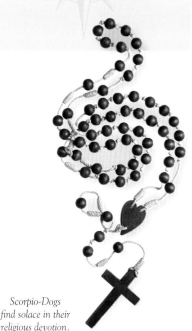

*Scorpio-Dogs
find solace in their
religious devotion.*

WORK, HEALTH, HOBBIES

Scorpio-Dogs are dedicated individuals, who will commit themselves body and soul to whatever career they decide to follow. A common theme among members of this twin sign is the desire to improve the human condition so many will turn to social work. Work among society's criminal element, the underprivileged or the disabled also draws Scorpio-Dogs. Moreover, as these can be religious people, sometimes fanatically so, some will feel a strong spiritual calling. On a another plane, contemplating the heavens can lead to a love of astronomy. Strong and wiry, they work hard for their living.

❤ ❤ ❤

LOVES, LIKES, DISLIKES

Underneath the Scorpio-Dog's crusty shell beats a warm heart. But reaching it can take time, since members of this dual sign build themselves a strong façade that only the most honest and pure can penetrate. Perhaps they are terribly afraid of being hurt, or fear that few can meet their rigorously high standards. Certainly, they are idealistic and their perfectionist eyes can spot microscopic defects at fifty yards away. Yet they are modest, too, and their tastes are quiet. A partner who teaches them to relax, laugh, and occasionally even to dance would be perfect.

CHILDREN AND PARENTS

From an early age, Scorpio-Dogs show a desire to make their own way in life. Fairly independent, they are not especially demanding of attention. Serious and self-driven, they are protective of their possessions and of their siblings and friends. Since the family is central to the Scorpio-Dog, they make dutiful, sincere, and conscientious parents.

SCORPIO-PIG

Scorpio-Pigs are ambitious creatures. They know from a very young age that success equals money and that money equals power. So the Scorpio-Pig sets his or her sights on the top. And, come hell or high water, however tough the trading conditions, the Scorpio-Pig strikes it rich at some point in his or her life. Partners are advised never, ever to cross the Scorpio-Pig in love because that sting in the Scorpion's tails can prove lethal! When these people love, it is exclusive and they expect their partners to make the same commitment. Sex is high on the Scorpio-Pig's agenda and, with their overt animal magnetism, they tend to attract suitors, like bees to a honey-pot. According to the Scorpio-Pig, only absolute loyalty and fidelity will make a relationship work.

Scorpio-Pigs are happy to put in all the hours necessary to achieve success.

EAST WEST FUSION

EAST
Scorpio brings to the Chinese Pig a seductive appeal

WEST
The Oriental Pig enhances Scorpio's dedication to the family

OBSERVATIONS
A volcanic temper is the fly in the ointment of this double sign

KEY CHARACTERISTICS
- popular
- outspoken
- trustworthy
- vindictive

YOUR COMPATIBLE SIGNS
Pisces-Rabbit
Cancer-Sheep

THE ESSENTIAL YOU

WORK, HEALTH, HOBBIES
Scorpio-Pigs don't take "no" for an answer. Once they have set their mind on a course of action, their motto is to keep on trying until they are satisfied with the results. This is as well, since these people set their sights on the highest rung of the ladder. For success, and the material prosperity that it brings, is paramount to the Scorpio-Pig's satisfaction in life and many will make their fortune in creative occupations. An exclusive business in interior design, for example, would suit. Running a five-star restaurant, frequented by the rich and famous, might do nicely too. Those with an interest in medicine will probably veer to the alternative kind, such as massage, aromatherapy, or osteopathy.

LOVES, LIKES, DISLIKES
Scorpio-Pigs are fun-loving creatures. They are supremely sensual and erotic people, and are usually stunning to look at. Both sexes of this sign would be welcomed by modeling agencies. Slinky and seductive, they enjoy dressing to thrill. Obviously money is important to support Scorpio-Pigs' expensive tastes and lifestyles. Certainly no Scorpio-Pig is happy living on the breadline. These people aspire to grand living and their homes reflect their luxury-loving lifestyles. Sex is a crucially important component in their lives because members of this sign are born with a healthy libido. A vibrant, intimate life with a partner is, therefore, essential to the Scorpio-Pig.

CHILDREN AND PARENTS
Young Scorpio-Pigs relish the good things in life. They have large appetites and a sweet tooth. They adore the sensual and comforting pleasure of snuggling up to their parents. These are refreshingly happy children, on the one hand amusing and yet themselves easily entertained. Scorpio-Pig parents are hugely loving—in fact, they are often prone to spoiling their children.

Scorpio-Pigs love stately styles festooned with the trappings of luxury.

SAGITTARIUS

BORN BETWEEN: NOVEMBER 22—DECEMBER 21
FIRE SIGN

*S*agittarius, the ninth sign of the Western astrological year, roughly corresponds to the Chinese month known as the Rat Moon.

If you were born at this time of the year you can either call yourself a Sagittarian, or a native of the Bulrushes Moon, which is a more poetic alternative Chinese name for this month.

According to the Chinese, this time of year is also broken up into two fortnights, each describing an aspect of the weather, or a feature relevant to the agricultural year. The first fortnight is called Lesser Snow and this corresponds to the first two weeks of Sagittarius. If you were born in the second half of the sign, though, you belong to the second Chinese fortnight, Greater Snow.

But it is, of course, when both your month and your year of birth are combined that the various influences begin to interweave themselves in a way that is essentially unique for you.

In whatever combination, Sagittarius, as an enthusiastic and expansive force, Sagittarius will add an element of optimism and far-sightedness to the mix.

SAGITTARIUS-RAT

Happy-go-lucky and full of the joys of Spring, Sagittarius-Rats breeze through life. They do not, however, live with their heads in the clouds for they are realists who couple wisdom with far-sightedness. People born under this dual sign can spot an opportunity at 30 yards. They will have sized up the implications and already decided whether or not to take any action before you can even say Jack Robinson. On the whole, Sagittarius-Rats are lucky creatures, but they all possess itchy feet and restless souls and will find it hard to make a commitment. Craving challenge and adventure, the last thing they want to do is settle down in some cozy, safe, suburban type of existence.

Sagittarius-Rats are not afraid of playing for high stakes.

EAST WEST FUSION

EAST
Sagittarius teaches the nervous Rat to be more carefree

WEST
The Rat quickens the Archer's thinking processes

KEY CHARACTERISTICS
- gregarious
- lucky
- incisive
- cheerful

YOUR COMPATIBLE SIGNS
Leo-Monkey
Aries-Dragon

Gifted players, young Sagittarius-Rats adore all forms of sports.

THE ESSENTIAL YOU

WORK, HEALTH, HOBBIES
Strong, energetic, and independent, these people like to live life on the hoof so a job in the same place from cradle to grave is unlikely to attract the Sagittarius-Rat. Change, diversity, and variety is what these workers call for, and if they can combine their job with traveling, preferably to foreign countries, the Archer born in a Rat year will be very happy indeed.

LOVES, LIKES, DISLIKES
Sagittarius-Rats enjoy company and are at their happiest when surrounded by people. They delight in having friends around for dinner, impromptu visitors, or family coming to stay for the weekend. Members of this sign are wonderful hosts, having the knack of making everyone feel relaxed and at home. Relationshipwise, Sagittarius-Rats have an aversion to being tied down and find it difficult to commit themselves to one partner for life. The world is a big place and there is so much else to do, to see, and to experience.

CHILDREN AND PARENTS
Youngsters of this dual sign are some of the liveliest children you will meet. They show signs of their independence from a very early age and will probably want to fly the nest in order to explore the world as soon as they are old enough. Sports of all kinds are their passion. They are keen to join activity groups and enjoy reading, both useful preparations for their active adult lives. Sagittarius-Rat parents teach their children good social skills and encourage them to become strong, independent people.

SAGITTARIUS-OX

Couple the Sagittarian vision and far-sightedness with the Ox's determination and tenacity, and it is easy to see why the world is the Sagittarius-Ox's oyster. Members of this dual sign are born lucky, which is just as well, since they are prone to taking the odd risk or three. Yet, they are shrewd and quick to assess a situation, so perhaps it is that those risks are really cleverly calculated strategies rather than apparently impulsive gambles taken on the spur of the moment. With talents such as these, it is little wonder that Sagittarius-Oxen reach prestigious positions in life and accumulate a goodly amount of money in the process.

The Archer's wide gambling streak is disciplined by the Ox, whose strength is strategy and forward planning.

KEY CHARACTERISTICS

- successful
- strong leaders
- articulate
- ambitious

YOUR COMPATIBLE SIGNS

Aries-Snake
Leo-Rooster

EAST WEST FUSION

EAST
The Archer brings the Ox.
speed of thought

WEST
The Ox blesses the Archer with the ability to focus on the task at hand

OBSERVATIONS

Impatience is perhaps one of the Sagittarius-Ox's worst faults.

Pundit, expert, guru, Sagittarius-Oxen are wise individuals.

WORK, HEALTH, HOBBIES

Perspicacity and an extraordinary talent for planning make Sagittarius-Oxen excellent leaders and directors. Brilliant at decision-making, powerful, and focused, many are in charge of extremely successful companies and steer their team with honesty and fair-play. Others look to members of this dual sign for guidance, and know that any advice they are given will be sound, sensible, and timely. It doesn't take long for the Sagittarius-Ox to become a respected person of influence.

♥ ♥ ♥

LOVES, LIKES, DISLIKES

With their powerful and driving egos, Sagittarius-Oxen keep busy and enjoy a wide range of interests. These are reflected in their living and working environments which they like to furnish not only practically and comfortably, but also with impeccable flair. To those they love, the Sagittarius-Ox is devoted and dedicated. Consequently, members of this sign find it easy to commit themselves to a lifelong partner.

CHILDREN AND PARENTS

Young Sagittarius-Oxen are solid young citizens, honest as the day is long. They do well in any situation where they can take charge—book monitor, class prefect, team captain, and the like. As achievement-motivated as their adult counterparts, these youngsters work hard to attain success in their studies. Sagittarius-Oxen take to parenting as efficiently as they do everything else in life. All is carefully planned in advance.

SAGITTARIUS: **NOVEMBER 22–DECEMBER 21**
YEARS OF THE TIGER: 1902 ✴ 1914 ✴ 1926 ✴ 1938 ✴ 1950 ✴ 1962 ✴ 1974 ✴ 1986 ✴ 1998 ✴ 2010
HOUR OF THE TIGER: 3AM – 4.59AM

SAGITTARIUS-TIGER

Of all the Tigers, those born under the influence of Sagittarius have to be the most far-sighted. And yet they are also perspicacious enough to catch every nuance, every tell-tale inflection of voice, which enables them to sum up a person or situation in a flash. With their colorful characters and huge appetites for life, Sagittarius-Tigers thrive on adventurous living and like to experience everything that life has to offer. On the negative side, they tend to be impulsive types, prone to putting their feet in their mouths, or charging in before having properly considered the consequences of their words or actions. Freedom and independence are vital ingredients for their well-being.

KEY CHARACTERISTICS

- 🐾 intelligent
- 🐾 aware
- 🐾 fortunate
- 🐾 day-dreaming

YOUR COMPATIBLE SIGNS
Aries-Dogs
Leo-Horses

Whatever their age, Sagittarius-Tigers never lose their love of learning.

EAST WEST FUSION

EAST
Sagittarius adds wisdom to temper the impetuosity of the Tiger

WEST
Tigers lend their inimitable magnetism to the Archer's armory

Whether physical or intellectual, Sagittarius-Tigers rarely pass up a challenge.

THE ESSENTIAL YOU

WORK, HEALTH, HOBBIES
The bigger the undertaking, the better the Sagittarius-Tiger likes it. For these people look at life as a broad canvas that needs to be filled with bold and colorful strokes. Jobs that require nitpicking attention to detail are definitely not for members of this sign. Nor are repetitive tasks that do not allow scope for sudden bursts of inspiration. But a career where their imaginations are given free rein, where they can find innovative solutions to old problems, and where they are given their own autonomy would be ideal for these types.

♥ ♥ ♥

LOVES, LIKES, DISLIKES
Eternal students, Sagittarius-Tigers spend a lot of time inside their own heads. They absorb facts, read books, and like to learn about anything and everything. Wise yet charmingly naive, spiritual yet interested in trivia, philosophical yet funny, and outwardly independent yet with an inner need to be secure and loved, the Sagittarius-Tiger personifies a working contradiction. In relationships, they need freedom but they don't necessarily want to act on it. Having the door open is enough to keep them contented, satisfied, and committed to the ones they love.

🐾 🐾 🐾

CHILDREN AND PARENTS
Youngsters belonging to this sign are so imaginative that they are never bored. Not that they are ever truly alone since their fertile imaginations constantly conjure up all sorts of games and imaginary friends to play with. These are protective young souls who will care tenderly for their younger siblings. Wiser than their years, Sagittarius-Tiger children are warm and cuddly, as well as good company. Sagittarius-Tiger parents never talk down to their children because they expect them to be grown-up even when still babies.

SAGITTARIUS-RABBIT

The Sagittarius-Rabbit is a talented individual and immense fun to be with. Unlike the domesticated nature of the average Rabbit-born individual, the Archer's influence here turns this Bunny into a bit of a wanderer so that members of this sign are far more vivacious and adventurous and less stay-at-home. In addition, the Sagittarian input injects a sense of levity into the normally sentimental Rabbit, with the result that these individuals are far less moody and much more optimistic and carefree. Both of these signs are far-sighted, which gives the Sagittarius-Rabbit a broad perspective on life as well as a visionary outlook. However, for these independent thinkers, relationships definitely need to be fluid.

EAST WEST FUSION

EAST
Sagittarius brings a sparkle of jollity to lift the Rabbit's spirits.

WEST
The Rabbit teaches Sagittarius to think before speaking.

KEY CHARACTERISTICS
- individualistic
- amenable
- self-controlled
- discerning

YOUR COMPATIBLE SIGNS
Aries-Sheep
Leo-Pig

Gifted with a prescient mind, Sagittarius-Rabbits often see the light long before less visionary colleagues.

OBSERVATIONS
Putting their eggs in too many baskets will lessen their chances of success

THE ESSENTIAL YOU

WORK, HEALTH, HOBBIES
Because Sagittarius-Rabbits like to do their own thing, they are perhaps better suited to working on their own, or at least in a position where they can call the shots. Yet when they do mix with others, they possess an extraordinary gift for dealing with people on whatever level the company requires, which means that members of this dual sign are easily accepted and assimilated into any society they choose. Every Sagittarius-Rabbit has the ability to become an expert in his or her own field just as long as they stick to doing what they know best.

Sagittarius-Rabbits fill their lives with refinement and style.

LOVES, LIKES, DISLIKES
Sagittarius-Rabbits like to roam—physically and sexually. In general, members of this duality are not the constant type. They are flirts who adore being admired, and the more admiring followers they collect the better. These are elegant people for whom image and presentation are important. So they are fussy about how they look, and they spend time and money on their appearance and on their environment in order to get it just right.

CHILDREN AND PARENTS
Young Sagittarius-Rabbits are beguiling creatures who need to try out a wide range of activities until each one finds his or her forte. Discovering at a young age where their of genius lies will make all the difference to these people in their future lives. Adult Sagittarius-Rabbits like to parent from a distance. Colicky babies and dirty diapers are to be kept at arm's length at all costs. But, as their offspring grow older and mature, then it is a completely different matter. For that is when these parents come into their own.

SAGITTARIUS-DRAGON

Sagittarius-Dragons never miss an opportunity to have fun.

Open and forthright, the Sagittarius-Dragon's honesty, though well-intentioned, can sometimes be inappropriate. A little more diplomacy certainly wouldn't go amiss! The snag is that each sign, independently, has a reputation for impulsiveness, for acting before fully understanding the consequences, and for blurting out indiscretions. Yet these are minor detriments in comparison to the Sagittarius-Dragon's ebullient personality and gusto for life, which sweeps up everyone and everything in his or her path. Sagittarius-Dragons can make the sun shine on the bleakest day. Their optimistic view on life is highly infectious and their happy demeanor cheers everyone who comes near. For the Sagittarius-Dragon, life is simply one broad and colorful canvas.

KEY CHARACTERISTICS
- ebullient
- unpredictable
- impatient
- Quixotic

YOUR COMPATIBLE SIGNS
Leo-Rat
Aries-Monkey

OBSERVATIONS
Naivety can take the Sagittarius-Dragon into complicated situations and lead to disappointment

Executive toys and gimmicky novelties make agreeable presents for the Sagittarius-Dragon.

EAST WEST FUSION

EAST
The Archer infuses the Dragon with a strong code of honor

WEST
The Dragon brings the Archer pizzazz

THE ESSENTIAL YOU

WORK, HEALTH, HOBBIES
There isn't anything a Sagittarius-Dragon cannot achieve. Or so he or she thinks. And it is this belief that brings members of this sign their phenomenal success. Their positive thinking can move mountains. And often it does, since the Sagittarius-Dragon thinks big—very, very big. Warm-hearted and imaginative, they are terrific leaders, respected for their gung-ho attitude and ability to inspire the troops. Blessed with immense vitality, they excel in areas where enthusiasm and new ideas are of the essence.

LOVES, LIKES, DISLIKES
Being in the thick of the action is the Sagittarius-Dragon's passion. These are people who throw themselves heart and soul into everything, and the busier they are, the better they like it. Full of dynamic energy and irrepressible cheerfulness, they are inevitably attractive and sought-after people. But it is essentially a soulmate, someone who shares their vibrancy and excitement for life, whom they seek. And, once they have found their match, these generous and passionate creatures are likely to stay constant for life.

CHILDREN AND PARENTS
Sparkling and vivacious, it is hard to deflate the spirits of the young Sagittarius-Dragon. Popular both with their teachers and their peers, children of this dual sign are like a breath of fresh air. Their enthusiasm is infectious, and their obvious appetite for life is a joy to behold. Sagittarius-Dragon parents never lose their childlike wonder and take an enormous interest in their offspring, launching themselves with equal glee into whatever game, activity, or latest fad their youngsters engage in.

SAGITTARIUS-SNAKE

The sagacity, moral integrity, and philosophical understanding of the Sagittarius-Snake are legendary. Far-sighted and highly intuitive, members of this combination succeed by following their instincts and their good taste, both in occupational matters in their private lives. Both signs are noted for their shrewd discernment, the Sagittarian instinctively shooting his or her arrows and uncannily finding the target, while the Snake senses the essence of a situation with almost clairvoyant vision. As such, Sagittarius-Snakes excel in occupations that require insight and the ability to analyze complex problems. Elegant and classy, or suave and debonair, in their personal lives Sagittarius-Snakes are searching for partners with whom they can share a deep and spiritual relationship.

KEY CHARACTERISTICS

- 🐍 knowledgeable
- 🐍 communicative
- 🐍 wise
- 🐍 visionary

YOUR COMPATIBLE SIGNS

Leo-Ox

Aries-Rooster

The Snake adds elegance and mystery to the Archer's philosophical musings.

EAST WEST FUSION

EAST
The Archer brings joy to warm the Snake's heart

WEST
The Snake's patience curbs the Archer's impulsiveness

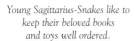

OBSERVATIONS

Self-satisfaction is a shortcoming associated with members of this dual sign

Young Sagittarius-Snakes like to keep their beloved books and toys well ordered.

WORK, HEALTH, HOBBIES

Quietly efficient, Sagittarius-Snakes make exceptional executives, able to organize their own and their clients' affairs, to advise discreetly, to anticipate events, liaise with colleagues, and generally run their businesses like well-oiled machines. With their intricate eye for detail and their zealous desire to help others, the legal profession is one that would meet a number of criteria. But, whatever career these highly motivated people choose to follow, they never mind starting from the bottom. They are happy learning the ropes so that they can get to know their job from the inside out.

♥ ♥ ♥

LOVES, LIKES, DISLIKES

Good manners are important to Sagittarius-Snakes and so is self-control. Indeed, members of this combination of signs prefer a careful, structured type of existence. Whether in terms of fashion, music, decor, dress, or tastes in general, they favor classical styles that never go out of style. In relationships, too, these people go for partners who have traditional values. To them, a commitment is a commitment for life.

🌹 🌹 🌹

CHILDREN AND PARENTS

Sagittarius-Snake children are neat and tidy and like to live in an ordered environment. In many ways, these are model youngsters, bookish and studious. Academic subjects pose no threat to them, and in class they turn in careful work, which, more often than not, merits good marks. In turn, Sagittarius-Snake parents are devoted to their children, although they have a tendency to wrap them up in a protective cocoon.

SAGITTARIUS: **NOVEMBER 22–DECEMBER 21**
YEARS OF THE HORSE: 1906 ✻ 1918 ✻ 1930 ✻ 1942 ✻ 1954 ✻ 1966 ✻ 1978 ✻ 1990 ✻ 2002 ✻ 2014
HOUR OF THE HORSE: 11AM – 12.59PM

THE ESSENTIAL YOU

SAGITTARIUS-HORSE

Essentially, this is the union of two Horses, and both have impulsive and free-wheeling spirits. On reflection, it is not a particularly beneficial pairing, since neither sign moderates the other's excesses. In combination, then, the dual sign produces characters who are irrepressibly enthusiastic, ever adventurous, and indefatigably optimistic. With a double helping of extroversion, Sagittarius-Horses tend to be larger than life. Moreover, their exuberance can blind them to their limitations and encourage them to overstretch their capabilities. Sagittarius-Horses need to learn to quit while they're ahead. In love, all Sagittarius-Horses enjoy the thrill of the chase, so a partner who gives them a good run for their money is essential to keep their interest alive.

Exuberant and irrepressible, Sagittarius-Horses are always amusing company.

KEY CHARACTERISTICS

- extroverted
- self-reliant
- daring
- out-spoken

YOUR COMPATIBLE SIGNS

Aries-Tiger
Leo-Dog

EAST-WEST FUSION

EAST
The Archer teaches the Horse to behave with integrity

WEST
The Oriental Horse polishes the Archer with panache

OBSERVATIONS

Impatience means that the Sagittarius-Horse often misses opportunities

With their busy lifestyles, Sagittarius-Horses often resort to fast food.

WORK, HEALTH, HOBBIES

With so much energy, the Sagittarius-Horse is made for sports. And, because these are social beings, team games would especially suit. Fast on their feet, they sprint—physically and metaphorically—so they work with great gusto but in short bursts. Time and time again, these people tend to overestimate their strength and take on too much. Understandably, they then get stressed out trying to meet their deadlines. Premature burnout is a distinct possibility for Sagittarius-Horses, so learning to pace themselves and prioritize are salutary lessons well worth learning early on in life.

LOVES, LIKES, DISLIKES

When they are young, Sagittarius-Horses gallivant a good deal which means they have little time to pay attention to the finer details of daily life. Fast food and fast living is what they like. And if some of their decisions in the emotional stakes are impetuous, relationships can backfire. Maturity unleashes greater common sense and changes their attitudes, behavior, and desires. Then, they decide to settle down, and seek a partner with the same exuberance, but who will provide them with a firm base.

CHILDREN AND PARENTS

No matter how often they are told that exam results count, the energetic children of this dual sign are sports mad, and to them, rushing around a field is so much more meaningful, (let alone preferable), than dry old academic lessons in a classroom. Still, they could always win a football scholarship or a handful of gold medals at the Olympic Games. Adult Sagittarius-Horses appear almost too busy to have time for a family.

SAGITTARIUS-SHEEP

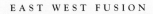

EAST WEST FUSION

With so many projects constantly on the boil, members of this duality tend to be a good deal busier than the average Sheep. And as long as they are free to pursue their own interests, Sagittarius-Sheep are content. The Archer's insistence on autonomy works well in this combination, giving the normally dependent Sheep greater confidence to stand on his or her own two feet. These are much more outgoing and tolerant Sheep, whose vision is considerably broadened by the Sagittarian's philosophical attitude to life. Creatively talented and with an eye on the distant horizon, Sagittarius-Sheep do well in any occupation that requires foresight and an instinctive feeling about future trends.

EAST
The Archer endows the Sheep with good judgment

WEST
The gentle Sheep bestows savoir faire upon the Archer

KEY CHARACTERISTICS
- imaginatively gifted
- far-sighted
- stylish
- eye for detail

YOUR COMPATIBLE SIGNS
Leo-Rabbit
Aries-Pig

The acquisition of creative skills comes as second nature to Sagittarius-Sheep.

OBSERVATIONS

The Sagittarius-Sheep all too often gives up before the end-game is reached

THE ESSENTIAL YOU

WORK, HEALTH, HOBBIES

In careers where the ability to tap into the zeitgeist is of the essence, Sagittarius-Sheep score top marks. With their talent for seeing far ahead, they do exceptionally well as fashion designers, where they have to launch ideas two to three seasons in advance. For the same reason, dabbling in the stock market can also also pay off handsomely for members of this double sign. Sagittarius-Sheep thrive in any career where their creative talents are given the freedom to shine—then they will always be one step ahead of the game.

LOVES, LIKES, DISLIKES

Sagittarius-Sheep do not possess logical, practical minds. They live by creative instinct instead. They particularly dislike getting their hands dirty. Partly because of this, and partly because this group is so security-oriented, a supportive partner, who can provide a safe domestic haven, and who doesn't mind picking up the clutter that members of this sign invariably scatter around them, is not only crucial for the Sagittarius-Sheep well-being, but will also free him or her to concentrate on earning the stacks of money members of this sign require to keep them happy.

The Sheep teaches Sagittarius the joys of a safe, happy, secure family home.

CHILDREN AND PARENTS

With their tender sensibilities, young Sagittarius-Sheep may be teased by their classmates. They shine in all subjects where their imagination is allowed free reign. Sagittarius-Sheep parents cherish their children, instiling good manners and encouraging their inherent skills.

SAGITTARIUS: **NOVEMBER 22–DECEMBER 21**
YEARS OF THE MONKEY: 1908 ✷ 1920 ✷ 1932 ✷ 1944 ✷ 1956 ✷ 1968 ✷ 1980 ✷ 1992 ✷ 2004 ✷ 2016
HOUR OF THE MONKEY: 3PM – 4.59PM

SAGITTARIUS-MONKEY

EAST
Sagittarius teaches the Monkey
to be less self-centered

WEST
The Monkey makes the
Archer street-wise

The Sagittarian and the Monkey make happy bed-fellows, producing lucky, cheerful personalities and clever individuals who are also deep-thinkers. Sagittarius-Monkeys like to think big. And why not, when the world is their oyster? With the Archer's far-sightedness and the Monkey's ingenuity, members of this dual sign will succeed at whatever they set out to do. And Sagittarius-Monkeys are indeed ambitious and perhaps occasionally bite off far more than they can comfortably chew. But this will not deter the Sagittarius-Monkey who believes that the bigger the challenge, the greater is the triumph. Sagittarius- Monkeys are so busy, they are unlikely to settle down until much later on in their lives.

Dreaming up new inventions is what the Sagittarius-Monkey does best.

KEY CHARACTERISTICS

- persuasive
- swift of thought
- unconventional
- restless

YOUR COMPATIBLE SIGNS

Leo-Dragon
Aries-Rat

Clear sight is the Sagittarius-Monkey's forté even when they are all at sea.

OBSERVATIONS

As youngsters, Sagittarius-Monkeys can be somewhat erratic

THE ESSENTIAL YOU

WORK, HEALTH, HOBBIES

Routine can dull the creative processes of the Sagittarius-Monkey. For these brilliant people need an environment which gives them the scope to act and think spontaneously. In an environment where news, views, and ideas are freely exchanged, the Sagittarius-Monkey shines and his or her brilliance overshadows everyone else in the team. Members of this dual sign are positive and energetic and do well in advertising, the media, politics, and all manner of advisory roles.

LOVES, LIKES, DISLIKES

The thought of the same old routine day in and day out spells misery for Sagittarius-Monkeys. These people need variety in both their interests and companions, so they tend to eschew committing themselves to one partner for as long as possible. Their soulmates, when they eventually find them, will have lively minds and will know precisely how to keep their Sagittarius-Monkeys guessing.

CHILDREN AND PARENTS

Equally interested in outdoor pursuits as they are in academic subjects, Sagittarius-Monkey children tend to be good all-rounders with excellent memories. They are bright and intelligent young people, able to see the whole picture and confident about giving their points of view in class discussions. Sagittarius-Monkey parents tend to prefer small families and so are able to focus a lot of time and attention on the few offspring they have. These are youthful parents who like to share their children's interests, and especially enjoy philosophical debates with them.

SAGITTARIUS: **NOVEMBER 22–DECEMBER 21**
YEARS OF THE ROOSTER: 1909 ✳ 1921 ✳ 1933 ✳ 1945 ✳ 1957 ✳ 1969 ✳ 1981 ✳ 1993 ✳ 2005 ✳ 2017
HOUR OF THE ROOSTER: 5PM – 6.59PM

THE ESSENTIAL YOU

SAGITTARIUS-ROOSTER

Cheerful and happy-go-lucky, the Sagittarian brings to the Rooster a lightness of heart, which lifts the spirits and puts a jauntier step into the Cockerel's gait. Moreover, the Archer's long-range vista on life draws the Rooster away from his or her more habitual punctiliousness and enables those born under this dual sign to see things from a broader perspective. Sagittarius-Roosters are more tolerant and philosophical than other Rooster groups. But since both in their own right are open, honest, and forthright, Sagittarius-Roosters also have a greater tendency to put their foot in their mouth. It is scrupulous honesty that these people look for in a relationship. The merest hint of deceit will be enough for them to lose faith in their partner. Sagittarius-Roosters are famed for their idealism and philanthropic instincts and they could never turn their backs on someone in need.

KEY CHARACTERISTICS

- conscientious
- trusting
- garrulous
- altruistic

YOUR COMPATIBLE SIGNS

Aries-Ox

Leo-Snake

OBSERVATIONS

Lack of tact is the Sagittarius-Rooster's downfall

Tact is not the Sagittarius-Rooster's strong point: what they see as plain speaking others may see as downright rude.

EAST WEST FUSION

EAST

Sagittarius puts a cheery jaunt into the Rooster's step

WEST

The Rooster brings a rigorous mental approach to the expansive Archer

Taking the car for a spin enables the Sagittarius-Rooster to unwind.

WORK, HEALTH, HOBBIES

A strong vocational instinct drives the members of this sign into social work or local politics. Because they are very community-minded, they may also be drawn to charitable organizations or follow careers that might be described as "worthy." These are restless and excitable people whose passion for roaming the world is matched by a prodigious talent for problem-solving. A job requiring an analytical eye and involving extensive travel, therefore, would suit them very well.

♥ ♥ ♥

LOVES, LIKES, DISLIKES

Sagittarius-Roosters like to be on the go. Happiest with the wind in their hair, they will take to the open road at the drop of a hat. Friendships are often formed on their travels or through their contacts at work. Partners must develop thick skins fast, since Sagittarius-Roosters, though well-meaning, are notoriously blunt. Transparent and honest in all their dealings, they cannot bear deception or disloyalty of any kind.

CHILDREN AND PARENTS

Sagittarius-Rooster children take their responsibilities seriously. At heart, though, they are high-spirited and enjoy rough-and-tumble games with their siblings and their peers. At school, they excel at sports and win trophies for their debating prowess. They tend to fly the nest at the earliest opportunity, not because they are desperately unhappy at home, but because they are driven by a strong sense of wanderlust. As adults, Sagittarius-Roosters are so busy with causes and vocational work that they hardly have any time to have children of their own.

SAGITTARIUS-DOG

Sincerity, warmth of character, and generosity guarantee the Sagittarius-Dog a loyal following. More adventurous and fun-loving than most other Dogs, these people like to look at life on a broad canvas. Although the Dog is essentially home-loving, the Archer's influence insists on a certain autonomy of action and being hemmed in, whether mentally or physically, makes the Sagittarius-Dog ill. Sports can provide the vehicle for the freedom that these people need, for both Sagittarians and Dogs enjoy the thrill of the chase. In fact, many who are born under this twin rulership make very fine athletes.

KEY CHARACTERISTICS
- imaginative
- popular
- friendly
- judicious

YOUR COMPATIBLE SIGNS
Leo-Tiger
Aries-Horse

OBSERVATIONS
A caustic tongue can at times be the Sagittarius-Dog's undoing

Young Sagittarius-Dogs do well in an academic environment.

EAST WEST FUSION

EAST
The Archer brings a sense of adventure to the otherwise cautious Dog

WEST
The Oriental Dog steadies the Archer's impulsiveness

A career in professional sports appeals to the Sagittarius-Dog.

THE ESSENTIAL YOU

WORK, HEALTH, HOBBIES
Sensible and down-to-earth, Sagittarius-Dogs are efficient and industrious workers who brook no interference and simply like to get on with the task in hand. Prone to calling a spade a spade, their no-nonsense approach can sometimes prove a little too blunt for colleagues with more delicate sensitivities. Perhaps, then, self-employment would be more suitable for the tough and resilient members of this group who would be able to call all the shots and not get disgruntled by the trivialities of other people's lives.

LOVES, LIKES, DISLIKES
In general, Sagittarius-Dogs like to keep busy so they probably arrange their lives around their jobs. These are serious-minded and committed people who are not prone to small talk or idle chitchat. Instead, they like to think things through deeply, religiously, or philosophically. In relationships, whether of the business or more intimate variety, it is sincerity that is of paramount importance to them. And if this means delivering the plain unvarnished—unwelcome—truth to their partner, so be it.

CHILDREN AND PARENTS
Sagittarius-Dog children take more to a classical upbringing than to modern, experimental ways. Not the most outgoing of the Sagittarian combinations, youngsters of this duality tend to be bookish and excel in languages and literature at school. They can make a significant impact on the sportsfield and especially when it comes to team games. Sagittarius-Dog parents lay down firm rules which they expect their youngsters to observe without question.

SAGITTARIUS-PIG

In this duality are joined the two most jovial, big-hearted, and extroverted signs of Eastern and Western astrology. The sign of the Sagittarius-Pig produces generous and genial personalities, who always attract a large and faithful following wherever they go. Generous Sagittarius-Pigs dispense largesse to all and sundry, scattering optimism and good cheer to all those around. No one ever leaves a Sagittarius-Pig's table hungry. No one goes without when a Sagittarius-Pig is around. For members of this dual sign everything always seems to turn out for the best because, according to the philosophies of East and West, they are born not only under one but two lucky stars.

OBSERVATIONS

The extravagant tastes of the Sagittarius-Pig can dig too deeply into his or her purse

KEY CHARACTERISTICS

- merry
- observant
- extravagant
- outspoken

YOUR COMPATIBLE SIGNS

Leo-Sheep
Aries-Rabbit

Sagittarius-Pigs spread joy, cheer, and largesse wherever they roam.

THE ESSENTIAL YOU

WORK, HEALTH, HOBBIES

With their open, friendly manner and confident attitude, the laid-back Sagittarius-Pig has no trouble putting others at their ease. This, of course, comes in handy when dealing with the public in whatever career these people choose to follow. As a rule, Sagittarius-Pigs are endowed with creative talents. But, given their enthusiasm coupled with a hearty constitution, it is the entertainment field, especially, that acts as a magnet for this group.

LOVES, LIKES, DISLIKES

Members of this sign appreciate a good joke. Sagittarius-Pigs who, for whatever reason, lose their sense of humor, are very unhappy creatures indeed. They are sensual beings and they take great comfort from all the pleasures of the flesh. Love comes very high on their agenda and when they do fall for the partner of their dreams, they tend not to stray but remain in contented bliss forever.

CHILDREN AND PARENTS

When they are with their friends, youngsters of this sign often like to clown around and make everyone laugh. They are very well-balanced individuals who always see the funny side of a situation, for they know instinctively the power humor holds. Children of this dual sign are drawn to the expressive arts and love to appear in school or amateur performances. Whether as children or parents, Sagittarius-Pigs love to snuggle up close to those they hold dear, for they are certainly loving in the extreme.

Children belonging to this sign are born entertainers, excelling in comedy.

CAPRICORN

BORN BETWEEN: **DECEMBER 22—JANUARY 19**
EARTH SIGN

Capricorn, the tenth sign of the Western astrological year, roughly corresponds to the Chinese month known as the Oxen Moon.

If you were born at this time of the year you can either call yourself a Capricorn, or you can say you were born at Youngest Winter Time, which is a much more lyrical alternative title given to this month in the East.

According to the Chinese, this time of year is also broken up into two fortnights, each describing an aspect of the weather, or a feature relevant to the agricultural year. The first fortnight is called the Winter Solstice and this corresponds to the first two weeks of Capricorn. If you were born in the second half of the sign, though, you belong to the second Chinese fortnight, Lesser Cold.

But it is, of course, when both your month and your year of birth are combined that the various influences begin to interweave themselves in a way that is essentially unique for you.

Whatever the combination, Capricorn, as a capable and industrious sign, will bring ambition and a strong desire to be upwardly mobile to the mix.

CAPRICORN-RAT

Capricorn-Rats like the cut and thrust of working in big business.

Life, for the Capricorn-Rat, is a serious business. Capricorn is the industrialist of the Western Zodiac, while the Rat is a prudent, tenacious creature and a born survivor. With a pedigree like this, it is not surprising that Capricorn-Rats are intensely ambitious and, moreover, that they make meteoric progress in their chosen occupations in life. These people are realists, however; they do not expect favors or kickbacks or need to take shortcuts in order to reach the top. But they do expect their hard work, practical application, and level-headed approach to be recognized and rewarded appropriately. Capricorn-Rats may not be the most romantic or sentimental of creatures, but they will be faithful and true as the livelong day.

EAST WEST FUSION

EAST
Capricorn reveals the benefits of organization to the Rat

WEST
The Oriental Rat tinges the Western Goat with charm

KEY CHARACTERISTICS
- ambitious
- materialistic
- realistic
- hard-working

YOUR COMPATIBLE SIGNS
Taurus-Monkey
Virgo-Dragon

OBSERVATIONS
Capricorn-Rats have a tendency to use others to help them get to the top

---

THE ESSENTIAL YOU

WORK, HEALTH, HOBBIES
Capricorn-Rats function much better as employers than they do as employees. They like being in charge and calling the shots. They don't take kindly to being ordered around. At work they are tough and go-getting, full of schemes, and bursting with ideas to organize and improve the system. These people rise to meet challenges, and though they are essentially conformists, they nevertheless like to go their own way, knowing that this will, sooner rather than later, lead to success. Capricorn-Rats excel in industry, business and high finance.

LOVES, LIKES, DISLIKES
Capricorn-Rats like to live in comfortable, well-appointed houses. A good address is important, since this will reflect their status and position in society. These people will not care to set up home in a run-down part of town. They have expensive tastes and will purchase only top-quality goods. Members of the Capricorn-Rat sign are tough, realistic creatures, who do not understand weakness or hesitation of any sort. However, they do need a partner, preferably a lifelong one, but it must be someone like-minded, who is strong, hard-working, and down-to-earth. Within such a partnership, Capricorn-Rats are highly unlikely ever to stray.

CHILDREN AND PARENTS
Young Capricorn-Rats like things done their own way and can therefore appear bossy toward their siblings and contemporaries. Having a goal to work toward is important for these children and they are prepared to work hard if they know that, in the end, they will be rewarded for their efforts. These children are tough and resilient but they must learn from an early age to respect the sensitivities of others. Adult Capricorn-Rats may not be the most cuddly of parents but nevertheless they are certainly devoted to their offspring.

With their track record of success, there will always be something to celebrate in the Capricorn-Rat household.

CAPRICORN-OX

If anyone is made of true grit, it has to be those born under the dual sign of the Capricorn-Ox. Resolute and implacable, once Capricorn-Oxen have made up their minds, nothing short of a tornado will prevent them steering their ship in their chosen direction, regardless of warnings and heedless of the elements. Just like the drip that gradually wears away the stone, so it is the sustained efforts of the Capricorn-Ox that enables him or her to accumulate wealth and achieve a comfortable lifestyle. They adorn their homes in a conservative style. Steady as a rock and thoroughly responsible, Capricorn-Oxen will work their socks off to provide the security and comfort they deem they themselves and their loved ones deserve.

OBSERVATIONS

Capricorn-Oxen believe in their own infallibility so are resistant to advice from outside

Capricorn-Oxen often find it hard to throw off the yoke of work at the end of the day.

KEY CHARACTERISTICS

- self-reliant
- practical
- logical
- dour

YOUR COMPATIBLE SIGNS

Virgo-Snake
Taurean-Rooster

EAST WEST FUSION

EAST
Capricorn invests the Ox with an appreciation for quality

WEST
The Chinese Ox endows the Western Goat with integrity

THE ESSENTIAL YOU

WORK, HEALTH, HOBBIES

Exceedingly industrious, Capricorn-Oxen are renowned workaholics. These people are tough and resilient, able to put in long hours at a stretch without tiring or losing momentum. Arch pragmatists, they are logical thinkers who take a systematic approach to everything they do. What Capricorn-Oxen lack in imagination, they certainly make up for in practical expertise. Their dour nature is best suited to working behind the scenes and preferably alone. They make excellent academics, government officials, scientific researchers, financial planners, computer analysts, and construction engineers.

❤ ❤ ❤

LOVES, LIKES, DISLIKES

Members of this duality are staunch traditionalists. They do not care for fads and trifles, but go for value and quality every time. In truth, they can be rather snobbish. Capricorn-Oxen tend to be set in their ways and take a somewhat dogmatic approach to life. Despite this obdurate nature, however, they do make solid and sincere partners and are at their best with a mate of like mind at their side. They are not fuzzy romantics but they have healthy libidos. Once they have pledged their troth, they will stand by their loved one through thick and through thin.

CHILDREN AND PARENTS

Capricorn-Oxen children work very conscientiously at school. They are achievement-motivated and invariably get the best grades in class. Whatever they do, they put tremendous effort and unfailing diligence into it and the results speak for themselves. As parents, Capricorn-Oxen take immense pride in their children's abilities but demand conformity and respect. They set the rules and their offspring must toe the line. No rebellion allowed.

Working with the irrefutable logic of computers is an ideal career for the members of this sign.

CAPRICORN-TIGER

EAST
The wise Goat tempers the
Tiger's impulsiveness

WEST
The Tiger empowers the Goat
with feline courage

People born under this dual sign are perhaps the most ambitious of the Tiger clan because, no matter what they do, they set their sights on reaching the very top. Capricorn-Tigers are not only high achievers, they are extremely clever as well. From an early age they realize that success comes through dedication and hard work, so they are prepared to put their shoulders to the grindstone in order to achieve the sort of status and position they believe they justly deserve. Conservative and law-abiding, members of this sign do not mind conforming and actively work to maintain the status quo. For the Capricorn-Tiger work comes first, love and relationships next.

Capricorn-Tigers juggle work and home with ease.

THE ESSENTIAL YOU

KEY CHARACTERISTICS

- keen
- motivated
- stubborn
- resourceful

YOUR COMPATIBLE SIGNS
Taurus-Horse
Virgo-Dog

OBSERVATIONS

Trying to do too many things at the same time means that, at times, Capricorn-Tigers can't see the wood for the trees

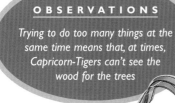

High-powered careers, especially if they involve lots of travel, suit Capricorn-Tigers well.

WORK, HEALTH, HOBBIES
Capricorn-Tigers are never idle. These people are physically and mentally strong and they like having plenty to do. Challenge is exciting and as long as the task stretches them just that little bit further and takes them forward along their chosen path, they're happy. For Capricorn-Tigers, learning something new, taking the next step, or acquiring another skill, is what life is all about. They are plain speakers and straight dealers. As honest and reliable as the day is long, they are just as suited to a creative environment as they are to a business or industrial setting. History and architecture are favorite subject areas. They like all kinds of music and take a keen interest in politics.

♥ ♥ ♥

LOVES, LIKES, DISLIKES
There is an interesting dichotomy in the make-up of the Capricorn-Tiger. One half likes stability and routine, but the other half demands thrills and adventure. To reconcile these two facets, members of this duality get the excitement from their work—which, with any luck, will take them here, there, and everywhere—while their cherished mate keeps the home fires burning for their return. As lovers, Capricorn-Tigers are warm and passionate people, loyal, and faithful in general, but they need just a little slack in the system to give them a psychological sense of freedom.

CHILDREN AND PARENTS
Capricorn-Tiger children are generally healthy and spirited young things who like to run around a great deal, and probably excel on the sportsfield. As long as the teacher is enthusiastic and able to capture their imagination, these youngsters should do well at school. Without a doubt, Capricorn-Tiger adults take their parenting duties seriously and are excellent providers for their young.

CAPRICORN-RABBIT

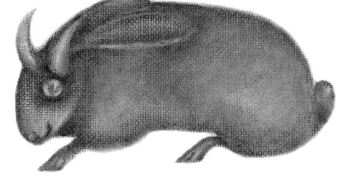

> **OBSERVATIONS**
>
> A cool approach in all aspects of their lives can make the Capricorn-Rabbit appear uncaring and aloof

Practical and ambitious, Capricorn-Rabbits are perhaps the most industrious of the Rabbit tribe. Capricorns are down-to-earth people with a strong materialistic streak. They are prepared to work hard in order to attain the high standards of living to which they aspire. Rabbits in their own way like to accumulate possessions too, so the acquisitive urge in members of this dual sign will be redoubled. Status is important to the Capricorn-Rabbit, whose patient efforts are eventually rewarded when they reach positions of power and prestige. In personal relationships, though Capricorn-Rabbits are none too demonstrative of their affections, they do make staunchly loyal partners and are steady as a rock.

Capricorn-Rabbits work hard to accumulate the creature comforts that are so important to their contentment in life.

KEY CHARACTERISTICS

- considerate
- wise
- cautious
- calm

YOUR COMPATIBLE SIGNS

Virgo-Sheep
Taurus-Pig

THE ESSENTIAL YOU

WORK, HEALTH, HOBBIES

Capricorn-Rabbits are intellectual people with creative appreciations. They certainly are reluctant to take on manual work, and are therefore best suited to desk jobs. They particularly excel as mediators. These are morally upright citizens who are respected for their honesty and integrity. Legal work, or else a career in the financial services would suit their talents. The diplomatic corps and Civil Service would certainly do well with a few of these calm and refined people on their staff.

LOVES, LIKES, DISLIKES

Members of this dual sign need their creature comforts. They also like their surroundings—at home and at work—to look expensive and refined. Capricorn-Rabbits enjoy displaying their wealth conspicuously. With their cautious mentalities, these people like to take their time to do things properly—they don't like to be rushed or forced to take shortcuts. This applies equally when making business decisions as it does in their personal lives when forming relationships. Since they are not given to open displays of affection, they have a tendency to come across as cool and detached. But under the exterior they are surprisingly passionate lovers.

CHILDREN AND PARENTS

Usually obedient and well-behaved, Capricorn-Rabbits are delightful youngsters and, whether at home or at school, present little difficulty to those bringing them up. They like to keep themselves neat and tidy, and their possessions well-organized. They work hard right across the curriculum and favor academic subjects best. Capricorn-Rabbits make loving and devoted parents, who nevertheless insist on good manners, politeness, and hard work at all times.

EAST WEST FUSION

EAST
The Western Goat toughens the normally mild-mannered Rabbit

WEST
The Oriental Rabbit refines the maladroit Goat

Children of this sign are some of the best-behaved youngsters in the zodiac.

CAPRICORN-DRAGON

The Capricorn-Dragon sign combines a practical, hardworking, and down-to-earth disposition with a driving desire for success. Little wonder, then, that members of this duality are prepared to work all hours to climb slowly but surely up every rung of the ladder to the top of their chosen professions. However, such dedication to their work comes at a price. Love and romance all too often have to take second place to their careers. Indeed, Capricorn-Dragons of both sexes are well known for putting their personal lives on hold in favor of their worldly aspirations. Once committed, though, Capricorn-Dragons can become some of the most responsible and dutiful soulmates of the combined astrological signs of East and West.

EAST WEST FUSION

EAST
The sure-footed Goat teaches perseverance to the impetuous Dragon

WEST
The fabulous Dragon imbues Capricorn with dynamism

KEY CHARACTERISTICS
- ambitious
- tough
- proud
- megalomaniac

YOUR COMPATIBLE SIGNS
Taurus-Rat
Virgo-Monkey

The Dragon transforms dour Capricorn into a popular office colleague who can enjoy the lighter side of work.

OBSERVATIONS

So focused are Capricorn-Dragons on their climb to the top that they often fail to see what else is going on around them

THE ESSENTIAL YOU

WORK, HEALTH, HOBBIES
Born leaders, Capricorn-Dragons are bound to achieve power and high status. They have spectacular ideas and believe they can move mountains with nothing more than their gusto and enthusiasm. And invariably they can. Far from being ruthless backstabbers, they remember those who have given them the breaks in their careers and are generous and loyal to them in return. These are strong and gutsy figures whose huge charismas inspire others to follower. Capricorn-Dragons are fascinated by the workings of the human mind and are drawn to psychological studies. They excel in occupations that are management-oriented, particularly in the capacities of personnel and public relations.

LOVES, LIKES, DISLIKES
Capricorn-Dragons like a bit of drama. They are social creatures, hospitable, generous, and loyal to their friends and loved ones. However, they cannot tolerate being deceived and will be vituperative to anyone who dares to cross them. Although they launch themselves with overwhelming enthusiasm into their projects or latest interest, they are oddly bashful when it comes to personal matters and affairs of the heart. Although they are prone to being a little backward in coming forward about their feelings, their emotions are entirely genuine.

CHILDREN AND PARENTS
With their boundless energy, children of this double sign are perhaps more suited to the sportsfield than they are to the more passive academic subjects. But whatever they do, they will strive to be the best, for they are born with one of the largest winning streaks ever dealt to a human being. Being elected the captain of any school sports team would be a fitting reward for their efforts. Capricorn-Dragons watch their offspring's development with interest and delight in their achievements.

Human psychology fascinates the natives of this sign.

CAPRICORN-SNAKE

It is with careful and meticulous planning and organization that Capricorn-Snakes build their reputation, position, and wealth in life. The combination of patience and efficiency enables them to soldier on, neither deterred by the vagaries of life nor deflected from their course by unforeseen obstacles. Capricorn-Snakes like to bide their time and inexorably plow their furrow until they reach their destination. Whether it is at home or at work, for themselves or for those they love, people born under the influence of this combination go for the best in everything. Capricorn-Snakes may be accused of snobbery, it is true, but their hearts are in the right place and their feet firmly planted on the ground.

OBSERVATIONS

A soft spot for picking up emotional strays can put a strain on the Capricorn-Snake

Because Snakes love beauty and Goats love tradition, an old-fashioned red rose is an ideal gift.

KEY CHARACTERISTICS

- classy
- haughty
- efficient
- tenacious

YOUR COMPATIBLE SIGNS

Virgo-Rooster
Taurus-Ox

EAST WEST FUSION

EAST

The Western Goat enhances the Snakes endurance

WEST

The Oriental Snake awakens Capricorn's sixth sense

Power dressing comes naturally to Capricorn-Snakes; quality before quantity every time.

WORK, HEALTH, HOBBIES

Clever by nature, Capricorn-Snakes know what they want and they know how to get it. It doesn't matter how long they have to wait, they will make their mark in the end. It is their intuition that wins the day and that ultimately leads to success in their career. For, whether they take up fashion design, advertising, or making movies for the big screen, they will always be one step ahead, always tuned into the zeitgeist, always aware of what the public will want next.

LOVES, LIKES, DISLIKES

Elegant and refined, Capricorn-Snakes adore beautiful clothes and, even if they had to paint the walls of their kitchen, they wouldn't be seen in less than designer label overalls. In fact, where they're concerned, it is designer everything, from interiors to exteriors, from gardens to cars. These people like the best. In love, they know how to use every wile in the book to get the object of their desire. And, of course, they win in the end.

CHILDREN AND PARENTS

Young Capricorn-Snakes respond well to a lot of pampering and petting. If they are made to feel wanted and special, they will give a lot in return. They have an uncanny knack for taking in stray cats or wounded birds, and nursing them back to health. Little Capricorn-Snakes have the ability to read people like books and learn early on in life how to manipulate people to their advantage. They must be encouraged to be honest to themselves and to tell the truth to others. As parents, Capricorn-Snakes will indubitably indulge their children.

EAST WEST FUSION

EAST
The Western Goat teaches the erratic Horse to be more reliable

WEST
The Chinese Horse graces the Goat with flexibility

CAPRICORN-HORSE

Achievement-oriented, the Capricorn-Horse is driven by a need to succeed. Money and status are all important. The industrious influence of the Goat steadies the erratic nature of the Horse, enabling these natives to apply themselves doggedly to their work. The Horse, on the other hand, brings to the duality greater flexibility, which can be applied to all areas of life. Stabilized by the Goat's input, Capricorn-Horses do achieve a great deal in their lives and many reach positions of immense responsibility and prestige. People of this combination are faithful and loyal, and they are loved and respected by all who make their acquaintance.

KEY CHARACTERISTICS

- talented
- fretful
- productive
- popular

YOUR COMPATIBLE SIGNS

Taurus-Dog
Virgo-Tiger

OBSERVATIONS

Despite their industriousness, Capricorn-Horses may have a long wait before they crown their achievements

Documentaries on geography, cosmology, and natural phenomena fascinate members of this group.

The scientific mind of the Capricorn-Horse is drawn to a career in industrial research and development.

THE ESSENTIAL YOU

WORK, HEALTH, HOBBIES

Not as austere as most Capricorns, nor as skittish as other Horses, the two combined produce a creative mind with the ability to hang on in there, which is guaranteed to get to the top of their chosen profession. Music is an abiding passion with Capricorn-Horses. They are curious people who want to understand how the universe is put together, and do well in research. In fact, science in all its manifestations is a big draw in the lives of Capricorn-Horses and, no matter what job they take on, they will apply a rigorous, analytical approach to their work. Success may be late in coming, but it does come in the end.

♥ ♥ ♥

LOVES, LIKES, DISLIKES

Capricorn-Horses take a practical approach to life. They are energetic people, who can get through a massive agenda of work each and every day. As such, they respect those who can match their industry and have little time for anyone who prefers to coast along. Members of this duality are as serious in life as they are when they give their affections. Now and again they like to let their hair down and kick up their hooves. A partner who can occasionally make them feel light of heart is worth untold riches.

🌸 🌸 🌸

CHILDREN AND PARENTS

Young Capricorn-Horses take life in their stride. They have no axes to grind and therefore no reason to rebel. They get on with their studies and generally do well at school. In so many ways, Capricorn-Horses are well-balanced and popular youngsters who look back on their childhood years as a positive and fulfilling time of their lives. Capricorn-Horses are loving parents, always offering a comfortable bolthole. They are good listeners and are ready with a much appreciated hug when needed.

CAPRICORN-SHEEP

The Capricorn provides the steadying influence to this duo. Duty and dedication, too, come high on the Goat's list of priorities. The Capricorn-Sheep fraternity are also very ambitious. Their strength of character, combined with industriousness and practical know-how, ensures that they will attain their worldly aspirations. It is true that, as a rule, those born under the Eastern Sheep sign like to take life at a more gentle pace than is customary for the Western Capricorn; the Sheep's philosophy is that all work and no play makes Jack or Jill very dull indeed. Interestingly, then, the Capricorn-Sheep dual sign produces people who, though on the whole are as steady as a rock and reliable, will occasionally want to let their hair down and behave, seemingly, quite out of character. Capricorn-Sheep are full of surprises!

KEY CHARACTERISTICS

- 🐑 industrious
- 🐑 sedate
- 🐑 surprising
- 🐑 vain

YOUR COMPATIBLE SIGNS

Virgo-Pig
Taurus-Rabbit

Children of this sign appreciate toys from a bygone age.

EAST WEST FUSION

EAST
Capricorn teaches the Sheep to stand on his or her own two feet

WEST
The Oriental Sheep mellows the brusque manner of the Goat

The Sheep brings a touch of the surreal to Capricorn's ordered existence.

OBSERVATIONS

Capricorn-Sheep always blame others for their own misfortune

WORK, HEALTH, HOBBIES

Capricorn-Sheep are sophisticates. They will work hard if they have to, but they usually gravitate only toward prestigious jobs. It's unlikely that they will want to put time and energy into grubby activities of any kind. A career where dealing with people is central, or one where they can apply their creative imagination would be ideal—making presentations is a particular skill they have. Running a museum, art gallery, or even an exclusive clothes shop would also all appeal.

♥ ♥ ♥

LOVES, LIKES, DISLIKES

When the rigors of work are done, nothing pleases the Capricorn-Sheep more than slipping out of the power suit and into something soft, comfortable, and definitely exotic. For underneath the cool, calm, industrious exterior beats a heart that likes some fun and frolics. Members of this sign also like spending money. They have expensive tastes and like to live in beauty and luxury. In their personal lives, they prefer not to have to do all the running. They are happiest with a stronger partner who makes the decisions and, if possible, keeps the Capricorn-Sheep in the manner to which he or she is accustomed.

🐑 🐑 🐑

CHILDREN AND PARENTS

Youngsters belonging to this sign are quite amazing. In their character the angelic is mixed with the scamp, so one minute they may be quietly practicing their scales on the piano and the very next they will be scrambling up trees with the local neighborhood gang. Adult Capricorn-Sheep perhaps relate better to older, more independent children than to the young babes-in-arms who are in constant need of attention.

CAPRICORN: **DECEMBER 22—JANUARY 19**
YEARS OF THE MONKEY: 1908 ∗ 1920 ∗ 1932 ∗ 1944 ∗ 1956 ∗ 1968 ∗ 1980 ∗ 1992 ∗ 2004 ∗ 2016
HOUR OF THE MONKEY: 3PM – 4.59PM

CAPRICORN-MONKEY

Intelligent and hard-working, the Capricorn-Monkey is perhaps more stable and resolute than most other Monkeys. As members of one of the Earth signs, Capricorns have a solidly determined and staunch approach to life. Such sterling qualities enable the Monkey to be less flighty than usual and to apply his or her talents consistently, plugging away at skills until they become honed, polished, and professional. With characteristics such as these, Capricorn-Monkeys make formidable businessmen and women and invariably become successful in life. Image and position in society are important to these people, so they are likely to be highly selective in their search for the perfect partner. Once they have found their soulmate, however, the Capricorn-Monkey need look no further.

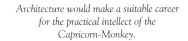

EAST WEST FUSION

EAST
Capricorn tames the
Monkey's impudence

WEST
The Monkey enlivens the stuffy
character of the Goat

KEY CHARACTERISTICS
- outspoken
- confident
- retentive
- even-tempered

YOUR COMPATIBLE SIGNS
Taurus-Dog
Virgo-Rat

*Architecture would make a suitable career
for the practical intellect of the
Capricorn-Monkey.*

OBSERVATIONS

*A tendency to exaggerate
can sometimes catch out the
Capricorn-Monkey*

THE ESSENTIAL YOU

WORK, HEALTH, HOBBIES
Capricorn-Monkeys are masters and mistresses of timing. Perhaps that is why they are so good at telling a joke, getting the punchline in just at the right moment. Musicians and singers need this sense of timing. And, of course, so do sportsmen and women. Interests and occupations in these fields obviously would admirably suit the strong and sinewy members of this dual sign. But Capricorn-Monkeys are also gifted wordsmiths with a memory equal to none. Couple this with a cheeky, caustic wit, and Capricorn-Monkeys become excellent writers, journalists, reporters, and television presenters.

LOVES, LIKES, DISLIKES
People born under this dual rulership do not like being fenced in. Physically and psychologically, they need room to breathe and maneuver. They like to keep abreast of trends and fashions. With their sharp, creative eye they can select at a glance what particular cut or style from the current season will suit their personalities and bodies. They are then able to create for themselves and their environment "the look" of the moment, yet somehow manage to retain an individual feel. Capricorn-Monkeys were born to communicate and spend long hours gossiping with friends.

CHILDREN AND PARENTS
Youngsters of this sign like their freedom, and ideally need a lot of space in which to roam and explore. They are terrific at making up stories and will probably excel in language and literature work at school. They will master a computer in the twinkling of an eye and will surf the net in rapt fascination for hours on end. Capricorn-Monkey parents are intelligent and will encourage their children to be independent.

*The Capricorn-
Monkey's keen sense
of timing is put to good
use both at work
and at play.*

CAPRICORN: **DECEMBER 22—JANUARY 19**
YEARS OF THE ROOSTER: 1909 ✻ 1921 ✻ 1933 ✻ 1945 ✻ 1957 ✻ 1969 ✻ 1981 ✻ 1993 ✻ 2005 ✻ 2017
HOUR OF THE ROOSTER: 5PM – 6.59PM

THE ESSENTIAL YOU

CAPRICORN-ROOSTER

Capricorn-Roosters are perhaps the most conservative of the clan. With the Capricorn tendency to keep his or her head down and shoulder to the grindstone, this Rooster has less time to stick his or her head over the parapet, and, consequently, is less in danger of having said head shot off. Ambition and worldly aspirations drive the Capricorn-Rooster to work hard and climb that ladder of success. Practical, super-efficient, and unflappable in a crisis, their superiors soon take note and recognize the sterling qualities of these dependable people. Status and reputation are top of the agenda for the Capricorn-Rooster and it is only a matter of time before these people are placed in a position of authority and become pillars of society.

*Immaculate grooming is essential
to the fastidious Capricorn-Rooster.*

KEY CHARACTERISTICS

- efficient
- fervent
- sober
- perceptive

YOUR COMPATIBLE SIGNS

Virgo-Ox

Taurus-Snake

EAST WEST FUSION

EAST
Capricorn confirms the
Rooster's integrity

WEST
The Rooster encourages
the Goat to socialize

*The Rooster's sharp eye for detail and
the Goat's practical skills make
tailoring a possible career choice.*

OBSERVATIONS

*"Sorry" is not a word that readily
springs to the lips of the
Capricorn-Rooster*

WORK, HEALTH, HOBBIES

With their exacting standards and exquisite eye for detail, Capricorn-Roosters are strict taskmasters. Quality control is their forte and they make excellent managers and supervisors. Though they may not be the most physically active of people, they do take pride in their organizational skills and will lick an office into shape before breakfast. Where the Capricorn-Rooster works, everything will be shipshape, spick and span, and running on oiled wheels. Scientific research draws these people and so does the world of finance.

♥ ♥ ♥

LOVES, LIKES, DISLIKES

Cleanliness and hygiene are next to the Capricorn-Rooster's heart, so these people ensure their homes are immaculately clean. Members of this sign take great pleasure in dusting and polishing their antique treasures until they sparkle and shine. Personal grooming, too, is diligently attended to and no Capricorn-Rooster worth his or her salt would ever be seen with dirty fingernails. In matters of the heart, Capricorn-Roosters find it difficult to express their emotion. They expect their partners to know they are loved without having to be told.

🌸 🌸 🌸

CHILDREN AND PARENTS

Youngsters of this duality work very hard at school and so tend to do well academically. They are not sports mad like so many of their peers. Instead, they enjoy mathematics and science and delight in geographical field studies and school trips. Capricorn-Rooster parents are deeply caring, though a little on the dry side. They cannot put up with a child's high jinx and insist with passion on clean hands and impeccably tidy bedrooms.

CAPRICORN-DOG

A Capricorn-Dog is like a mountain—solid and enduring. Wherever a Capricorn is found, a prodigiously hardworker will follow. Couple that with the unwavering dedication of the Dog, and it is not difficult to understand why people born under this dual sign are caring, dutiful, and utterly responsible. Capricorn-Dogs make thoroughly good providers for their loved ones. They run their businesses efficiently, keep their accounts meticulously, and their homes impeccably neat and tidy. Moreover, they guard their families assiduously. Capricorn-Dogs are not the most emotionally expressive of people but they certainly have hearts of gold. Nevertheless, the Capricorn-Dog could be accused of being a little prudish.

OBSERVATIONS

Capricorn-Dogs say exactly what they mean and their caustic tongue can make them unpopular

KEY CHARACTERISTICS
- truthful
- anxious
- reserved
- systematic

YOUR COMPATIBLE SIGNS
Taurus-Tiger
Virgo-Horse

Archives, lists, information retrieval systems, the Capricorn-Dog knows how to keep them all meticulously.

EAST WEST FUSION

EAST
Capricorn encourages the Dog to pursue his or her ambitions

WEST
The Oriental Dog helps to make Capricorn's character more malleable

THE ESSENTIAL YOU

WORK, HEALTH, HOBBIES
Members of this sign can be rather intolerant. Their brusque manner and blunt approach does not make for easy relations with work colleagues, so perhaps Capricorn-Dogs are happier in a self-employed capacity. Academic studies suit them well, particularly if they can specialize in research or writing text books. Literature is a love of theirs, so library work, perhaps in a career as a curator or as keeper of archival records, would please them too. Interestingly, many Capricorn-Dogs turn to sports, either professionally or as a hobby, for these are sinewy people, who possess the stamina and determination to hang on in there and don't give up easily.

LOVES, LIKES, DISLIKES
With feet firmly planted on the ground, Capricorn-Dogs are essentially pragmatic people. They are not given to flights of fancy, they dislike pretence, and they can't be doing with sloppy shows of romance. In love, as in life, they can be rather prim and proper. But they are honest-to-goodness types, with a penchant for all that is wholesome and natural. Home and family get top priority, for these are domestically-oriented people who like to make jams, bake pies, and serve their own home-grown vegetables for dinner. Reading a book beside a roaring log fire is a favorite pursuit of the Capricorn-Dog.

CHILDREN AND PARENTS
Young Capricorn-Dogs excel on the sportsfield and they make particularly fine athletes. Not that they want to skip lessons necessarily—in fact, they like learning in class and acquiring knowledge. It's just that in sports, these youngsters find freedom and independence. As parents, Capricorn-Dogs are dutiful and try to teach their children by example.

Members of this sign like to prepare wholesome, home-made food for their families.

CAPRICORN-PIG

Capricorn-Pigs are solid citizens. Industrious, responsible, and down-to-earth, they are staunch upholders of values and tradition. All Capricorns work extremely hard for their living and Pigs are certainly no slackers when it comes to hard graft. Equally, neither would shrink from his or her duty, especially when family security and well-being are at stake. People who are born under this twin sign are ambitious. Capricorn-Pigs know exactly what they want and how to go about getting it. And this applies as much to the man or woman in their lives as it does to their worldly aspirations! However, unlike the workaholic Goat, Pigs tend to know when enough is enough. At this point, they will put down their tools and put their feet up to relax, in the interest of gathering enough energy for the next day's industry.

KEY CHARACTERISTICS
- scrupulous
- decisive
- traditionalist

YOUR COMPATIBLE SIGNS
Virgo-Rabbit
Taurus-Sheep

OBSERVATIONS
Putting blind trust in others can work against the Capricorn-Pig

EAST
Capricorn curbs the Chinese Pig's profligacy

WEST
The Oriental Pig boosts the Goat's imagination

Young Capricorn-Pigs tend to be possessive and must be taught to share with others.

THE ESSENTIAL YOU

WORK, HEALTH, HOBBIES
To feel happy and truly fulfilled in their work, Capricorn-Pigs should choose a career in which art and science combine. Too dry an occupation, such as finance perhaps, will frustrate the creative side of this duality. Equally, a purely artistic profession will make the Capricorn-Pig feel that there is little substance in what he or she is doing. A balance would be ideal, so careers in art history, for example, or perhaps a humane science, such as medicine, might therefore suit these people. Equally, a career in music, which blends theory and practice, or work in the theater will appeal to this group. So might interior design, as well as work with computers.

LOVES, LIKES, DISLIKES
Traditional styles please the Capricorn-Pig. Members of this dual sign appreciate quality in all things and will invest in exquisite artworks and antiques. Capricorn-Pigs love to have and to hold. What is theirs is theirs and let no man dare take it away from them. This applies as much to their possessions as it does to those they love. Once they have given their hearts they are faithful and true, and they demand absolute fidelity in return.

The Capricorn-Pig finds a relaxing drink in convivial company a just reward after a hard day's work.

CHILDREN AND PARENTS
Youngsters of this double sign will show their mettle from their very early years. They are hard-working at school and will enjoy drama, pottery, cooking, and other technological subjects. They can be jealous creatures and will suffer terribly if "best friends" move their allegiances elsewhere. Uncontrollable rage will ensue if siblings take their toys away, so, from the beginning, these children must learn to share. Capricorn-Pig parents have a tendency to wrap their offspring in a protective cocoon.

AQUARIUS

BORN BETWEEN: JANUARY 20—FEBRUARY 18
AIR SIGN

A*quarius, the eleventh sign of the Western astrological year, roughly corresponds to the Chinese month known as the Tiger Moon.*

If you were born at this time of the year you can either call yourself an Aquarian, or you can say you were born at the Time of Natural Radiance, which is a much more poetic alternative name given to this month in the East.

According to the Chinese, this time of year is also broken up into two fortnights, each describing an aspect of the weather, or a feature relevant to the agricultural year. The first fortnight is called Greater Cold and this corresponds to the first two weeks of Aquarius. If you were born in the second half of the sign, though, you belong to the second Chinese fortnight, Beginning of Spring.

But it is, of course, when both your month and year of birth are combined that the various influences begin to inter-weave themselves in a way that is essentially unique for you.

In whatever combination, Aquarius, as the sign of humanitarianism and advanced ideas, will contribute a very large pinch of idealism to the mix.

AQUARIUS-RAT

Original and individualistic, Aquarius-Rats take a liberal, laid-back attitude to most things in life, their supreme philosophy being one of live and let live. By other people's standards, members of this twin sign may appear somewhat unconventional and definitely more tolerant of human ways and foibles than most other Animals. By nature, Aquarians possess a strong humanitarian instinct, which restrains considerably the self-interested, opportunistic tendencies normally associated with members of the Rat sign. In short, this East and West dual sign produces outgoing individuals, people who are able to see life's bigger picture and are given to acts of spontaneity. Aquarius-Rats like to feel part of the community in which they live, and they are always striving to work for the betterment and well-being of mankind.

KEY CHARACTERISTICS
- inventive
- keen
- individualistic
- undisciplined

YOUR COMPATIBLE SIGNS
Gemini-Monkey
Libra-Dragon

Like opening Pandora's box, Aquarius-Rats need to discover the mysteries of the universe.

EAST WEST FUSION

EAST
The Western Water-bearer increases the Rat's generosity toward others

WEST
The Chinese Rat brings charm to grace the Aquarian's personality

OBSERVATIONS
A tendency to change their mind in mid-stream can affect the Aquarius-Rat's chances of success

---

THE ESSENTIAL YOU

WORK, HEALTH, HOBBIES
As long as the Aquarius-Rat is allowed free rein at work, he or she is happy. The limitation of strict rules thwart their imagination. And imagination is precisely what they have plenty of. Yet these people must learn to channel their talents and focus on the job in hand. With such discipline, Aquarius-Rats would make fine technical designers, academics, professors, or inventors.

Driven by their desire to be original, Aquarius-Rats like to stand out from the crowd.

LOVES, LIKES, DISLIKES
Unique, singular, and different, Aquarius-Rats like to stand out from the crowd. Plowing the same furrow day in and day out is anathema to them. Instead, the Aquarius-Rats' tastes tend toward originality, minimalism, and chic. They create their own dress style, which never appears old hat. In their relationships, Aquarius-Rats need partners who will offer both love and intellectual companionship.

CHILDREN AND PARENTS
Young Aquarius-Rats are full of bright ideas. Each one is a budding genius, able to see solutions that escape other people. However, they do need to learn the importance of concentrating on their tasks and seeing projects through to the end. Aquarius-Rat parents are loving people. They treat their offspring as individuals right from birth and ensure they receive a broad education.

AQUARIUS-OX

Oxen by nature are solid, constant, and predictable. In contrast eccentric Aquarians, ruled by the unpredictable planet Uranus, are much lighter of spirit and, as such, unlikely to lose too much sleep if they have not exactly paid attention to every detail. Such diametrically opposed attitudes to life, then, are not easily reconciled, and must account for the push-me-pull-you qualities of the Aquarius-Ox that gives this individual such a colorful personality. Members of this dual sign may be described as laws unto themselves. Free-thinking and intelligent creatures, Aquarius-Oxen need variety—both at work and in their love lives—if they are to fulfill their true potential.

KEY CHARACTERISTICS

- honest
- hard-working
- nonconformist
- eccentric

YOUR COMPATIBLE SIGNS

Libra-Snake
Gemini-Rooster

EAST WEST FUSION

EAST
Aquarius frees the Ox from his or her conventionality

WEST
The Chinese Ox brings stability to the Water-bearer

OBSERVATIONS
Aquarius-Oxen are sorely divided between unconventional drives and a need to uphold the status quo

Aquarius encourages the hide-bound Ox to shed some inhibitions.

THE ESSENTIAL YOU

WORK, HEALTH, HOBBIES
Outdoor jobs suit the Aquarius-Ox. As a group, these people are conscious of environmental issues, way ahead of the rest in the world in understanding the need to maintain the delicate balances of Nature. As such, research and work in biological studies and natural sciences attract them. Being altruistic souls, social concerns, too, occupy the minds of Aquarius-Oxen, and many will gravitate toward a career in charitable institutions. These people are practical when it comes to applying their manual skills and take relish in home renovation or mending equipment. Working with technical machinery will also satisfy them, be this in the printing industry, radiology, or air traffic control. Piloting radio or television broadcasts would also make good use of their skills.

♥ ♥ ♥

LOVES, LIKES, DISLIKES
Aquarius-Oxen don't like to show off. Nor do they like anyone else to show off. Rather, these are temperate people, who like to do their own thing and go their own way without having to explain themselves to others. At home, their style is very much their own—a mixture of comfort and classic. In relationships, they are not the most romantic of people and they tend to go more for mental stimulation than sexual excitement. A partner, therefore, who is their intellectual equal is what they seek.

CHILDREN AND PARENTS
Though not always possible, young Aquarius-Oxen fare considerably better when taught in smaller classes. They need lots of attention, not because they are egocentric, but because their numerous ideas flourish best in the hothouse climate of a small gathering. Adult Aquarius-Oxen take on the parenting role with great gusto. They instil into their children the belief in free speech combined with consideration for others, and they teach their children by example.

The Ox's personality and the water-bearer's creative flair come together well in home improvement projects.

AQUARIUS: **JANUARY 20—FEBRUARY 18**
YEARS OF THE TIGER: 1902 * 1914 * 1926 * 1938 * 1950 * 1962 * 1974 * 1986 * 1998 * 2010
HOUR OF THE TIGER: 3AM – 4.59AM

THE ESSENTIAL YOU

AQUARIUS-TIGER

EAST WEST FUSION

EAST
Aquarius extends the Tiger's
visionary powers

WEST
The Chinese Tiger brings courage of
conviction to the Water-bearer

*Aquarius-Tigers like to keep in touch
with friends and acquaintances.*

WORK, HEALTH, HOBBIES
Members of this sign like to philosophize. Being socially aware, they are prepared to take a reduced salary in order to work in careers that benefit the community at large. Living as they do on high octane, they have extraordinary drive and masses of initiative. It is their hatred of rules that means they are probably happier working on their own. Aquarius-Tigers are ingenious people, mavericks in the workplace, and invaluable as members of a think tank. New ideas, new solutions, and a brand new approach are their stock-in-trade. Travel is a favorite pastime, and if they can combine this with a career, so much the better.

♥   ♥   ♥

LOVES, LIKES, DISLIKES
Adventure attracts the Aquarius-Tiger, who, metaphorically and especially in their youth, like nothing better than to set sail on uncharted seas. They not only take change in their stride, but they actually court the thrill and challenge of the new and the unknown. The same applies in life as in love. For Aquarius-Tigers, infatuations and the grand passion tend to be many and frequent.

🐾   🐾   🐾

CHILDREN AND PARENTS
Young Aquarius-Tigers are interested in everything and anything, and will stretch the knowledge of both parent and teacher to the limit with their constant stream of questions. Mentally and physically, these children never seem to tire. At school they will shine in information technology and computer work. Adult Aquarius-Tigers are in no hurry to start a family, but when eventually they do, they make good parents, who bring up intelligent young people.

A quarius-Tigers are born with a double helping of eccentricity. Unpredictable by nature, they flout all the rules and regulations. Nor are the members of this sign great upholders of tradition and convention. Indeed, these people are veritable laws unto themselves, and as such incredibly unpredictable. Thus unhindered by the constraints to conform, the Aquarius-Tiger has the advantage of being able to take a dispassionate view of his or her world. Moreover, with their clear-sightedness, they have a knack of bypassing perplexing emotions in order to get to the heart of the matter. However, it is this very ability to intellectually rationalize their feelings that makes the Aquarius-Tiger come across as emotionally distant.

OBSERVATIONS

*Rushing through with little heed of the
consequences undermines the performance
of the Aquarius-Tiger*

KEY CHARACTERISTICS
- adventurous
- spontaneous
- optimistic
- unconventional

YOUR COMPATIBLE SIGNS
Gemini-Horse
Libra-Dog

*Exploring distant lands and
different climes is a passion of
the Aquarius-Tiger.*

AQUARIUS-RABBIT

EAST
Aquarius endorses the Rabbit's
quest for knowledge

WEST
The Chinese Rabbit tempers Aquarius'
eccentric tendencies

Less introverted than most Rabbits, the merging of these two signs produces intelligent individuals, blessed with imagination and great vision. These people like to play with ideas and appear to be well ahead of their time. Aquarius is the sign of the intellect and its members have a reputation for the acquisition of knowledge rather than of material possessions. Rabbits, on the other hand, appreciate life's little comforts and like to surround themselves with beautiful things. Aquarius-Rabbits, therefore, will work with their brains and because their far-sightedness enables them to steal a march on others in their same profession, these people invariably end up very comfortably off indeed.

OBSERVATIONS

An occasional tinge of haughtiness can sometimes peep through the Aquarius-Rabbit's level-headed character

KEY CHARACTERISTICS
- far-seeing
- humanistic
- imaginative
- knowledgeable

YOUR COMPATIBLE SIGNS
Libra-Sheep
Gemini-Pig

*Members of this sign always look
on the sunny side of life.*

THE ESSENTIAL YOU

WORK, HEALTH, HOBBIES
Aquarius-Rabbits do well in professions where they can give advice to others or help people to work out their problems. Essentially practical people, Aquarius-Rabbits are capable of seeing solutions to problems or offering innovative answers to old dilemmas. In addition, members of this dual sign are blessed with a strong intuitive sense. Combine this with a creative mind and strong intellect, and it is easy to see why Aquarius-Rabbits are guaranteed to go far in life. They excel as fashion designers, software engineers, and political advisors.

*Aquarius-Rabbits don't shy away from
scientific subjects—software engineering
appeals to their gifted intelligence.*

LOVES, LIKES, DISLIKES
Aquarius-Rabbits like to be chic and ultra-modern—a combination which invariably ends up giving their environment an unusual yet timeless feel. Natives of this dual sign enjoy relaxed dinner parties in elegant surroundings, where guests are encouraged to engage in intelligent discussion and philosophical debate. Heated arguments are avoided at all cost, since these people have a horror of disputes and unpleasant situations of all kind. Generous-spirited, intellectual, and idealistic, Aquarius-Tigers are happiest with clever, even-tempered partners.

CHILDREN AND PARENTS
Young Aquarius-Rabbits have an immense curiosity about their world. These little ones, however, are not risk-takers and seem to be aware of their limits from a very young age. Their capacity for acquiring knowledge is huge and they will delight in being taken to museums, art galleries, and exhibitions of all kinds. At school, the library will be a favorite haunt. As parents, Aquarius-Rabbits tend to invest a great deal, both in terms of time and money, into their children's education. They will hot-house their youngsters and introduce them to as many avenues of science and culture as they possibly can.

AQUARIUS-DRAGON

The Water Carrier's altruistic drive and the Dragon's inherent nobility make these individuals both idealistic and capable of realizing their ideals.

OBSERVATIONS

A staunch need for independence can preclude Aquarius-Dragons from forging strong friendships

KEY CHARACTERISTICS

- influential
- deep
- hard-working
- crusading

YOUR COMPATIBLE SIGNS

Gemini-Rat
Libra-Monkey

EAST WEST FUSION

EAST
Aquarius brings the Dragon clarity of thought

WEST
The Dragon endows the Water-bearer with popularity and success

I dealistic and unconventional, members of this duo are perhaps the most unorthodox of all the Dragons. With their outlandish tastes and far-sighted views, Aquarius-Dragons delight in the shock of the new. Without doubt, Aquarius-Dragons are intellectuals first and foremost, individualistic, and eccentric in both their opinions and behavior, as if born well ahead of their time. They have an uncanny ability to see beyond today's laws and morality and they endeavor to chip away at the boundaries that limit our understanding. Tolerant and broad-minded, Aquarius-Dragons fit into any sphere of life and are generally well-loved by all.

Young Aquarius-Dragons dream of becoming airline pilots.

WORK, HEALTH, HOBBIES

Aquarius-Dragons are driven by an intellectual curiosity to discover what makes people tick. They are interested in dynamic situations, coincidence, chaos theory, and in what makes the world spin on its axis. Then Aquarius-Dragons want to put that knowledge toward improving the world. These are confident and energetic people, who get on with their tasks cheerfully and enthusiastically. Suited to a diverse range of careers from aid worker to archeologist, travel agent to aviator, Aquarius-Dragons make it the top of their chosen profession sooner rather than later in their lives.

LOVES, LIKES, DISLIKES

Aquarius-Dragons adore magic and illusion, and indeed are quite adept at creating some of their own. They take great pleasure in surprising people, lending a helping hand and cheering those whose spirits are low. Making the world a brighter place gives Aquarius-Dragons enormous satisfaction. Moreover, they are idealistic in the main, and any kind of duplicity upsets them deeply. In love, these people need a solid partner who is honest and straight-forward.

CHILDREN AND PARENTS

Young Aquarius-Dragons are intelligent and quick to learn. They like taking things to pieces in order to find out how they work, although they are not always as interested in putting the pieces back together again! Aquarius-Dragons make dutiful parents and they take the responsibility of raising their children seriously.

AQUARIUS-SNAKE

Intellectual but idealistic, broad-minded but possessive, open but prone to withdrawing when upset, the Aquarius-Snake is full of contradictions. What is more, Snakes need to feel they have a supportive partner by their side, but on the other hand, the bright and breezy Aquarian hates to feel shackled and refuses to be tied down. Thus it is that the Aquarian and the Snake do not altogether make happy bed-fellows. Nevertheless Aquarius-Snakes have a lot going for them, for these are outward-looking people, with a flexible and philosophical approach to life. Their ability to take bad news on the chin ensures they will make the best of every situation. Communication—both intellectually and in a practical way—is their raison d'être.

KEY CHARACTERISTICS
- realistic
- observant
- adaptable
- articulate

YOUR COMPATIBLE SIGNS
Libra-Rooster
Gemini-Ox

EAST WEST FUSION

EAST
The Water-bearer deepens the Snake's intuitive processes

WEST
The Chinese Snake bestows wisdom upon Aquarius

These contradictory people are possessive of their loved ones, yet demand their own space.

OBSERVATIONS
A tendency to nervous tension can sometimes adversely affect the Aquarius-Snake

THE ESSENTIAL YOU

WORK, HEALTH, HOBBIES
Aquarius-Snakes are more cerebral than they are physical. If they could, they would live inside their heads and generate ideas and fantasies the whole day long. Such talents would be well employed in research laboratories where pioneering breakthroughs take place, in psychological work, or in universities and other places of learning. Coupling this imaginative potential with their articulate skills can take the Aquarius-Snake into advertising, public relations, and copy-writing. The media, too, holds lots of attractions for this group.

LOVES, LIKES, DISLIKES
Mystery movies, detective fiction, and crossword puzzles all please the acquisitive nature of the Aquarius-Snake. As long as they can keep their imaginations stimulated, they are happy. Amassing great wealth or surrounding themselves with creature comforts are not top of the agenda here. But personal freedom is a must, and Aquarius-Snakes like to be able to come and go as they please. This especially applies to their intimate relationships, since nothing turns them off faster than a partner who is clingy and dependent.

Imaginative young Aquarius-Snakes, will spend hours with their heads in the clouds.

CHILDREN AND PARENTS
Day-dreaming is characteristic of young Aquarius-Snakes, who may spend a lot of time staring out of the classroom window. But this activity merely reflects a fertile imagination, which needs to be encouraged, honed, and directed. These children have the ability to shine across most academic subjects, but especially in literature and language work. Young Aquarius-Snakes learn the art of being economical with the truth fairly early on in life. Needless to say, this is a tendency which should be discouraged kindly but firmly. Adult Aquarius-Snakes have winning ways with their offspring and are adept at bed-time storytelling.

EAST WEST FUSION

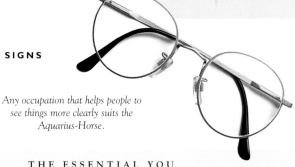

EAST
Aquarius teaches the Horse to
be more tolerant

WEST
The Oriental Horse brings
Aquarius speed of thought

AQUARIUS-HORSE

The Aquarius-Horse is perhaps the most colorful of all the Horses: zany, unconventional, unorthodox, funny, and uniquely eccentric. Born ahead of their time, with philosophies and ideas that transcend the present, they are indeed far-sighted, forward-thinkers. Possessing immense creative flair, they make talented inventors. Wherever there is an affiliation with the Water-bearer, there will usually be strong humanitarian links, which in this duality manifests itself in an instinct for working toward the improvement of the lot of mankind.

KEY CHARACTERISTICS
- dramatic
- enthusiastic
- humanitarian
- resourceful

YOUR COMPATIBLE SIGNS
Gemini-Dog
Libra-Tiger

Any occupation that helps people to see things more clearly suits the Aquarius-Horse.

THE ESSENTIAL YOU

Their love of experimentation puts the Aquarius-Horse at the forefront of scientific research.

OBSERVATIONS
A lack of forward planning can seriously catch out the Aquarius-Horse

WORK, HEALTH, HOBBIES
No matter what occupation Aquarius-Horses take up, they will always bring to it a uniquely original approach. Even the most run-of-the-mill sort of job will be stamped with their offbeat flair. In general, these are clever people, abounding in energy and suited to a wide range of professions. They possess a strong vocational instinct, which might take them into social work or into allied medical fields, such as optometry. The life of academia could also be a draw, perhaps lecturing in scientific subjects or social policy. On the other hand, their creative talents might take them into the world of film, and specifically into production or direction. Whether professionally or as a spare-time pursuit, though, New Age practices and therapies, such as aromatherapy, are bound to intrigue and provide pleasure.

♥ ♥ ♥

LOVES, LIKES, DISLIKES
Attracted by the weird and the wonderful, Aquarius-Horses have some pretty unusual tastes. These people are positively eccentric, proud of their original turn of mind and Bohemian lifestyle. Indeed, they are freethinkers, not bound by traditional conventions and ways, which they believe stifle creative imagination and hamper the march of progress. Moreover, they are not interested in possessing luxuries or in vulgar displays of wealth. They do want to do good, though. And they want to have fun. As far as affairs of the heart are concerned, Aquarius-Horses don't always get it right the first time around. They fall passionately in love, but as soon as the novelty wears off, they gallop away to seek fresh challenges elsewhere. Many have several attempts at relationships before finally settling down.

CHILDREN AND PARENTS
There are bound to be problems if an Aquarius-Horse child is born into a very strict family because these youngsters rebel against rules and regulations. Allowed to roam free, at least intellectually, young Aquarius-Horses will make and create, working hard and achieving results at school, both in academic subjects and on the sportsfield. As parents, Aquarius-Horses are easy-going, fair-minded, and tolerant.

AQUARIUS-SHEEP

Couple the Aquarian's originality with the Sheep's intuition and it is not difficult to understand why many Aquarius-Sheep have brilliantly inventive minds. They are zany people, given to acts of spontaneity and unconventional behavior. No one should attempt to pin down an Aquarius-Sheep. For here is a colorful character and one of Nature's free spirits—ethereal, elusive, and electric. Aquarius-Sheep are something of a paradox. Although they work best in a partnership, whether of the intimate or business kind, their need to be free makes them fight against commitment or restraints. Moreover, Aquarius-Sheep live for the moment and expect others to do the same.

Ideas flow readily through the inventive minds of the Aquarius-Sheep.

KEY CHARACTERISTICS

- insightful
- whimsical
- tolerant
- ephemeral

YOUR COMPATIBLE SIGNS

Libra-Pig
Gemini-Rabbit

EAST WEST FUSION

EAST
Aquarius encourages the Sheep
to become self-confident

WEST
The Oriental Sheep brings stylishness
to the Water-bearer

OBSERVATIONS

Aquarius-Sheep can be headstrong and not prepared to take any advice or criticism from others

Aquarius-Sheep find it easy to absorb themselves in a good book.

WORK, HEALTH, HOBBIES

Spontaneous creativity is the mark of the Aquarius-Sheep. These people can come up with inspirational ideas, but unless they can put these instantly into motion and see results pretty quickly, they will lose all enthusiasm and leave the project in mid-air. Consequently, they need to work in a partnership or team, so that others can see the project through to its conclusion. The worlds of fashion and the arts draw these beautiful people. Theater, too, is a love. Millinery, floristry, secretarial, reception, or library work equally appeal.

♥   ♥   ♥

LOVES, LIKES, DISLIKES

Aquarius-Sheep find making commitments quite unthinkable. After all, who's to know how they will be feeling tomorrow, let alone next month? No, *carpe diem* is their motto: seize the day, enjoy the present, do it now. This philosophy does, of course, have repercussions in their emotional lives. It also means a relaxed attitude toward personal loyalties and ties. On the other hand, Aquarius-Sheep don't expect partnerships to be exclusive. Indeed, if they do settle for a relationship, they will demand that it must be fluid and open at all times.

CHILDREN AND PARENTS

With their winsome ways, children born under this dual sign are attractive and engaging characters. They excel in the creative and expressive arts—for instance, painting, writing poetry, or playing a musical instrument. If they get involved in an activity they enjoy, they can lose themselves for hours, and become totally oblivious to everything else that is going on around them. Aquarius-Sheep are fun-loving and laid-back parents.

EAST WEST FUSION

EAST
Aquarius soups up the Monkey's
flair for originality

WEST
The Chinese Monkey contributes a
playful spirit to this partnership

AQUARIUS-MONKEY

Colorful and eccentric is perhaps the best way to describe the Aquarius-Monkey. They are also intelligent and laid-back individuals, and they seek like-minded company—both at work and home. Aquarius-Monkeys are born with a powerful streak of curiosity. They are the tiresome children who never stop asking questions. They are the people who pick up rocks simply to find out what is crawling underneath. In adult life, Aquarius-Monkeys are the ones who ask the probing questions, challenge opinions, generally digging and delving. They are also the ones who want to know how people tick or what keeps the universe from spinning out of control. In short, Aquarius-Monkeys are the world's problem-solvers.

OBSERVATIONS

Riding rough-shod over other people's beliefs can be a failing of this dual sign

KEY CHARACTERISTICS
- ingenious
- outgoing
- curious
- fair

YOUR COMPATIBLE SIGNS
Gemini-Dragon
Libra-Rat

Aquarius-Monkeys are driven by their curiosity to scrutinize the world around them.

THE ESSENTIAL YOU

WORK, HEALTH, HOBBIES
Natives of this dual sign are strong, active people, full of initiative and blessed with vigorous minds. They like to pour their abundant energies into their work. Whether as employer or employee, Aquarius-Monkeys are conscientious workers, honest, cooperative with their colleagues, and staunch supporters of justice and equality in the workplace. They are intelligent people, free thinkers who are hardly ever lost for words. As professions go, the judiciary attracts them, and so does politics. However, another of the Aquarius-Monkey's talents is as a wordsmith, so any sort of oral or literary career suits them well— from lecturing and making presentations, to writing and broadcasting.

LOVES, LIKES, DISLIKES
Aquarius-Monkeys like to get around. Travel pleases them and the more dramatic the scenery the better. Indeed, they are fascinated by the spectacular, be it the Egyptian Pyramids, technological wonders, or lavish theatrical performances. Hi-tech gadgets amuse them greatly and there will be plenty of computers, gizmos, and other space-age appliances in their homes. And, because Aquarius-Monkeys are verbally skilled, they will enjoy all manner of games, puzzles, and brain-teasers, too. Intelligent ideas and stimulating conversation are important to Aquarius-Monkeys, so a partner who is able to share their intellectual interests is a must.

CHILDREN AND PARENTS
Young Aquarius-Monkeys are linguistically advanced. They begin to talk very early in their lives, and from then on hardly ever seem to stop! These children are sunny, energetic young scamps, with a cheekiness that just adds to their charm. Clever, versatile, and wise beyond their years, these happy youngsters generally do well at school.
Aquarius-Monkey parents believe in reasoning with their children, so there will be plenty of discussion, moral tales, and stories at bedtime in this household.

A career in law suits the intellectual and verbal skills of the Aquarius-Monkey.

EAST WEST FUSION

AQUARIUS-ROOSTER

EAST
Aquarius encourages the Rooster
to be more broad-minded

WEST
The Chinese Rooster introduces the
Water-bearer to swanky style

Roosters tend to do quite a lot of strutting around in order to show off their beautiful plumage. Aquarians are outgoing and distinctively stylish in their own way. The combination of these signs produces a group of people who like to stand out from the crowd—to be different, or even downright eccentric. The drab, dull, and mundane is certainly not for them. Intellectually, people born under this twin sign are way ahead of everyone else. In the emotional stakes, they cannot bear to be tied down. With one of the lowest boredom thresholds around, Aquarius-Roosters need to seek out fresh challenges on a daily basis if they are to avoid their fertile imaginations going stale.

OBSERVATIONS

*Aquarius-Roosters can be
brutally frank*

KEY CHARACTERISTICS

- inquisitive
- pushy
- efficient
- resolute

YOUR COMPATIBLE SIGNS
Libra-Ox
Gemini-Snake

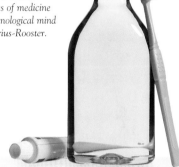

*Orthodontics and
other branches of medicine
attract the technological mind
of the Aquarius-Rooster.*

THE ESSENTIAL YOU

*Aquarius-Roosters are always ready to move on to
seek new challenges, whatever field they work in.*

WORK, HEALTH, HOBBIES

Since Aquarius-Roosters like giving orders and doing things their own way, perhaps they do better as bosses than employees. These people want to see their achievements crowned with financial rewards, so they will seek out careers that offer high salaries. Aquarius-Roosters excel in draftsmanship and technical design. Other good career avenues are the law and diplomatic services. Radiography and orthodontics also attract. Let it be noted that, no matter what career they choose, it is certain that Aquarius-Roosters will strive to break new ground.

LOVES, LIKES, DISLIKES

Aquarius-Roosters like to think of themselves as controversial figures with the power to shock. They like nothing better than to see their ideas met with a few raised eyebrows. They feel that their mission in life is to push against the boundaries of convention in order to

allow in a breath of the future. Above all, they dislike sentimentality, which they believe impedes progress. But at the same time, these people also like their creature comforts. They are conscious of their image so are regulars at the gym, and they do like a good income to support their lifestyle. Emotionally, Aquarius-Roosters tend to be cool. A partner who can maintain a sense of mystique will stand a good chance of winning an Aquarius-Rooster's heart.

CHILDREN AND PARENTS

Young Aquarius-Roosters are unique people with a very clear idea of what they want. And they can be quite headstrong about getting it. Their tendency to buck against rules and regulations is probably more bravado than anything else. Whatever, they court attention by showing off. Adult Aquarius-Roosters can be somewhat aloof and make better parents to older children than they do to babies.

AQUARIUS-DOG

OBSERVATIONS

Aquarius-Dogs have a tendency to mighty bossy

Original and somewhat eccentric people, Aquarius-Dogs are the least materialistic people in the world. Both signs, independently, have a reputation for addressing humanitarian concerns, and both are staunch upholders of a person's democratic rights. One person, one vote, is their tenet in life—and even the underdog must be given his say. In fact, in the Aquarius-Dog's idealistic and egalitarian world, there simply would not be such a thing as an underdog. In life, it is spiritual fulfilment that the Aquarius-Dog seeks, not dazzling wealth or the legacy of enduring fame. Caring for others is their mission in life and Aquarius-Dogs can dedicate themselves altruistically to anyone they consider to be worse off than they are.

KEY CHARACTERISTICS

- helpful
- faithful
- kindly
- caring

YOUR COMPATIBLE SIGNS
Gemini-Tiger
Libra-Horse

A strong desire to help urges the Aquarius-Dog to take up humanitarian causes.

EAST WEST FUSION

EAST
Aquarius encourages the Dog to be more flexible

WEST
The Oriental Dog brings a stabilizing instinct to the Water-bearer

Aquarius-Dogs do not seek vast wealth—but just enough to ensure a comfortable existence.

THE ESSENTIAL YOU

WORK, HEALTH, HOBBIES
Curiously, Aquarius-Dogs need people to rely on them, so they offer their services to all and sundry and heap responsibilities on themselves. The problem is that they soon become snowed under and, when they find they can no longer cope, they develop nervous conditions and then start to bemoan their fate. Learning when enough is enough is a good lesson for the Aquarius-Dog. Whatever career they pursue, however, these people make trustworthy and conscientious workers. Whether they work on their own or for a company, as boss or as employee, they can be relied on to perform their duties without making a fuss. Nursing, the teaching profession, and social welfare would all suit. Aquarius-Dogs would also make fine town planners and laboratory technicians.

LOVES, LIKES, DISLIKES
Members of this twin sign love to bestow on others the benefit of their experiences and opinions. They will strive to take control of any and every situation. At home, they like to have things done their way. Aquarius-Dogs don't much care for "roughing it" through life, so home comforts and a full complement of modern conveniences will be essential. Money, therefore, is important, and Aquarius-Dogs will fret if they don't have a tidy nest egg growing steadily in the bank. In relationships, Aquarius-Dogs need to have a bit of freedom so they don't feel too hemmed in. For them, the course of true love does not always run smoothly; in fact, it can sometimes prove to be a somewhat bumpy ride.

CHILDREN AND PARENTS
Young Aquarius-Dogs are dutiful and responsible young people, with an innate instinct for protecting their siblings. They construct a tough façade behind which they hide their sensitivities and anxieties. For all their show of independence and maturity, these are anxious children who need masses of reassurance and tender loving care. Aquarius-Dog parents care deeply for their children even if they don't always express their love openly.

AQUARIUS: **JANUARY 20—FEBRUARY 18**
YEARS OF THE PIG: 1911 ✳ 1923 ✳ 1935 ✳ 1947 ✳ 1959 ✳ 1971 ✳ 1983 ✳ 1995 ✳ 2007 ✳ 2019
HOUR OF THE PIG: 9PM – 10.59PM

THE ESSENTIAL YOU

AQUARIUS-PIG

Being born under the dominion of the Aquarius-Pig makes these natives bright and breezy to be around, chatty, sociable, and outgoing. As such, Aquarius-Pigs are popular and sought after by friends and acquaintances alike. This is just as well, since communicating is what the Aquarius-Pig does best. People tend to listen to Aquarius-Pigs, take their advice on board, even imitate their habits and their styles. They are never fashion victims, they do not follow trends—they set them. The problem is that Aquarius-Pigs get bored too easily. No sooner have they set a trend than they want to move on.

KEY CHARACTERISTICS

- persuasive
- fortunate
- brash
- prosperous

YOUR COMPATIBLE SIGNS

Libra-Rabbit
Gemini-Sheep

Only the best will do for the discerning Aquarius-Pig.

EAST WEST FUSION

EAST
Aquarius teaches the Pig the value of independence

WEST
The Oriental Pig makes the Water-bearer more assertive

OBSERVATIONS
Greed can be a failing among the members of this dual sign

Aquarius-Pigs have empathy to spare and make good counselors.

WORK, HEALTH, HOBBIES
Members of this dual sign are highly ambitious—born to rule. Bureaucratic red tape drives them mad. Aquarius-Pigs want both success and a high income, and so they will make a speedy rise to the top of whatever career they choose to follow. Articulate and persuasive, they do well in any occupation where verbal skills are a prerequisite. Many gravitate toward a career in sales or commerce, and a seat on the company board would particularly suit them. Other appropriate occupations might include printing, photography, electronics, and quantity surveying.

♥ ♥ ♥

LOVES, LIKES, DISLIKES
Aquarius-Pigs don't like other people spoiling their mood, getting in their way, or raining on their parade. It is just as well that Aquarius-Pigs have the Midas touch when it comes to money-making because they enjoy expensive tastes, filling their homes with beautiful things. Indeed, Aquarius-Pigs have a creative eye and many are artistically gifted. Fortunate in love as well as in life, Aquarius-Pigs are passionate creatures and usually strike it lucky when it comes to relationships. Most will have happy, successful and long-lasting marriages.

CHILDREN AND PARENTS
Young Aquarius-Pigs are gregarious little children, blessed with a knack for making friends easily. They enjoy school life and work hard at their studies. Challenge spurs them on to great heights and they will want to acquit themselves well in every subject. Adult Aquarius-Pigs are not the most cuddly of parents. They can be strict and insist that rules and regulations are adhered to stringently.

PISCES

BORN BETWEEN: **FEBRUARY 19—MARCH 20**
WATER SIGN

Pisces, the twelfth sign of the Western astrological year, roughly corresponds to the Chinese month known as the Rabbit Moon.

If you were born at this time of the year you can either call yourself a Piscean, or a native of the Apricot Blossom Moon, which is a far prettier Chinese name for this month.

According to the Chinese, this time of year is also broken up into two fortnights, each describing an aspect of the weather, or a feature relevant to the agricultural year. The first fortnight is called Rain Waters and this corresponds to the first two weeks of Pisces. If you were born in the second half of the sign, though, you belong to the second Chinese fortnight, Insects Awaken.

But it is, of course, when both your month and your year of birth are combined that the various influences begin to interweave themselves in a way that is essentially unique for you.

Whatever the combination, Pisces, as a dreamy and intuitive sign, brings both romance and compassion to the mix.

PISCES-RAT

The Piscean brings a marked sensitivity to the Oriental Rat, imbuing this twin sign with insight and receptivity. At the same time, the gutsy Rat adds a certain brio to the normally timid disposition of the Piscean character. In union, then, the Pisces-Rat is a caring, perceptive individual who especially excels as a personal consultant or in the counseling profession. Equally, Pisces-Rats are highly artistic and creatively talented, though they do tend to lack self-confidence in their own abilities. It is for this reason that members of this twin sign are able to function much better as part of a team than they do living or working on their own.

KEY CHARACTERISTICS

- affable
- intuitive
- creative
- supersensitive

YOUR COMPATIBLE SIGNS

Cancer-Monkey

Scorpio-Dragon

EAST WEST FUSION

EAST
Gentle Pisces mellows the Oriental Rat's assertiveness

WEST
The Chinese Rat intensifies Pisces' ambitious drive

THE ESSENTIAL YOU

WORK, HEALTH, HOBBIES

At work, Pisces-Rats abide by the philosophy of "all for one and one for all," because team spirit is important to these people who do so much better working in a cohesive group of like-minded people than they do alone. Indeed, self-employment is not recommended for the highly strung Pisces-Rat. However, a partnership with one other person is often the ideal. Travel is a favorite pastime and, combined with their business, satisfies these people no end. Creatively inspired, Pisces-Rats are blessed with imagination and gifted with sensitive ideas. Literary skills are innate so work in journalism or publishing would suit. Illustrating, too, is an appropriate profession here. Child care, importing art, or the wine and spirit trade attract too.

LOVES, LIKES, DISLIKES

Pisces-Rats like collecting pretty things and their homes will be filled with an eclectic assortment of exotic artifacts, antique furniture, porcelain, paintings, brocades, and souvenirs of all description.

These are very accommodating people who like to please their friends and loved ones. Sharing is a natural instinct for Pisces-Rats, perhaps because they dislike the thought of living on their own so much. Members of the opposite sex find it easy to fall for these people who are devoted to the ones they love.

CHILDREN AND PARENTS

Since both Pisces and Rats like cuddles, youngsters of this dual sign will need double the average dose of cossetting. At school, they shine in creative subjects and have no problems making friends. Pisces-Rats are responsible and deeply caring parents to their children.

Sharing a drink with a loved one gives the Pisces-Rat great pleasure.

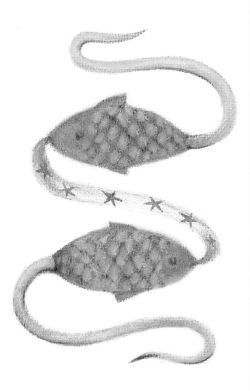

The Rat teaches vacillating Pisces to focus on a direction.

EAST WEST FUSION

PISCES-OX

EAST
Pisces teaches the Ox to be
more compassionate

WEST
The Chinese Ox strengthens Pisces'
delicate sensitivities

Moderated by gentle Pisces, sensitivity and introspection temper the normally craggy toughness that is so characteristic of the Ox. An intricate personality this, the Pisces-Ox has a bottomless well of creative talent and a perspicacity that enables him or her to get right to the heart of the matter or to read a person like a book. Artistic occupations attract members of this dual sign and, since Pisces-Oxen have no burning drive for power and glory, they are perfectly contented to work behind the scenes or in a supportive capacity. Having a romantic and sentimental character, it is not so much a partner as it is a soulmate that the Pisces-Ox seeks out in life.

OBSERVATIONS

Pisces-Oxen never forget the smallest slight—it may take years but they will get even sooner or later

KEY CHARACTERISTICS
- honest
- reserved
- sentimental
- persevering

YOUR COMPATIBLE SIGNS
Scorpio-Snake
Cancer-Rooster

The Ox encourages the inconstant Fish to settle down to a happy life in the family.

THE ESSENTIAL YOU

WORK, HEALTH, HOBBIES
Dependable and trustworthy, Pisces-Oxen are responsible people, who handle their duties with integrity, and who work with a quiet dignity which earns respect from fellows and colleagues alike. They couple considerable artistic talent with practical expertise and, whatever career they choose to follow, they produce work of a consistently high standard. Pisces-Oxen are drawn to outdoor work and make fine garden designers, or else find satisfaction as administrators of historical houses. Other suitable careers might include nursing, the brewery trade, or marine insurance. Pisces-Oxen enjoy a strong constitution and aspire to a good standard of living.

LOVES, LIKES, DISLIKES
Maintaining traditions is important to the Pisces-Ox and members of this dual sign will display classic tastes. A quiet life in the country is preferred to the hubbub of the city. But deep comfort at home is essential—these people will not make do with tea-chests for tables! In love, Pisces-Oxen are profoundly passionate, though reticent in coming forward, and their emotions lie just beneath the surface, ready to be triggered into expression by a like-minded soulmate.

CHILDREN AND PARENTS
Young Pisces-Oxen are endearing individuals—hard-working, serious, responsible, and sensitive toward their siblings and friends. At school, these youngsters will hand in work that is neat and carefully done. Reading, writing, and handicrafts especially will be preferred. Family life is central to both young and adult Pisces-Oxen and parents of this sign will delight in their children and follow their development closely. Stories at bedtime are a favorite pastime in this household.

When it comes to upholding traditional values Pisces-Oxen take the biscuit.

PISCES-TIGER

Pisces-Tigers possess a natural rapport with animals, large and small.

The soft, tender, and genteel influence of the Piscean nature acts to moderate the Tiger's aggression and hot-headedness. But, though tempered, the spirit and the verve is nonetheless present in this big cat's makeup and should never be underestimated. Still, it is fair to say that Pisces-Tigers are more amenable than most, despite the fiery passions that lurk beneath the surface. Patient and sensitive, these people prefer to watch from the wings rather than push themselves forward. Pisces-Tigers are adept at playing a subtle game since, when they do set their sights on a partner, they will use their sharpest insights and cleverest wiles to ensure that they stake their claim.

EAST WEST FUSION

EAST
Pisces teaches the impulsive Tiger to act with subtlety

WEST
The courageous Tiger breathes fiery vigor into Pisces' veins

KEY CHARACTERISTICS
- attractive
- charming
- competent
- proud

YOUR COMPATIBLE SIGNS
Cancer-Horse
Scorpio-Dog

OBSERVATIONS

Pisces-Tigers have a tendency to take on far more work than they can comfortably handle.

Dramatically creative, Pisces-Tigers can achieve success in costume or set design.

THE ESSENTIAL YOU

WORK, HEALTH, HOBBIES
Blending passion with sensitivity can take the Pisces-Tiger into the realms of dance, music, and the arts. From make-up artist to set designer, jeweler to thriller writer, costumier to fashion photographer, Pisces-Tigers will create with their souls. They are not, as a rule, drawn to tasks that require extreme precision, for members of this sign prefer to paint on a broad canvas. And they are happier self-employed than bound by the rules and regulations of permanent employment. Pisces-Tigers are energetic and enthusiastic and throw themselves one hundred percent into any work they undertake.

♥   ♥   ♥

LOVES, LIKES, DISLIKES
The accumulation of wealth or of material possessions are not top of the agenda for Pisces-Tigers. In fact, it is spiritual well-being that takes priority, for Pisces-Tigers are fundamentally helpful people, with chivalry as their code of honor. Yes, they do seek new experiences and they do like the freedom to come and go as they please, but they are essentially driven by a compulsion to uphold the just cause so they try to be as honest as they can. However, they are idealistic enough to expect the same in return from others—especially from a partner. Deceit and disloyalty from their loved ones smites them to the core. Tender yet ardent lovers, when they find their soulmate, they remain loyal and true.

CHILDREN AND PARENTS
Active and athletic, young Pisces-Tigers will enjoy energetic activities such as gymnastics, swimming, and dancing. These are warm and affectionate children with lots of love to give. Pisces-Tigers are good parents and ensure that their youngsters receive the best possible grounding and education for life.

PISCES: **FEBRUARY 19–MARCH 20**
YEARS OF THE RABBIT: 1903 ✴ 1915 ✴ 1927 ✴ 1939 ✴ 1951 ✴ 1963 ✴ 1975 ✴ 1987 ✴ 1999 ✴ 2011
HOUR OF THE RABBIT: 5AM – 6.59AM

THE ESSENTIAL YOU

PISCES-RABBIT

Mix sensitivity with astuteness, idealism with adroitness, loving kindness with finesse and the resulting Pisces-Rabbit is a creature of infinite complexity. These two signs are a happy merger since both have sensitivity and strong creative talents in good measure. Pisces-Rabbits are not high-powered individuals and are much more comfortable in low-key professions, or in occupations where they can put their creative skills to good use. Able to pick up mood and vibration instinctively, members of this sign are easily influenced by people and by the atmosphere around them. They thrive best in peaceful, harmonious settings in which they can set their own deadlines and work at their own pace.

The gentle healing properties of complementary medicine suit the sensitive systems of Pisces-Rabbits.

KEY CHARACTERISTICS
- talkative
- agreeable
- cautious
- artistic

YOUR COMPATIBLE SIGNS
Scorpio-Sheep
Cancer-Pig

Painting is both an ideal occupation and excellent therapy for the Pisces-Rabbit.

OBSERVATIONS

Pisces-Rabbits find it difficult to recover after a set-back

EAST WEST FUSION

EAST
Pisces deepens the Rabbit's understanding of others

WEST
The Chinese Rabbit heightens Pisces' creative talents

WORK, HEALTH, HOBBIES
Dealing with members of the general public is the Pisces-Rabbit's specialty in life. These folk are blessed with a comforting bedside manner so they make terrific medical practitioners or counselors. Medicine, psychiatry, and complementary therapies are fields that appeal to this group. But, because Pisces-Rabbits are nervous worriers, any conflict or criticism at work will seriously upset them. Working in a gentle and harmonious atmosphere, perhaps as a potter, artist, designer, or illustrator, could be ideal.

♥ ♥ ♥

LOVES, LIKES, DISLIKES
Pisces-Rabbits want a smooth ride on their journey through life. They find sudden change unsettling. Unpleasantness disturbs them and arguments make them ill. Tranquility is what they seek, so a comfortable house in a safe environment will be essential to their happiness and well-being. At home, their refined tastes will be evident all around with exquisite items of furniture and delicate artwork on the walls. In affairs of the heart, Pisces-Rabbits are notoriously tender romantics and seek a gentle and supportive partner with whom to share their lives.

CHILDREN AND PARENTS
Young Pisces-Rabbits are gentle, well-mannered children with good imaginations and a talent for art. Security is an uppermost need followed closely by plenty of cuddles and reassurance. A creative environment, music and dancing lessons as well as trips to the theater and museum will build their confidence and stimulate their minds. As parents, Pisces-Rabbits are deeply loving and tend to worry and fret about their children.

PISCES-DRAGON

A mutually advantageous combination, the Piscean input brings sensitivity to the brashness of the Dragon, while the Dragon part of the equation bolsters Pisces' tender emotions. Together, the mixture produces Dragons who are no less colorful of character and as ardent as any self-respecting Dragon can be, but with the added benefit that these people are less self-centered and far more responsive to the needs of others. Nevertheless, the Dragon's drive is always present for, while members of this dual sign may appear calm and placid on the surface, underneath their feelings and ambitions are smoldering. The Pisces-Dragon may be described as working with an iron fist in a velvet glove.

KEY CHARACTERISTICS

- 🐉 inventive
- 🐉 creative
- 🐉 enterprising
- 🐉 sentimental

YOUR COMPATIBLE SIGNS

Cancer-Rat

Scorpio-Monkey

Pisces-Dragons delight in sleight-of-hand, and make excellent magicians.

EAST WEST FUSION

EAST

Pisces enfolds the Chinese Dragon with gentleness and kind dreams

WEST

The Dragon breathes vibrant color and life into the Fish

The Dragon brings laughter and joy to gladden Pisces' spirits.

THE ESSENTIAL YOU

WORK, HEALTH, HOBBIES

Because Pisces-Dragons are multi-gifted individuals, they may have difficulty deciding which of their talents to develop. The desire may be to juggle as many talents as possible but, in reality, focusing their attention on fewer activities is more likely to bring success. Pisces-Dragons are blessed with original mentalities and endowed with profound imaginative powers. They prefer to work unfettered by routine but need to ensure they are motivated in their job. Pisces-Dragons are excellent performers so the entertainment business is a suitable avenue—as magicians they would certainly pull the crowds. A job in an industrial setting, perhaps in the petrochemical field, would appeal.

❤ ❤ ❤

LOVES, LIKES, DISLIKES

Dreams of courtly love and romantic adventure fill the minds of Pisces-Dragons. The harsh reality of day-to-day living can be hard for them to bear, so these people tend to live with their heads in the clouds. In matters of the heart, they must be constantly in love and when the romance fades with one partner, they will look around for another to take its place. In a very sweet way, however, Pisces-Dragons like to remain friends with all their exlovers. They don't want any hard feelings to spoil their lives.

🐉 🐉 🐉

CHILDREN AND PARENTS

Young Pisces-Dragons are irresistibly beautiful and therefore easy to spoil. They have a soft, complacent nature though they can be prone to angry outbursts when they feel hurt or their loyalty has been betrayed. Daydreaming is typical of this dual sign and they should be encouraged to use their imaginative talents constructively. Pisces-Dragon parents are loving and entertaining. A serious generation gap is rare.

PISCES-SNAKE

Perhaps the most sensitive of the Snake clan, these people are soft and sensual, dreamy and kind. Unfortunately, they also have a highly delicate emotional system which is very easily wounded since they take even the merest slight deeply to heart. Being so sensitive themselves, however, makes the members of this sign acutely receptive and compassionate toward others so they excel in the caring professions where they concern themselves with the welfare of others. Being ruled by their feelings, whenever Pisces-Snakes fall in love, they tumble hook, line, and sinker. And when Pisces-Snakes commit themselves to a partner, it is definitely for life—no questions asked.

Feelings run very deep in the beautiful, cool-headed, mysterious Pisces-Snake.

EAST WEST FUSION

EAST
Pisces enhances the Oriental Snake's intuitive powers

WEST
The Snake brings the wisdom of the ages to Pisces

KEY CHARACTERISTICS
- introspective
- sceptical
- ultrasensitive
- private

YOUR COMPATIBLE SIGNS
Scorpio-Rooster
Cancer-Ox

OBSERVATIONS
Taking a negative view of things can blight the Pisces-Snake's outlook on life

---

THE ESSENTIAL YOU

WORK, HEALTH, HOBBIES

Pisces-Snakes are cerebral people, deeply interested in psychological issues and in asking questions about the meaning of life. As such, members of this dual sign make excellent philosophers and academics, especially the sort who like to live in ivory towers. These people are thinkers and dreamers, suited to intellectual or white collar occupations. They are not physically robust types and so are unlikely to be attracted to heavy, manual jobs. Clinical psychology, psychiatry, and occupational therapy will appeal to them. But Pisces-Snakes are also most intuitive and are interested in the spiritual side of life, in mystical matters, and even in magic. In general, these people prefer working quietly and undisturbed on their own.

LOVES, LIKES, DISLIKES

Deep thinking and reflective, Pisces-Snakes are attached to their roots. They do not like too much physical exertion; being in loud, noisy, and crowded places gives them a headache; and the idea of masses of material possessions weighing them down is not what they aspire to in life at all. But members of this duality are family oriented and like nothing better than being surrounded by the people they love. Home is the center of their universe and, if they could, that is where they would stay.

Pisces-Snakes are drawn to the spiritual and the mystical in life.

CHILDREN AND PARENTS

Youngsters belonging to this double sign are extremely easy to raise. They are quiet, polite children and often shy and retiring. Reading is a great passion. As parents, Pisces-Snakes are deeply loving. Quiet, well-behaved children is what they need. Raucous ones will jangle their sensitive nerves.

PISCES: **FEBRUARY 19–MARCH 20**
YEARS OF THE HORSE: 1906 ∗ 1918 ∗ 1930 ∗ 1942 ∗ 1954 ∗ 1966 ∗ 1978 ∗ 1990 ∗ 2002 ∗ 2014
HOUR OF THE HORSE: 11AM – 12.59PM

THE ESSENTIAL YOU

PISCES-HORSE

Pisces, synonymous with sensitivity, adds gentleness, empathy, and a deeply caring instinct to the Horse's brio. In its turn, the Horse strengthens the Fish's emotional resolve so that those who are born under the influence of this combination will be romantic individuals but not, however, overly sentimental nor quite so prone to mood swings. Pisces-Horses are nevertheless impressionable people and can all too easily become swept along by ideals. Or else they fall for a sob story or spend their lives collecting lame ducks. Adventure does call the Pisces-Horse but all too often this is pursued in the imagination. Loving and giving, when Pisces-Horses find the partner of their dreams, they devote themselves entirely to the service of love.

Pisces-Horses always find time to listen to their friends.

KEY CHARACTERISTICS

- patient
- generous
- suggestible
- visionary

YOUR COMPATIBLE SIGNS

Cancer-Dog
Scorpio-Tiger

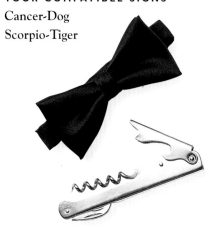

Dressing up, an elegant cocktail bar, and a romantic evening with a lover greatly pleases the Pisces-Horse.

EAST WEST FUSION

EAST
Pisces instills a strong altruistic spirit into the Horse

WEST
The Chinese Horse encourages Pisces to become more gutsy

OBSERVATIONS
Erratic and changeable, Pisces-Horses can be somewhat capricious creatures

WORK, HEALTH, HOBBIES

Receptive to other people, Pisces-Horses possess innate sympathy, seemingly endless patience, and are always prepared to listen. With their quiet wisdom, members of this dual sign are able to penetrate the very heart of a problem and are thus born counselors and therapists. The cut and thrust of big business, however, disturbs the Pisces-Horse's fragile nervous system. They tend, rather, to be drawn either to therapeutic occupations or careers in the creative or artistic world. Fine Arts, literature, and design appeal, as do all forms of handicraft. Many do well in the food business, horticulture, and music.

LOVES, LIKES, DISLIKES

There's a certain charming naivety about Pisces-Horses. They are hugely idealistic and romantic, and somewhat divorced from the reality of everyday existence. They like to fantasize, to put their lovers on pedestals, and to dream dreams of what could be. In matters of the heart, Pisces-Horses are attractive to the opposite sex but they tend to be fickle in love. Though they like their independence, they can be emotionally clingy and, whether morally, physically, or financially, they like to be looked after by other people.

CHILDREN AND PARENTS

Gentle and tender-hearted, young Pisces-Horses are supersensitive people with a huge capacity for loving. With such affectionate, well-behaved children, it can be easy to overindulge them. At school, these youngsters will perform best at art and music and will excel at writing stories. As parents, the love of the Pisces-Horse for his or her offspring knows no bounds. They must take care, however, not to let their emotions swamp their children.

PISCES-SHEEP

Two very soft creatures come together here to form the Pisces-Sheep. Neither are particularly pushy signs, their natives preferring to take a back seat on life. Both do better in partnership than alone so Pisces-Sheep are doubly in need of a supportive partner or at least of a mentor who can both guide them through life's trickier moments and help them to bring their potential to fruition. Left to their own devices, Pisces-Sheep are in danger of neglecting their very considerable talents. Sensitivity always accompanies the Piscean temperament and this, coupled with the Sheep's creativity, combine to make members of this dual sign highly accomplished artists. Love, for the Pisces-Sheep, is most definitely seen through rose-colored spectacles.

Love is always in the air as far as the Pisces-Sheep is concerned.

KEY CHARACTERISTICS
- kind
- peace-loving
- complacent
- capricious

YOUR COMPATIBLE SIGNS
Scorpio-Pig
Cancer-Rabbit

THE ESSENTIAL YOU

WORK, HEALTH, HOBBIES
In the universal scheme of things, Pisces-Sheep are not movers and shakers. Instead, they prefer to stand on the periphery of the action and cheer the players on. In terms of career, Pisces-Sheep are not generally attracted to industry. There is, though, something essentially glamorous about these people and they won't be found in menial drudgery. However, when it comes to creative talent, Pisces-Sheep are awash, and they will live and die for their art. A career in the field of music or dance certainly appeals to them and so do painting and creating of all kinds. Pisces-Sheep will be found in the beauty and fashion business or, if drawn to social work, they make good advisors and sound marriage guidance counselors.

LOVES, LIKES, DISLIKES
Pisces-Sheep like to sit in contemplation of the world. These are beautiful and dreamy people, not given to organizing their affairs. They much prefer leaving the details of daily living to other people. As long as they are surrounded by beauty, live in sumptuous surroundings and have gorgeous clothes to wear, they will be happy. In love as in life, there is much of the fey and ephemeral in this dual sign. Pisces-Sheep do not want to be pinned down. They waft gently through life on a cloud of scented rose petals fanned by the delicate warmth of the Zephyr breeze.

CHILDREN AND PARENTS
Young Pisces-Sheep are hugely gifted children who will delight everyone with their ability to sing, dance, and draw. But they are very laid-back children—they hate tidying up after themselves—and unless they are guided with a firm but gentle hand, they may squander their talents and fail to achieve their true potential in life. Adult Pisces-Sheep tend to take the glamorous approach to parenting and like to do it from a distance.

EAST WEST FUSION

EAST
Pisces brings out the Sheep's genius for art

WEST
The Sheep enhances Pisces' originality

Colors inspire the creative minds of young Pisces-Sheep.

OBSERVATIONS
Pisces-Sheep are too easily swayed by the opinions of other people

PISCES: **FEBRUARY 19–MARCH 20**
YEARS OF THE MONKEY: 1908 ∗ 1920 ∗ 1932 ∗ 1944 ∗ 1956 ∗ 1968 ∗ 1980 ∗ 1992 ∗ 2004 ∗ 2016
HOUR OF THE MONKEY: 3PM – 4.59PM

THE ESSENTIAL YOU

PISCES-MONKEY

There is a whimsical delicacy about the Pisces-Monkey that belies a clever and calculating mind. Members of this sign are blessed with Piscean intuition and the Monkey's intelligence. Above all, Pisces-Monkeys are sophisticates. Now, sophistication has several meanings. It can indicate a person who is worldly, cultured, and refined, something which does indeed apply to the Pisces-Monkey. It can also imply something that is complex or highly developed and that, too, describes the Pisces-Monkey's talents. However, sophistication can also suggest a certain artificiality or an economy with the truth and no other sign is as adept as the clever Pisces-Monkey when it comes to fabricating stories with words.

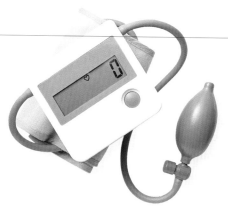

Intelligent and compassionate, the medically minded Pisces-Monkey has a wonderful bedside manner.

KEY CHARACTERISTICS

- friendly
- articulate
- elegant
- skillful

YOUR COMPATIBLE SIGNS

Cancer-Dragon
Scorpio-Rat

OBSERVATIONS

A failure to keep their word can undermine the Pisces-Monkey's credibility

EAST WEST FUSION

EAST
Pisces brings integrity to this partnership

WEST
The Monkey teaches Pisces to be more logical

The bright, articulate minds of the Pisces-Monkey can produce works of literary genius.

WORK, HEALTH, HOBBIES

Couple the colossal intelligence of the Monkey with the profound intuition of Pisces, and it is easy to see that a person born under this twin sign has the potential to go far. Add a large helping of verbal skill and a liberal sprinkling of charm and the recipe guarantees success. Pisces-Monkeys are high-profile people—not at all the sort who like sitting in the wings. Whatever career they choose to follow, they will be driven by an imaginative creativity that can come up with brilliant solutions on the spot. Their articulacy and keen minds will take them into almost any occupation from sales to politics, dancing to medicine, writing to gambling.

♥ ♥ ♥

LOVES, LIKES, DISLIKES

Pisces-Monkeys have expensive tastes. They like to dress elegantly and to live in luxurious surroundings. Meeting friends for an evening out, gossiping over dinner, going to parties, attending premiers, or being invited to an exclusive art or fashion show will all delight the members of this sign. Misery for this group includes living on the breadline, disloyalty from loved ones, and being used by friends and acquaintances. Sexually, they are beautiful and seductive and inevitably surrounded by scores of admirers.

CHILDREN AND PARENTS

Young Pisces-Monkeys are bright and engaging. They're quick to learn to read and write and both their intelligence and imagination will be impressive. They have innate psychological skills, can read people like books, and know how to wind their parents around their little fingers seemingly without effort. Adult Pisces-Monkeys are good providers and make intelligent parents.

PISCES-ROOSTER

A paradoxical mixture of hard-headed pragmatism and sensitive romanticism, the Pisces-Rooster is more amenable and less abrasive than other members of the Rooster clan. All Roosters enjoy their own rhetoric and they relish an intellectual argument or debate but, if these should turn into disagreements, the Pisces-Rooster will definitely want out. Bad feelings and emotional friction of any sort upsets these tamer Cockerels who are inclined to see the world around them through rose-colored spectacles. Moreover, in order to keep life sweet, Pisces-Roosters may sometimes bend reality in order to fit their own idealistic picture of life. More flexible than the average Rooster, those born under the influence of Pisces will happily slot into almost any job that is going.

KEY CHARACTERISTICS
- self-motivated
- conservative
- independent
- exacting

YOUR COMPATIBLE SIGNS
Scorpio-Ox
Cancer-Snake

EAST WEST FUSION

EAST
Pisces rounds off the
Rooster's sharper corners

WEST
The Rooster encourages Pisces
to become more resilient

Sudden mood swings may disturb the Pisces-Rooster's path to true love.

OBSERVATIONS
The Pisces-Rooster's tendency to boast can be off-putting

THE ESSENTIAL YOU

WORK, HEALTH, HOBBIES
At work, the Pisces-Rooster's motto must surely be, "if a job's worth doing, it's worth doing well." So they will have high standards and stake their reputations on the quality of their workmanship. Members of this twin sign are essentially practical types who like to see tangible results from their efforts. Veterinary work, horticulture, or pharmaceuticals would suit. Electronics or computer engineering might also attract. Prone to stress, classical music matches these people's robust temperaments and helps them unwind.

For Pisces-Roosters, music eases the tensions of a stressful day.

LOVES, LIKES, DISLIKES
Pisces-Roosters like to feel close to nature and enjoy long rambles through the woods, moonlit strolls on the beach, or bracing walks along the cliffs. Life in the country with time to potter in a garden suits these people well. At home, the uncluttered, classical tastes of the Pisces-Rooster will be apparent everywhere. They spend a long time coordinating style and color. Relationships with Pisces-Roosters can be difficult because, not only are these proud and fussy people, but they are also prone to dramatic mood swings.

CHILDREN AND PARENTS
Young Pisces-Roosters can be little bundles of nerves, constantly fretting about this and that. They do have tremendous talent but, because their standards are high, people (including themselves) rarely come up to their expectations. Teaching these children to believe in themselves, encouraging them to develop their interests, and boosting their morale will stand them in good stead for life. In truth, adult Pisces-Roosters are neither the cuddliest of parents nor, on the whole, the sort who blindly dote on their little ones.

PISCES-DOG

Happiness for the Pisces-Dog centers around a quiet, restful environment, a loving home, and a devoted partner. These are essentially peace-loving, sensitive souls, but both in the Western as well as in the Eastern tradition, the Fish and the Dog are somewhat prone to over-anxiety. Neither push themselves forward; each likes to go with the flow and both enjoy being part of the crowd. These are not leaders of men, they prefer to wait in the wings and to take their cues from more forceful types. Gentle, creative, and poetic, harmony and security are paramount to the Pisces-Dog's happiness and well-being.

KEY CHARACTERISTICS

- serene
- earnest
- neurotic
- family-oriented

YOUR COMPATIBLE SIGNS

Cancer-Tiger
Scorpio-Horse

A sense of security in a happy family setting keeps the Pisces-Dog content.

EAST WEST FUSION

EAST
Pisces encourages the Dog to become more trusting

WEST
The Chinese Dog teaches Pisces to become more steadfast

Pisces-Dogs have an innate understanding of animals and love to work with them.

THE ESSENTIAL YOU

WORK, HEALTH, HOBBIES

Though they may not show it, Pisces-Dogs are ultrasensitive and possess fragile egos that need constant shoring up. Perhaps this is what makes them so understanding of people with physical or psychological problems and why they are drawn to working with the underprivileged or in centers with alcoholics, drug addicts, or excriminals. Alternatively, working with animals also brings the Pisces-Dog fulfillment.

Career-wise, they are happier working as part of a team than on their own. They make cooperative employees and are always ready to help when colleagues are in need.

LOVES, LIKES, DISLIKES

Material possessions, luxuries, or sumptuous surroundings are not top-of-the-agenda requirements for the Pisces-Dog. However, security, a contented family life, and enough money to provide the basic comforts in life are absolute essentials. Tranquility and peace of mind are also important since the Pisces-Dog finds confrontations upsetting and he or she will do almost anything to keep on everyone's good side. In relationships, partners who are calm and who will help to remove the burdens from the shoulders of these sensitive souls, will be valued beyond compare.

CHILDREN AND PARENTS

Young Pisces-Dogs are tender little flowers that need careful nurturing. Teaching them to relax, perhaps massaging them with aromatherapy oils even when they are babies, or introducing them to yoga or meditation as they approach their teenage years, will be of inestimable help to them later on in life. Pisces-Dog parents adore their children and engross themselves body and soul in their families.

PISCES-PIG

Pisces and the Pig have much in common and thus the two can work well in combination. Not only do they share the distinction of coming last in both the Western and Eastern astrological traditions, but they each in their own way stand for sensuality. Thus it is that, multiplied by two, the Pisces-Pig's tendency to indulge themselves in the pleasures of the flesh are considerably strengthened. Equally, both are creative signs and together this can produce individuals with remarkable artistic talents. Indeed, many Pisces-Pigs are drawn either to the arts or to the beauty industry. Being loved, being attached, and feeling secure are fundamental to the Pisces-Pig's well-being and these people will do anything to keep a relationship alive.

EAST WEST FUSION

EAST
Pisces expands the Pig's intuitive awareness

WEST
The Oriental Pig brings both serenity and optimism to the sign of the Fish

The exuberance of the playful Pisces-Pig is always ready to burst to the surface.

KEY CHARACTERISTICS
- sensual
- confident
- determined
- fortunate

YOUR COMPATIBLE SIGNS
Scorpio-Rabbit
Cancer-Sheep

OBSERVATIONS
Extravagance can be the major fault among members of this dual sign

THE ESSENTIAL YOU

WORK, HEALTH, HOBBIES
Pisces-Pigs are such multitalented creatures that their skills can take them far and wide. The Chinese Pig half of this duality is a practical technologist while the Western Fish side is essentially creative. Putting these two together, then, will enable the Pisces-Pig individual to take ideas and translate them into reality. Their expensive tastes, however, will draw them to occupations offering attractive salaries. Architecture and design are ideal occupations. Many, too, become wine merchants or dealers of art and antiques. Exclusive fashions and five-star catering also attract.

LOVES, LIKES, DISLIKES
Pisces-Pigs love to bask in opulence. Deep, deep comfort is prerequisite. The larder will groan with good food, the cellar will be filled with rich wine, and the table laden with silver and crystal. Antiques, paintings, porcelains, and brocades will be matched and positioned just so. They have a strong feeling for the past and many have a tendency to theme their interiors to a particular period. For Pisces-Pigs, their homes are very much their castles. Self-indulgence is strong in this sign and physical pleasures are never stinted—making unhurried, passionate love is a special joy.

Pisces-Pigs are happiest surrounded by their families in the security of their own homes.

CHILDREN AND PARENTS
Young Pisces-Pigs tend to be sensitive—both emotionally and physiologically. These youngsters need lots of love and reassurance at home and at school. They love their families and a happy, settled home life will give them the sense of security and stability that children of this double sign so desperately need to boost their confidence in the outside world. Big appetites and a sweet tooth are characteristic of Pisces-Pig children. Adult Pisces-Pigs are some of the happiest parents in the world. They live for their families and are completely in love with their children.

EAST WEST FUTURE FORECASTS

THE NEXT TWELVE YEARS

According to Western astrology, the transiting effects of the slow-moving planets through the different signs of the Zodiac have an impact on human affairs and usher in the changes that affect the course of history.

Shifting cosmic patterns herald the changes that will be felt on Earth.

Each of the planets is said to exert a specific action and each astrological sign is linked to a different aspect of life. The planets travel through the signs at different speeds. Some whiz in and out in a matter of months while others, like the slower-moving ones, remain in a sign for many years.

As these slower-moving planets—Jupiter, Saturn, Uranus, Neptune, and Pluto—leave one sign and move into another, we experience a shift of emphasis, a change of awareness, or a new direction concerning those aspects of life represented by the signs involved.

As an example, Pluto's move into the sign of Scorpio in the early 1980s coincided with the development on a global scale of the AIDS virus. The planet Pluto is associated with death, regeneration, and the organs of reproduction, while Scorpio is the sign that represents sexual matters and mores. Therefore it comes as no surprise at all that such a life-threatening sexually transmitted disease should have presented itself to the world during that time.

In the same manner, the other slow-moving planets activate the astrological signs through which they pass in their own unique way. Therefore, as the new millennium gets under way, so the planets will progress a little further and, in changing signs, they will herald a fresh approach for the new age.

These same changing patterns are marked by the Chinese astrological system, which recognizes recurring themes over a cyclical timespan of sixty years.

World economies, for example, see an upward trend in the years of the Rat. Issues concerning women, children, and the home are likely to come to the fore in Rabbit years. Adverse weather conditions and political unrest may be expected during the Year of the Tiger. Scandal and intrigue rock the nations in the Year of the Snake. Marriages and mergers that take place in the Year of the Dog tend to be solid and long-lived.

Locked as they are into the repeating rhythms of the heavens, the Chinese Animal Years introduce one by one their own trends according to the prevailing planetary influences of the year.

By understanding these shifting patterns, and fusing the astrological systems of both the East and the West, we have the ability to begin not only to recognize the sequence of events that is likely to govern global trends, but also to glimpse the changing fortunes that will shape our own destinies in the years to come.

1999

EASTERN ASTROLOGY	WESTERN ASTROLOGY
1999 Year of the Rabbit Feb 16th, 1999–Feb 4th, 2000 Element—Earth Yin	Jupiter moves into Aries Saturn moves into Taurus

 The Year of the Rabbit is often described as a peaceful time and this year does offer some solace considering its situation between the dramatic signs of the Tiger and the Dragon. According to the Western system, Jupiter, the planet of expansion, will this year move into the aggressive sign of Aries, so rumblings created by religious fundamentalists may be felt. However, Aries is also a pioneering sign and since the Rabbit governs health matters, medical advances are likely and orthodox and complementary therapies may also move closer together. Politically, diplomacy will be the key. Matters which are likely to come to the fore in 1999 concern family welfare, houses and the home, children, and women's issues. The arts, too, should gain prominence.

2000

EASTERN ASTROLOGY	WESTERN ASTROLOGY
2000 Year of the Dragon Feb 5th, 2000–Jan 23rd, 2001 Element—Metal Yang	Jupiter moves through Taurus and Gemini

 High drama typifies the Year of the Dragon when grand projects and magnificent spectaculars will bring in the new millennium with style. New excitement should stimulate the money markets, which will profit from the vogue for lavish schemes. As a result, international economies bounce back from the doldrums and standards of living will generally rise. Jupiter in Taurus helps to generate wealth and well-being, and augurs well for commerce and trade. New businesses set up in 2000 promise success. As Jupiter also moves into Gemini, a boom in the communications industry can be expected. Publishing, education, and the world of ideas will flourish. Moral issues will be aired. Fashion and the performing arts will prosper. Children born in the Year of the Dragon are said to bring good fortune to their families. Energy and enthusiasm are required to make full use of the year's potential—those who are daring and bold fare best.

2001

EASTERN ASTROLOGY	WESTERN ASTROLOGY
2001 Year of the Snake Jan 24th, 2001–Feb 11th, 2002 Element—Metal Yin	Jupiter moves into Cancer Saturn moves into Gemini

 Following the excesses of the Dragon year, the Snake redresses the balance with a dose of restraint. Flamboyance is this year replaced by economy and ideas err on the side of conservatism. With Saturn's move into Gemini, discipline and the serious application of one's talents win the day. Mathematics, engineering, and science will come to the fore, although we may also experience frustration and breakdown in communications. Often duplicity, chicanery, and deceit are rife in the Year of the Snake and an undercurrent of suspicion and distrust permeates the year. Jupiter's move into Cancer highlights matters concerning the home and family, traditions, and questions on morality. The food industry, farming, and real estate should all find favor now.

2002

EASTERN ASTROLOGY	WESTERN ASTROLOGY
2002 Year of the Horse Feb 12th, 2002–Jan 31st, 2003 Element—Water Yang	Jupiter moves into Leo

 In 2002 the emphasis will be on freedom and fun. The Year of the Horse is typically fast-paced, emotions are volatile, and energies are high. The travel industry will fare well this year, with more people than ever taking adventurous holidays. Spontaneity will be the key with many short breaks taken on the spur of the moment. This year, attention will turn to recreational pursuits and sporting events. With Jupiter moving through Leo, the entertainment business and the performing arts will enjoy patronage. Gambling fever could strike although speculation is generally unwise this year. As optimism returns, passion and romance are high on the agenda. Businesses connected with romance—roses, jewelry, wedding gowns, exotic holidays— will have a heyday. However, in the Year of the Horse, while romantic overtures are abundant, one is warned that true love and marriage contracted this year may not last the course.

2003

EASTERN ASTROLOGY
2003 Year of the Sheep
Feb 1st, 2003–Jan 21st, 2004
Element—Water
Yin

WESTERN ASTROLOGY
Jupiter moves into Virgo
Uranus moves into Pisces

 After the frenetic speed imposed by the Year of the Horse, 2003 brings in a more sedate pace. This, the Year of the Sheep, switches the focus of attention onto family life. With Saturn also moving into Cancer, the sign associated with domestic matters, our awareness of family responsibilities, and in particular of our duties toward the elderly, will be raised this year. Reconciliation and peacemaking, both politically and in terms of our own personal relationships, are the order of the day. Many olive branches offered in the Year of the Sheep will be accepted and old rifts will be healed. As Uranus, the Great Awakener, begins its long stay in Pisces, the sign associated with imagination and the subconscious, so new interest will be sparked in mysticism and in the workings of the mind. Commercially, fashions will accent the chic and the sophisticated.

2004

EASTERN ASTROLOGY
2004 Year of the Monkey
Jan 22nd, 2004–Feb 8th, 2005
Element—Wood
Yang

WESTERN ASTROLOGY
Jupiter moves into Libra

 The question of justice, as well as issues concerning the legal system, come to prominence when Jupiter enters the sign of Libra this year. Any partnerships forged, whether of the intimate or business variety, come under good auspices. The three heavyweights—Uranus in Pisces, Neptune in Aquarius, and Pluto in Sagittarius—continue to stimulate intellectual matters and to promote interest in education and new ideas, so imaginative projects are encouraged, communications flourish, and spiritual issues are given a higher profile. Questions on religion and morality will be asked; political, philosophical, psychological, and mediating skills will all be in demand. Scientific research and professions that require manual dexterity will also prosper. And though this sign is notorious for its mischievousness, 2004 promises to be a progressive, up-beat year with much to be enjoyed.

2005

EASTERN ASTROLOGY
2005 Year of the Rooster
Feb 9th, 2005–Jan 28th, 2006
Element—Wood
Yin

WESTERN ASTROLOGY
Jupiter moves into Scorpio
Saturn moves into Leo

 Image matters in Rooster Years and in 2005 the fashion industry will ride high. The uniform look could stage a comeback; tailoring and attention to detail will be all-important. Saturn's transit through Leo suggests children's affairs will come to the fore with perhaps the passing of new laws to protect their interests, while tough measures to deal with young offenders will be called for. Since Leo is the sign of authority and leadership, and Saturn is the herald of restriction and control, this year could see the rise to power of a dictatorial force. With Jupiter moving into the intense sign of Scorpio, religious fundamentalism could again be at the root of international disquiet. Interestingly, however, Rooster Years are also times when the oppressed make their voices heard. This year, businesses dealing in financial services, accountancy, insurance, and taxation should do well. Everywhere, bureaucracy will rule.

2006

EASTERN ASTROLOGY
2006 Year of the Dog
Jan 29th, 2006–Feb 17th, 2007
Element—Fire
Yang

WESTERN ASTROLOGY
Jupiter remains in Scorpio
for most of the year

Since relationships forged in the Year of the Dog are blessed with happiness and prosperity, 2006 appears to be an excellent year for commitment and marriage. Animal welfare and environmental issues, too, come under the aegis of the Chinese Dog, so measures to improve the countryside may well be set in place. Moreover, a sense of social responsibility pervades political thinking in Dog years and moves to raise the standard of living will be introduced. Security, both national and personal, is another theme likely to gain in prominence. With Jupiter's progress through Scorpio, a resurgence of interest in mystical matters gains strength. Mystery and magic captures the imagination of the people and scientific research will turn its attention to subconscious issues and the investigation of mystical beliefs. A taste for detective stories will be reflected in movies and literature.

2007

EASTERN ASTROLOGY	WESTERN ASTROLOGY
2007 Year of the Pig Feb 18th, 2007–Feb 6th, 2008 Element—Fire Yin	Jupiter transits through Sagittarius for most of the year Saturn moves into Virgo

 Deep philosophical questions about the nature of the universe will be uppermost in intellectual minds as Jupiter moves through the sign of the Archer. Socially, improvements in higher education can be expected and sports events are likely to make the news. The travel industry, too, should profit from people's desire for freedom and sense of adventure. Since the sign of the Pig is the last in the cycle, this is a time for reaping rewards for past efforts—or to be found wanting if we have failed to pull our weight. Bringing projects to a conclusion will be favored in 2007, next year will be more favorable for new starts so for now we must simply make plans for taking action. As Saturn moves into Virgo, we can expect medical advances and improvements in the health service. As this is the sign of the family, having a baby in 2007 is considered highly auspicious.

2008

EASTERN ASTROLOGY	WESTERN ASTROLOGY
2008 Year of the Rat Feb 7th, 2008– Jan 25th, 2009 Element—Earth Yang	Jupiter begins the year in Capricorn Pluto moves into Capricorn

 As the first of the twelve Animal signs, the Year of the Rat kicks off a new cycle and encourages us all to begin afresh. Interestingly, this year sees Pluto, the planet of change and regeneration, commence a sixteen-year stay in Capricorn. Jupiter, too, moves into Capricorn for the year, bringing with it a new wave of conservative thinking and the return of traditional values concerning education, morality, and law. Pluto in this sign stimulates organization and matters relating to the process of government. Perhaps, then, in 2008 we can expect the first stirrings of new political thinking, serious moves toward international accord, and the foundation of an innovative system of government on a global basis? A feel-good factor usually accompanies the Year of the Rat, market economies take an up-turn, and all new ventures prosper on a tide of optimism and hope.

2009

EASTERN ASTROLOGY	WESTERN ASTROLOGY
2009 Year of the Ox Jan 26th, 2009–Feb 13th, 2010 Element—Earth Yin	Jupiter moves into Aquarius Saturn moves into Libra

 Consistency and consolidation are the key words associated with the Year of the Ox, a time when hard work is recognized and we are given the opportunity to achieve our aims. Integrity will be rewarded and loyalty will be expected of us. Markets continue the growth spurt initiated last year, and businesses connected with farming, gardening, and real estate do well. Jupiter moves into the high-minded, idealistic sign of Aquarius, sweeping in a new religious and social tolerance, and a spirit of humanitarian zeal. Philosophical and intellectual truths are pursued, improvements to the lot of mankind are encouraged, and great scientific advances are made. Saturn, the stabilizing influence, moving into Libra promotes cooperation. Laws regulating contracts and agreements are likely to be implemented and a desire to strike an entente cordiale will underscore international politics.

2010

EASTERN ASTROLOGY	WESTERN ASTROLOGY
2010 Year of the Tiger Feb 14th, 2010–Feb 2nd, 2011 Element—Metal Yang	Jupiter moves into Pisces Uranus moves into Aries

 Years of the Tiger enter with a roar and are notoriously fast-paced and turbulent. Weather conditions are unusual, political situations are volatile, and financial markets fluctuate dramatically. Catastrophic losses can be made in Tiger years but, for those with nerves of steel, stupendous gains can be achieved. To heighten the drama further, this is the year when Uranus, the great awakener and planet of sudden change, enters the pioneering but daring sign of Aries. Thus, in 2010, we can expect widespread social and legal reforms, while innovation and adventure will blaze new trails that will affect us all. Jupiter's presence in Pisces will encourage new techniques in healing, and foster a spirit of charity. This transit, however, will also stimulate a deep devotional need that may find an outlet in a figure destined to become a modern-day idol.

Chinese Astrology, **Derek Walters**
(Aquarian Press, London, U.K., 1987)

Chinese Horoscopes, **Lori Reid**
(Ward Lock, London, U.K., 1992)

Chinese Horoscopes for Lovers: The Rat, **Lori Reid**
(Element Books Limited, Shaftesbury, U.K., 1996)

Chinese Horoscopes for Lovers: The Ox, **Lori Reid**
(Element Books Limited, Shaftesbury, U.K., 1996)

Chinese Horoscopes for Lovers: The Tiger, **Lori Reid**
(Element Books Limited, Shaftesbury, U.K., 1996)

Chinese Horoscopes for Lovers: The Rabbit, **Lori Reid**
(Element Books Limited, Shaftesbury, U.K., 1996)

Chinese Horoscopes for Lovers: The Dragon, **Lori Reid**
(Element Books Limited, Shaftesbury, U.K., 1996)

Chinese Horoscopes for Lovers: The Snake, **Lori Reid**
(Element Books Limited, Shaftesbury, U.K., 1996)

Chinese Horoscopes for Lovers: The Horse, **Lori Reid**
(Element Books Limited, Shaftesbury, U.K., 1996)

Chinese Horoscopes for Lovers: The Sheep, **Lori Reid**
(Element Books Limited, Shaftesbury, U.K., 1996)

Chinese Horoscopes for Lovers: The Monkey, **Lori Reid**
(Element Books Limited, Shaftesbury, U.K., 1996)

Chinese Horoscopes for Lovers: The Rooster, **Lori Reid**
(Element Books Limited, Shaftesbury, U.K., 1996)

Chinese Horoscopes for Lovers: The Dog, **Lori Reid**
(Element Books Limited, Shaftesbury, U.K., 1996)

Chinese Horoscopes for Lovers: The Pig, **Lori Reid**
(Element Books Limited, Shaftesbury, U.K., 1996)

Do it Yourself Astrology, **Lyn Birkbeck**
(Element Books Limited, Shaftesbury, U.K., 1997)

Elements of Astrology, **Janis Huntley**
(Element Books Limited, Shaftesbury, U.K., 1990)

Lovers' Horoscopes, **Lori Reid**
(Ward Lock, London, U.K., 1992)

Moon Magic, **Lori Reid**
(Carlton Books, London, U.K., 1998)

Parkers' Astrology, **Julia and Derek Parker**
(Dorling Kindersley, Shaftesbury, U.K., 1991)

Star Signs, **Lori Reid**
(Scholastic Publications, London, U.K., 1996)

The Complete Book of Chinese Horoscopes, **Lori Reid**
(Element Books Limited, Shaftesbury, U.K., 1997)

The Handbook of Chinese Horoscopes, **Theodora Lau**
(Fontana, London, U.K., 1997)

INDEX

INDEX